'I was touched by this journey from loss and separation, through grief and pain to a place of truth, love and acceptance. A story of sadness and joy which could just as easily be entitled *The Power of Love*'

Kathy Gore OBE DL, chair of Friends of Sussex Hospices

'This is a wonderful memoir that is funny, moving, and ultimately life affirming. It addresses emotional wounding and male depression in ways that millions of us can understand and relate to. Andrew might be writing about dogs, but his real topic is how to find the courage to open up to love again'

Jed Diamond, psychotherapist and author, *My Distant Dad: Healing the Family Father Wound and Surviving Male Menopause: A Guide for Women and Men*

The
Power
of Dog

How a puppy helped heal
a grieving heart

ANDREW MARSHALL

RedDoor

Published by RedDoor
www.reddoorpublishing.com

ISBN 978-1-910453-60-5

A CIP catalogue record for this book is available
from the British Library

Cover design: Emma Graves

Typesetting: Tutis Innovative E-Solutions Pte. Ltd

Printed and bound by Nørhaven, Denmark

To Ignacio

'Any action is often better than no action, especially if you have been stuck in an unhappy situation for a long time. If it is a mistake, at least you learn something, in which case it's no longer a mistake. If you remain stuck, you learn nothing.'

Eckhart Tolle, The Power of Now: A Guide to Spiritual Enlightenment

BEFORE

What I wanted most and what frightened me most, when I was a child, turned out to be the same thing. Every year as I blew out my birthday cake candles, I'd wish for a puppy – with my eyes tightly closed to maximise the magic. But while my daydreams were full of adoring Labradors fetching sticks, my nightmares were stalked by their distant relatives: wolves.

My parents belonged to the 'comfortably off' middle classes and were only too happy to pay for tennis lessons, new bikes and summer camp – indeed they were particularly keen to send me to these. My birthday cake was always home baked, a fruit cake decorated with teddy bears sitting in a spiky snow scene. Despite the growing number of candles and my entreaties, the gods of birthday wishes were unmoved. Although my mother agreed first to guinea pigs and later mice, she remained firm about getting a dog: 'I'll be the one who ends up walking it.'

I can pinpoint the exact moment the nightmares started. Our next-door neighbours, whom I'd christened H'auntie and H'uncle, had retired to Bournemouth and one summer we stayed overnight at their house. I must have been four or five and already possessed a vivid imagination. In the middle of the night, I had to tiptoe across an unfamiliar landing to the lavatory – never toilet because my mother considered the term vulgar. Returning,

I closed the bedroom door as quietly as possible and revealed a large hairy wolf ready to pounce. I can't remember if I screamed or whether anybody came. Maybe my mother pointed out that the wolf was really a man's woollen winter dressing gown hanging on a hook; all of those details have been forgotten but I can still remember the nightmares.

Back home in Northampton, I slept in a tall wooden bed which had originally belonged to my father. The mattress and the springs were so old that they had sunk to form a hollow which fitted exactly around my small body. I felt safe nestling between the two hills on either side. However, the old-fashioned design left a large amount of space under the bed. By day, this space housed a box of favourite toys, but at night I never had the nerve to lift the white candlewick counterpane. I instinctively knew the wolves had set up camp there. The rules of engagement were simple: I was safe in bed, but they could pounce and catch me if I didn't run fast enough back from the loo – an acceptable abbreviation. On particularly dark nights, the wolves would emerge from their lair and dance round the room with their teeth glinting in the moonlight. I'd scream out and Mummy would come and reassure me:

'The wolves will not get you.'

She would lift the counterpane and show me.

'There's nothing there.'

It was easy for her to say – the wolves would disappear as soon as she'd open my bedroom door. But after she'd told me to 'sleep tight' and gone back to bed, they would rematerialise, slink back into the lair and an uneasy truce would be established.

Wolves did not have a monopoly on my fears. For a while in the sixties a 'cop killer' called Harry Roberts evaded the police by haunting my nightmares. If there was a strange-looking man drinking alone at the rugby club bar – where my father was treasurer – I would sidle up to one of my parents and whisper:

'THERE'S HARRY ROBERTS.' It must have been embarrassing for my parents, but in defence of my seven-year-old self, the rugby club did attract an odd crowd.

Fortunately, my fear of Harry Roberts was easy to cure. One night in 1966, I was allowed to stay up late to watch his capture on the news. I can still picture the small makeshift camp in the woods – the blanket strung between three trees and the discarded tin cans – but not where (except it was many miles from my home). I slept soundly that night.

Flushed by her success with Harry Roberts, my mother took me to London Zoo. I was softened up with lions, monkeys and possibly even a ride on an elephant. Next, she casually mentioned that they had wolves too. I can't remember what I was wearing but I can picture myself in an anorak so large it came down past my knees – 'you'll grow into it' – being taken to an enclosure hidden in some back alley of the Zoo. Did I actually look at the wolves? Perhaps I refused. Perhaps they were asleep in their den. Whatever happened next, the pack under my bed would not be exorcised so easily.

At that age it was impossible to believe I would ever reach ten; but I did. I even turned eighteen and left home for university, where I studied Politics and Sociology. After graduating, I got a job first at BRMB Radio in Birmingham (in the newsroom) and then Essex Radio in Southend (as a presenter and producer) and Radio Mercury in Crawley (where I rose to become deputy programme controller). My nightmares about wolves had long since ended, but if they appeared on TV they would still make me feel uneasy and I would switch channels. I still wanted a dog, but I was far too practical. I had a career to pursue. Who would walk the dog? Would it be fair to leave it alone while I worked? I couldn't be tied down by such responsibilities.

At thirty, I fell in love with Thom and we talked about getting a dog together. However, for the first four and a half years, he lived in Germany and I lived in Hurstpierpoint (a small Sussex village). In the spring of 1995, Thom finally moved over to England with plans to set up an interior design company. However, six months later, he fell ill. All our plans for dog-owning were put on hold, while we concentrated on getting him better. He spent months in hospital first in England and then in Germany and I spent a lot of time flying backwards and forwards between the two countries. I loved Thom with a passion that sometimes terrified me, so when he died, on 9 March 1997, I was completely inconsolable.

I moved into the office he'd created in our spare room, but I couldn't stop the computer from still sending faxes from Andrew Marshall and Thom Hartwig. As far as Microsoft Word was concerned, he was immortal. I tried various strategies to cope with my bereavement but three different counsellors did not shift it. Two short-term relationships made me feel worse, not better. I had just turned forty. My regular sources of income – being Agony Uncle for Live TV and writing a column for the *Independent* newspaper – were both terminated. My grief was further isolating me and many of Thom and my couple friendships had just withered away.

Approaching the Millennium, something had to change but what?

PART ONE

The Puppy Years

Yesterday, I flew to Germany for Thom's father's eightieth birthday celebrations. Over the past two and a half years, I've been over three times to visit his parents and his mother regularly calls to check how I'm doing. We've tried to look after each other and it certainly helps me to talk to people who loved Thom and miss him as much as I do.

Erwin was thrilled that I could make his birthday supper and despite having to retire somewhere quiet for a weep, I was pleased to be there too. Looking round the family lunch table at Thom's parents, brother, nephews, aunts and uncles, I felt a warm glow which could not entirely be put down to the champagne, venison and strudel. Despite our different cultures and my shaky German, I felt truly included. But I couldn't help feeling, without Thom beside me, I no longer truly belonged to this family. As I said my goodbyes, Ursula hugged me and pulled me closer:

'Don't be alone.'

If an elderly woman, so crippled with arthritis that she can barely leave her apartment, could move on – what is holding me back?

— ✄✄ —

I have been staying with Jürgen and Gabi, Thom's brother and sister-in-law, just outside Frankfurt. Jürgen had to work and Gabi was busy preparing for Christmas Eve, Germany's main focus of the celebrations. Rather than being in the way, I decided to visit the city's modern art gallery. I borrowed a map, was given detailed instructions on how to navigate their train system and wrapped myself up against the gathering winter gloom.

Everything started fine. Line 8 – direction of Wiesbaden – arrived punctually. What else would you expect in Germany? However, once inside the carriage, I was confused by the train map, which looked like a child had thrown spaghetti at the wall. I couldn't find either Mülheim, where I'd boarded, or Konstablerwache, my destination. With little idea how long the journey would take, I settled down with my book. At each stop I glanced up and checked the station name, but as we crawled through the suburbs the storyline in my book became more and more gripping. I looked up so late at Konstablerwache the doors almost trapped my coat as I leapt on to the platform. Trying to work out which exit to use, I realised I was holding my book, my street map of Frankfurt, but only one glove. I'd left the other one, along with the Kangol rapper-style hat I'd bought especially for the trip, on the carriage seat opposite me. Outside the blackness had turned to sleet, and I trudged around the corner to Museum für Moderne Künst Frankfurt am Main cursing both my forgetfulness and my lack of hair.

The gallery boasted a good collection of Andy Warhol hand-drawn male nudes, a Hockney, Lichtensteins and a fascinating collection of Japanese photography. Two hours later, I emerged back into the cold. Found Stadtbahn 8 from the multitude of options – this time heading towards Hanau – and opened my book again. On the return journey I had a good idea how long it would take and had finally worked out the train map, so I could concentrate on my book. It was only as the train pulled into Mülheim that I looked round the carriage. I had begun to mentally prepare for the unprotected tramp through the snow when I suddenly spied one black hat and one grey glove on the seat opposite me! Many trains must ply that route – and, of course, there are many carriages – but by some strange coincidence I'd returned to exactly the same spot and my belongings were waiting for me. Lost and found. Returning much warmer to Jürgen and Gabi, I felt like I was in a waking dream. Somewhere in these last two days, and in that slightly surreal experience, is a profound truth – all I've got to do now is unravel it.

Boxing Day, Sunday 26 December

I spent a quiet companionable Christmas with my two closest friends: Gary, whom I met at university and accompanied me to Sitges, where I first met Thom ten years ago and my best friend Kate, who had been Agony Aunt to my Agony Uncle on a cable TV station and was a huge support while Thom was ill and in the first difficult months after his death.

This morning, Gary opted for a lie-in but Kate needed a break from rich food and TV, so I suggested a walk along Brighton seafront. Despite being a bright morning, the only people at Hove lawns were the families of children with new bikes and the occasional dog walkers. Kate and I linked arms and we took stock of the past year. She told me about the ashes of her long-term relationship and I shared my hat and glove story.

'Have you any idea what it means?' I asked. We stood at the railings and looked out over the choppy seas.

'Everything happens for a reason,' she replied, 'but what?'

'All my life, like the Frankfurt train system, is a circle?' I asked – trying to push away the lyrics to a seventies pop song by The New Seekers.

'How's about this? You found your new hat and your glove, because you opened your eyes and looked around.'

I nodded.

'Well, that's it. We spend too much time with our nose buried in old scripts. Look around. The last time, what you needed the most – your hat and glove against the cold – was right there waiting for you. What do you want most now?'

'I don't want to be alone any more,' I replied, almost without thinking.

We turned around and looked over the esplanade. An elderly man was throwing a ball for an equally old Golden Retriever. The dog ran stiffly to fetch the blue ball, lolloped back, dropped the ball at his master's feet and started barking wildly.

— ✤ —

Four months after Thom had died, I had met Tyson – not so much a dog, more a force of nature. I'd been visiting friends and he kept shoving his hairy black nose into my hands and rubbing against my legs like a cat. In fact, he made such a fuss my friends suggested that I took Tyson home with me. I laughed but offered to look after him when they went on holiday. It was perhaps the lowest point of my bereavement and Tyson's visit, back in July 1997, had proved a turning point. He was an unusual combination of Parson Jack Russell and Black Labrador, and even with two long walks a day he was still full of energy. He had such an unusual face that strangers would stop and talk to us. While my friends peered at me anxiously – as if bereavement was some kind of dance where it was imperative to master all the steps – out dog-walking, I was no longer a grieving widower but just 'Tyson's owner'. His visit worked a miracle. The house no longer felt empty and some of his exuberance had rubbed off on me – along with lots of black hairs and his fleas!

'I'd like to get a dog of my own.' I'd finally said it aloud.

'So what's stopping you?' Kate was watching the teenage couple in one of the seafront shelters. He had his right arm round her shoulders and was using his left hand to push strands of blonde hair away from her face. They kissed.

'Is this the right time?' I asked.

'Don't wait around for your real life to start.'

Monday 3 January 2000

With New Year's Day falling on a Saturday, I had Sunday and a bank holiday Monday to recover from partying from one millennium into another. The hype had suggested that we'd finally come round from our hangovers to find the collapse of the banking system and planes falling from the sky because computers could not cope with the transformation from 1999 to 2000. However, the new millennium seemed remarkably similar to the last one. I went up to my office, opened my diary and began to write:

Every time I confess my New Year's resolution is to become a dog owner the responses, in order of popularity, are:

1. *It's a huge responsibility.*
2. *It's a terrible tie.*
3. *You don't know what you're taking on.*

Maybe it would be less controversial if my resolution had been to try crack cocaine. I expect I'd receive fewer warnings. So dogs are a tie and a responsibility. At the moment I'm entirely free to do exactly as I please. I can stay out all night and nobody cares. I can stay in bed all day and nobody moans. Don't fancy working today? No problem. I just don't phone anybody, and don't sell a newspaper or magazine article. My problem is not having *enough* ties or responsibilities. I tried to see my resolution from all the angles.

1. *What if I move somewhere without a garden (because I don't know if I can still live in this house without Thom)?*

2. *What if I suddenly land a full-time job (because I certainly need the money)?*

3. *What if I fall in love with someone who owns a cat (because my last boyfriend had been allergic to pet hairs)?*

4. *What if Hollywood calls to buy my film script and I have to hop on the next plane?*

OK, the last item is particularly unlikely, but I do need to be flexible – ready to take on board whatever direction my life is going to take next – and how flexible can you be with a dog in tow? Perhaps the doubters are right, I don't know what it's like to own a dog full-time. Unlike Tyson, I won't be able to return it.

Except it's not just a new year but a whole new millennium and finally it's truth time: these are all excuses to stay exactly where I am. So on 3 January I have finally decided:

I WANT A PUPPY.

After I finished typing this entry. I start dancing round the house like a demented Kylie Minogue, singing 'I want a puppy… puppy, puppy, puppy' to the tune of 'I Should Be So Lucky'.

I have finally gone mad.

Friday 7 January

I spent the day in London at the sales with Brandon. We had a short and painful affair last spring but now we are just 'friends'.

He suffers from multiple allergies and I should have known our relationship was not meant to be, when he told me:

'Of course we can have a dog but it would have to live outside in a run.'

Brandon is still prepared to be my style guru – a role Thom had performed – because I have no idea what to wear and left to my own devices I'd probably never go clothes shopping again. We trekked round Gap, H&M and Habitat before resting with espresso and *pains au chocolat*. Finally, I had the courage to tell him about my intended furry purchase. He had a different take:

'You want a dog because you want unconditional love.'

I never knew I had so many failings, but took comfort in also having bought a beautiful Linea black V-neck jumper – reduced by £10.

Brandon was tired of shopping, so he got a bus to go home and I went to Borders bookshop to look at their dog training section. After forty-five minutes flicking through various guides, I finally opted for *Complete Idiot's Guide to Choosing, Training, and Raising a Dog*, although I was almost put off the whole idea by one of the nuggets of information highlighted in the book:

'The fancy name for dogs is *Canis domesticus*, while wolves are *Canis lupus*. Although now considered two different species, based on their common ancestry, they can still interbreed.'

I shuddered and made a mental note to have my dog neutered.

— ⁂ —

On the train home, I faced the next difficult choice – what breed? My book catalogued the various vices, health problems and temperaments of hunters, herders, retrievers, fighters, rescuers and toy dogs – but I was totally perplexed. Surely there must be one just for me? Something manageable but with spirit, intelligent enough to be easily trained but not needing constant stimulation, neither a house dog nor one needing a garden the size of a prairie. Although the more I thought about it, the more I wanted just a dog – not a Labrador or a Golden Retriever or a Yorkshire Terrier, but a mutt. The book claimed pure breeds are predictable: chuck a ball into a pond for a retriever and you know happens next. However, life, as I've discovered, throws up some unpredictable turns. However much we believe it should be different, however much we rebel against the curveballs, we have no option but to take life as it is bowled. So I'd decided on a crossbreed, but how to find one?

When I got home I read the local advertising free sheet. There were plenty of pedigree puppies but mine was more likely to be the result of unbridled passion behind the park bushes than selective breeding. Healthier for the puppies, and certainly more fun for the parents. There must be hundreds of unwanted puppies that fitted the bill, especially after Christmas, but how to track them down?

My next door neighbours, Valerie and Michael, a couple in their mid-fifties whom I often turn to in a crisis, had a brainwave: the RSPCA.

Wednesday 12 January

The lady who answered the phone at the RSPCA was exceedingly vague – to the point of giving two addresses for rehoming centres. However, she did explain that I needed to visit to register. Hoping the signs I'd spotted, when taking the A27 to Lewes, might have been for the RSPCA, I set off full of excitement. Indeed, there was a sign to 'ANIMAL CENTRE' at the foot of the South Downs. I knew I was definitely heading in the right direction when I passed a man rather self-consciously walking a Weimaraner. They had all the awkwardness of a couple on a first date trying to simultaneously assess each other and enjoy themselves. The dog held itself a little too high while the man steadfastly avoided making eye contact with me.

As I pulled into the car park at Patcham, I had visions of playing with a swarm of adorable dogs while a kindly old RSPCA inspector chuckled and offered helpful hints. In the background, my imagination was playing sentimental music, as I coaxed a shy puppy centre stage. The internal orchestra had reached an emotional climax as I pushed open the front door, and then came to an abrupt stop.

There were more people waiting than in an NHS Accident and Emergency department during a winter flu epidemic. I almost expected a dog to be sleeping on a trolley in the corridor. The next shock was the chest-high reception counter. The message was clear – Keep Out. Four or five women were dealing with the throng of customers. The staff fitted into two categories: inept volunteers who cowered in the corner and handed out the wrong forms, and loud women who would have solved Third World debt before lunch if only they had not devoted themselves to animals. I was only too familiar with the latter. My mother had been a school games teacher with a voice that carried over four hockey pitches and never needed a whistle to referee.

Obediently, I joined one of the queues. In front of me, a distraught twenty-something woman was answering questions about her two cats. I had arrived too late to discover why she was forced to give them up, but from the tart expression on the RSPCA officer's face it was considered not good enough. All the cats' foibles, and by extension their owner's failings, were mercilessly exposed while the queue examined their shoes. Mine were well overdue their January polish.

Finally, one of the volunteers, probably the one who gave out directions, handed over a form for a home visit. I needed one of these before they would even consider showing me a dog. The questions were incredibly detailed. 'Which vet are you going to register with?' 'Who will look after the animal when you are ill?' I doubted that '*I'll cross that bridge when I come to it*' would be an acceptable answer. Except, on second thoughts, if I lost the use of my legs and hands, Valerie and Michael could probably open a can of dog food. But did they need to sign an affidavit?

It was now the turn of an elderly man to entertain the queue. He had already completed his form, survived a home inspection and was finally ready to collect his new pet.

'I'm afraid you're too old for this cat,' the officer announced to the whole room.

I could picture her as a schoolgirl brandishing her hockey stick and charging. The opposing team would probably have quaked in a similar way to the elderly man beside me. But to his credit, he rallied slightly:

'But we've had cats all our lives.'

'This one is really only a kitten – too much for you.' She clobbered him round the ankles.

'Perhaps I could come through and see it again.'

I was beginning to think it would be easier to adopt a child as a single gay man than rescue a dog.

When I reached the front of the queue, being no fool, I gave my form to one of the inadequate volunteers. I was a little bit anxious over the question about gardens. I had one – hurrah – so no problem there. Except there was a minimum height requirement for the fence: four feet at the lowest point and no cheating. To be honest, I'm not certain how big it is – I've never measured it. So I decided to be bold and write down four feet. I could always rectify it.

My volunteer had to ask one of the Gruppenführers what happened next, so there was another wait. Finally, she found the name of my local home visitor and wrote it, along with her telephone number, on my form.

I was about to leave but she stopped me:

'By the way, you could speak to her now,' she said and pointed to a moderately scary woman behind the counter. I joined her queue. It was just as well I didn't phone because she took one look at my form:

'Where did she get that number from − it's not even close − and you don't spell Pauline with two "e"s.' She made a ticking noise between her teeth.

'Is this all correct?' She gave me a withering look and pointed to the question about the fence.

I immediately confessed everything:

'It's about three feet, could be four, but there's a wood behind, so it's not dangerous, you see…' I babbled to a stop. '…the fence,' I finally finished in case there was any confusion.

Pauline was not a woman who got confused. She ploughed on:

'Have you ever had a dog before?'

'No, but…' How can you explain the deep longing, the birthday candles, the lifetime spent waiting?

'A puppy.' She looked down at the form again. 'Do you know what you're taking on?'

I would have liked to reply: does anybody ever know? Does life hold any certainties? But I knew Pauline would not be interested in a philosophical debate. I could have been assertive and told her we could discuss this in private at my home visit. However, I'd reverted to being seven years old and the only refuge at that age is silence.

'I could do a home visit in two days' time,' she said.

I nodded.

As I drove out of the car park, the prospective owner whom I'd spotted on my arrival was now walking a three-legged Boxer dog. I looked at him with new respect. He had been tested and risen to the challenge; he had been approved.

Friday 14 January

After a disturbed night filled with visions of Pauline casting me into outer darkness, I got up early to make another tour of the garden and tried to prepare my defence. Unfortunately, my case was severely compromised by the previous owners who had cut a hole in the fence to allow their children easy access to the thicket behind the house. Up to now, I'd had no reason to close the gap. Trees and brambles had grown closely enough to put off any opportunist burglars and I enjoyed the occasional wildlife visitor. One morning, I came down to the kitchen and was startled to see a deer drinking from my pond. On another occasion, I'd watched a litter of fox cubs playing on the lawn.

By the time Tyson came to visit, the pond had been turned into a flower bed, so there was no danger of any puppy drowning. See, I am beginning to think like a respectable dog owner. I know just how many scrapes a dog can get himself into. Once, I took Tyson over to a friend who had a swimming pool. Being the sort of dog whose mission is to explore, Tyson decided to test whether the pool cover could take his weight. As it was a flimsy plastic affair, designed to keep leaves out and heat in, Tyson sank slowly into the water and had to be dragged out by the scruff of his neck. For a second he looked a bit shocked, but then set off to discover how absorbent their white thick-pile carpet could be.

Fortunately, I headed him off before any lasting damage could be done.

The gap in my fence had not proved a problem with Tyson.

'No, Tyson,' I had said firmly – using the tone my mother would use to control a class of unruly teenagers – as he sniffed his escape route.

He had just finished charging around the house, so I was not feeling particularly confident. However, miraculously, Tyson obeyed and we set up an understanding. He never went through the gap. OK, I'll be honest, he followed the rules, except when the temptation was just too huge – like when I'd had a heavy night and he needed to be let out in the morning but instead of coming back to the bedroom got through the forbidden gap and escaped into the neighbourhood. I was woken by a ring of the doorbell and found the woman across the road holding an apologetic-looking dog by the collar.

'I think he's staying with you.'

After that, I had accepted my limitations in controlling Tyson, and Tyson accepted my limitations of his territory. A good English compromise.

— ❧ —

It was hard to settle down to any work that morning. Every noise was Pauline's car pulling up outside. In fact, I felt so tuned into her movements, I sensed her climbing into the car three villages away. When the doorbell finally rang, she was somehow smaller than the woman who had chased me through my nightmares. There was even something approaching a smile on her lips.

'Good morning.' I felt ashamed that I could ever have been frightened of anyone called Pauline.

She refused my offer of a coffee and asked for my form.

'You've never had a dog before,' she said icily, scanning my details.

I explained about looking after Tyson and how he had become my official 'god dog'. I thought it sounded better than claiming I was his godfather, although Tyson would have been delighted to find a tasty horse's head in my bed. I showed her a framed photo of Tyson and me and Pauline softened. We headed for the garden. She paced around like a general inspecting troops. Through her eyes, I knew my fence was hardly three feet tall. But in my defence, m'lud, if a dog is really determined to escape it will take a lot more than four feet to stop them. At least, near to my house, there are no main roads.

'I'm having the gap closed up,' I called out.

'What gap?' She peered at the wilderness behind my garden. The bushes had almost totally obscured the hole.

Oops, I should have kept my mouth shut.

'Here.' I pointed it out, and tried to distract my tongue from bringing up the dreaded four-foot rule by remembering the names of all my form mistresses and masters from five to eighteen.

Back in the kitchen, Pauline looked at my form again and muttered:

'Everything seems to be in order. Have the gap closed up and I will approve you.'

'Fine, I was going to do that anyway.'

'But I'll need to come back to check.'

'You don't trust me?'

She gave me the sort of look my mother would have reserved for pupils claiming to have accidentally forgotten their gym kit:

'Give me a call when it's done.'

So I had survived, hurrah! However, it would be at least a week before the local odd job man could come to secure the garden.

It feels like for ever.

Saturday 22 January

I was so pleased with the new fencing that I made several extra trips round the garden to admire the neat handiwork. Pauline from the RSPCA was satisfied too and took out her pen to complete my home visit form. While I tried to chat naturally about my dog-sitting experiences with Tyson, she would seize on a particular comment and start scribbling. My brain was trying to perform three tasks at once: read her handwriting, edit out Tyson's most terrible escapades and send out properly formed sentences. Finally, she finished her inquisition and I was handed back the form:

'Take this down to the centre and they will take you through to look at the dogs.'

Too shocked that I had finally made the grade to read her comments. I babbled:

'Have you got any puppies at the moment?'

'Don't know, haven't been down there since Thursday.'

My brain might have been grappling with the idea of being allowed past the front desk, but before Pauline left I really should check her report before it was too late to complain. In the comments box she had written: 'nice home'. I felt as pleased as a six-year-old who had clocked up three 'goods' in a row in their workbook and was entitled to a red star from Mrs Ward.

'Thank you.'

'Just one piece of advice, don't take the first puppy you see, unless it is what you want.'

I was supposed to be waiting in for a phone call from the British psychotherapist Susie Orbach – best known for treating Princess Diana. I was due to interview her about her book, *The Impossibility of Sex*, for a magazine article. The last thing I wanted to talk about was penises, vaginas and all that stuff; I wanted to look at puppies.

Pauline had hardly left the end of my road before I leapt in the car. At the roundabout by the church, I remembered my mobile phone and turned back again, although who knows what Susie Orbach would make of an interview surrounded by barking dogs.

The sanctuary was much quieter this time round. No queue. Wordlessly, I handed over my form to the grim-faced receptionist. I still felt like I'd pushed a note at the teller in the bank: 'I've got a gun, hand over the money or I'll shoot'. Instead of pressing an alarm, she smiled. Somehow, I must have graduated from 'reckless – most likely to cause trouble' to 'responsible potential adopter'. Perhaps she too had been impressed by 'nice home' on my form.

'If you'd like to walk through to the kennels and have a look around. See anything you're interested in, come back and I'll tell you all I know about it. There's one puppy, Dasher, a Collie cross, and some other younger dogs which might take your fancy.'

It was easy to find the kennels. I just followed the frantic barking. With the annual campaign that a dog was for life, not just for Christmas, I had expected the centre to be full of unwanted presents, so I was surprised to find about half of the thirty-odd runs empty. Each dog had his or her name and a short biography posted on the door. Unfortunately, my view of Dasher was completely blocked by a mother, father and two children. From the little girl's excited squeals, he must have been gorgeous. I had to resist an urge to behave like a bargain hunter at the January sales and dive between their legs. I hadn't jumped through all the RSPCA hoops to watch my puppy being stolen.

I paced the narrow walkway between the rest of the runs, looking at the remaining dogs. I had imagined smaller dogs were easier to control, yet while an Alsatian stared passively through the bars, a tiny Jack Russell which never stopped barking leapt three feet in the air over and over again. With Tyson being half Jack Russell ancestry, I had considered the breed as a possibility but made a quick mental note to think again. I went back to the friendly-looking Alsatian and smiled at him. 'Lure' seemed docile but his biography described him as 'only for an experienced owner'. Choosing a dog was more complicated than I had imagined.

The family had left Dasher's run, but when I went over there was no sign of him. I guessed that auditioning must be very wearing and the star had retreated to his kennel. I walked up and down past all the dogs a couple of times and tried to screw up my courage to ask for help. The door to the site office was ajar. Nobody was in there, so I could glance at their instructions for who could walk which dogs. Lure was categorised as 'staff only'. I returned to Dasher's run, still no sign. Really, I should speak to someone, but I didn't want to be any trouble. Finally, I returned to the front desk, where I expected to find the family completing Dasher's ownership papers – at least I could give them a sour look. However, the officer on the front desk was alone and only too happy to give out information about the puppy. Dasher was the oldest boy from a litter of six who arrived at the centre just before Christmas. The owner had been thinking of giving them away, but the RSPCA considered this inadvisable. So the puppies were split into two groups of three and fostered by the staff until they could be put up for adoption.

'He's ten weeks old. The mother was a Collie but we're not certain about the father. Collies are working dogs, so they're easy to train but need lots of stimulation.'

'What do you mean?' I asked.

'Walking is not enough, you need to provide activities like retrieving sticks, dog agility classes or Flyball.' I had no idea what the last could be, but decided it was wiser not to show too much ignorance. 'Let's go out and meet him,' she finished.

The officer unlocked the padlock on Dasher's run and made a gentle clicking noise. In the basket at the back of the kennel, two black ears pricked up. I was amazed that her signal could even be heard above the cacophony of barking. A black and white Border Collie, but with a short coat, leapt on a fluffy stuffed lion.

'This is his best friend,' explained the officer. 'He's already began to engage with toys, so he's going to be very intelligent.'

Dasher was so excited, he seemed able to move in three directions at the same time. His oversized paws scrabbled on the concrete as he charged around. How could anybody not instantly love him? But after all the lectures about being a responsible dog owner, I was trying to be rational. Would he grow up too big for the house? Could I cope with a clever hound? What personality traits had he inherited from his parents? What on earth breed had been the father?

My *Complete Idiot's Guide* sets out a lot of valuable tips on choosing a puppy. The author stresses the importance of assessing the litter hierarchy and grading them from leader of the pack to the shyest. Apparently, the first is in danger of becoming a tyrant and the latter of cowering in the corner. All very difficult when the litter has just one puppy left. I had studied the tests: uplift (picking the puppy up by its middle), flip-flop (what happens when you cradle it in your arms), back to earth (stroke it at least fifteen times to judge willingness to be handled). So, trying to look as if I knew what I was doing, Dasher and I started on the first test. I picked him up; skin-to-fur, we finally began to communicate and somehow I instantly knew he had the sweetest nature. Next, I swivelled him round in my arms; he instantly licked my face and I laughed. Perhaps choosing a puppy need not be such a serious business.

My book also recommends performing a wacky walk, fooling around like a monkey tapping two spoons together, and finally a crash test, which involves pretending that I've fallen and hurt my knee. These are supposed to test whether the puppy is Active (Top Dog or Next in Line), Neutral (Middleman) or Passive (Shy).

The author is American and my British middle-class reserve rules out her more bizarre tests. So I just placed Dasher back on the ground.

He would make a wonderful pet for someone, but am I the right owner? In all the pet rescue television programmes, the glowing new owners talk about instantly falling for their dog – some even claim the dog chose them. I told the officer I would think it over and get back to her.

Why can't I be spontaneous and know my own mind? Or am I just being sensible and taking Pauline's advice not too leap in too quickly?

— ❧ —

Yesterday evening, I had been to the cinema in Brighton – Johnny Depp in *Sleepy Hollow* – and picked up the local edition of the *Friday Ad*. In the dogs' section, I had ringed: 'For Sale Boarder [sic] Collie/Brittany Spaniel cross pups, fully vaccinated'. On my return home, with no message from Susie Orbach, I decided to phone and fix a viewing of these puppies too. Forty minutes later, I rang the doorbell of an ordinary bungalow in a neighbouring village. There was an explosion of barking and the sounds of dogs being locked away. Mr Foster, a grey-haired man in his sixties, answered and I was ushered into the kitchen. There were obviously three generations living in the house because I was joined by what I took to be his son and two grandchildren. All eyes were on me – particularly his granddaughter, who gave me a look normally only seen in documentaries where social workers are about to prise children from their mothers' arms.

The door from the conservatory to the kitchen was flung open and out poured a river of black and white fur. Once the barking had subsided and the mother expelled, I could make out two adorable puppies – a bitch and a dog. Both had the traditional Border Collie black and white markings but with a

Spaniel's ears. Most attractive of all, they had black spots on their legs and noses.

I picked up one of the puppies and was about to follow the tests laid out in my puppy training book, but Mr Foster handed me a towel:

'Put that on your knee.'

I looked down at my smart new trousers and designer sweatshirt. Perhaps I was not giving out the right message.

'You have owned a dog before?' he asked tentatively.

I changed the subject.

'It's an unusual combination. Did you choose it deliberately?'

'I thought the mother was safely in the conservatory. What I didn't know was that my neighbour's Spaniel had broken in.' He pointed to a snapshot of the father on the kitchen table and I recognised the same stockiness in the puppies.

'Can I have a closer look at their mother first?' All the dog books, and the *Friday Ad*, are firm about checking she appears 'healthy and of sound temperament'.

We walked into the garden and the mother started barking fiercely – not a good sign. But when I looked more closely at her stance, weight back on haunches, the dog body language seemed more defensive than aggressive.

'She was a rescue dog, doesn't like strangers,' Mr Foster explained.

'What's the father's personality like, beyond being a bit of an adventurer?'

'If you look quickly, you'll spot him. There, he's being taken on his afternoon walk.'

Across the field, behind the house, ran a dog which to my untutored eyes looked like a Springer Spaniel. He was a picture of health and vitality.

Back inside the kitchen, I put first one puppy and then the other on to my knee. They had been playing out in the garden, so I was soon muddy and covered in hairs. There had been six puppies in their litter, but these puppies were two weeks older than Dasher. Whether it was being twelve weeks or staying longer with their mother, both pups seemed much more confident. As I put each of them back on the floor, they wandered back over to Mr Foster's granddaughter for a cuddle. They were certainly used to being handled and would be no problem around children – both good signs. After half an hour playing in the kitchen, I was relaxed enough to ask for advice on the Collie temperament and the personality of each puppy. The granddaughter had lavished her attention equally, but I sensed this was a ruse.

'Bitches are more biddable,' explained Mr Foster and his granddaughter's shoulders relaxed ever so slightly. She had betrayed her favourite.

I put the dog puppy down and watched it wander round the kitchen. He stopped just by their white convector fan heater and looked over his shoulder directly into my eyes. What should I do?

I thought my indecision at the RSPCA rescue centre had something to do with having a choice of only one puppy. The dog runs, with their locks, had the air of East Berlin – before the wall came down – which had not been helped by Pauline's casual remark:

'I'll see you again – at the follow-up home visit.'

A picture of her in an East German Stasi uniform had instantly sprung into my head.

In the West, we are constantly told: choice is good. I had seen three adorable puppies, all guaranteed to send the Pet Rescue phonelines into meltdown, but I was still dithering and more confused than before.

Finally, I told Mr Foster I would think about it. After all, I had waited forty years so there was no rush.

— ❧ —

When I finally spoke to Susie Orbach, it was difficult to tussle with her theory that the better you know somebody, the harder it is to be intimate. Half my brain was wondering if the more you know about puppies, the harder it is to choose. Perhaps I should trust my gut instinct – whatever that is.

After finishing the interview, I popped next door to talk my dilemma over with Valerie and Michael, who've had Dalmatians since they got married over thirty years ago. Our relationship is stronger than just neighbours. They were a great support when Thom was very ill, always anxious for the next bulletin about his health, and were two of the few people from whom he did not hide the full extent of his problems. It was good to sit at their kitchen table, with a cup of coffee, and discuss the pros and cons of each dog. Lily – their latest Dalmatian – sat beside Valerie, intently following our conversation.

'Perhaps one of the dogs will speak to you,' Valerie explained. 'When we went to the animal sanctuary to inspect Lily, I told Michael we wouldn't have her if she was an ugly dog and there she was, with all her spots in the wrong place. But we took her out for a walk, and by the time we'd returned the staff had filled out all the paperwork. I believe we were fated to rescue her. Despite her fear of other dogs, and her tendency to run home alone, we love her dearly.'

—— ✺ ——

In the evening, I drove up to London to visit a friend. Normally, I would have listened to the radio, but my head was too full for even music. However, by the time I reached Steve Leder's house, I had made a decision: if I wasn't sure it was probably because I hadn't met the right dog. I would wait.

So we drank beer, chatted over Steve's house-moving problems and generally chilled out. Maybe it was the alcohol, or maybe sleeping in a strange bed, but my dreams were full of one particular puppy. I kept returning to Mr Foster's kitchen and the intelligent, over-the-shoulders stare from the male puppy. His eyes seemed to bore through the mists of sleep and I found myself imagining him in the car, driving away from Henfield. He whimpered slightly about leaving his mother, but was really more excited about his new life. Next, I pictured myself taking him for walks around the village. A few moments later, he was at the bottom of my garden, where he fixed me with another meaningful stare. It seemed to say:

'Don't be surprised to find me in your garden, I belong here.'

In the next subliminal message the puppy was curled up at my feet while I watched *Coronation Street*. I would lean down to tickle him and he would roll over to expose his white warm tummy.

Monday 24 January

Almost forty-eight hours after viewing the Border Collie/Brittany Spaniel puppy and my strange dream, I was still convinced he *had* spoken to me. I'd planned to wait till 9 a.m. before phoning Mr Foster, but by 8.50 nerves got the better of me. Pushing down a fear that someone else had already bought him, I phoned and said as nonchalantly as possible:

'I've decided I'd like to take your male puppy, please.'

I become terribly polite when nervous. Once when I was walking back to my hotel in Manchester, through what I later learned was the red light district, I was approached by a street walker. 'No, thank you,' I replied as if the vicar had offered me a second slice of Battenberg cake.

'You do realise the problems, don't you?' Mr Foster replied.

'In what way?' I thought he was referring to breaking the news to his granddaughter.

'Puppies, they are a lot of work.'

'Of course,' I replied a little more forcefully than I felt.

Surprisingly, he backed down:

'That's OK then.'

I fixed to visit at lunchtime and leave a deposit, but we agreed I would not collect the puppy until Friday. Partly because I had a full day's training course at Relate (the UK's largest couple counselling charity) on Thursday, but mainly because I needed time to prepare, mentally and practically (purchase basket, food, lead, etc.).

I took Valerie on the visit. Partly for a second opinion and partly to reassure Mr Foster that even if I was not the ideal owner, there would be a safe pair of hands next door. In the car over to Henfield, Valerie asked what I planned to call my puppy.

'I've always thought that dogs should have doggy names, rather than human ones.' I tried to tread carefully because before Lily, the Dalmatian, there had been Daphne and Deirdre. 'I don't want to shout out his name and have half the male population of Hurstpierpoint turning round.'

It is not just human names that cause problems. My niece, who was then nine, phoned to tell me they were the proud owners of a black Labrador puppy. 'What's it called?' I asked, and she replied: 'Saddo.' What had this dog done to be saddled with a name like that? So I double-checked: 'Saddo?' 'No,' she replied, annoyed, 'Saddo.' We went back and forth like that until I realised she meant Shadow! Apparently, the children had wanted to call him 'Blackie' but my sister had decreed it non-PC.

'So, what have you decided?' Valerie interrupted my thoughts.

'Bonzo – short for Bonzo Dog Doo-Dah Band.' They had featured weekly in my favourite TV show as a kid: *Do Not Adjust Your Set*.

Valerie was very polite and said nothing.

Maybe she was right – perhaps Bonzo did not suit my puppy. But I didn't worry. He'd found a way of communicating that we belonged together, perhaps he'd also tell me his name.

Once again we were greeted by riotous barking, although the mother dog was not so distrustful of Valerie as she was of me. Watching the puppies play tag and tumble in the hallway, it was clear that the larger bitch was the boss. On one occasion Mr Foster had to separate them when she became too rough-house. However, the dog puppy gave as good as he got. I had told Valerie to be frank if she saw any defects or had any doubts about him.

Fortunately, she was enchanted and I think her presence reassured Mr Foster.

'I'd been thinking of keeping him,' he said, 'but I'm sure that Lady here will make a fine companion.' He stroked the bitch puppy wistfully.

Before he could change his mind, I handed over £50, as a deposit, and a couple of Thom's old hand towels. I reasoned that if they were left in Bonzo or whatever-his-name's basket, by the end of the week they would be covered with familiar smells and help the transition to his new home.

Mr Foster looked a bit doubtful but humoured my attempts at dog psychology. He disappeared off to find some paper to write me a receipt and within two seconds of his back being turned, the bitch leapt on his slippers and started gleefully ripping them apart. I winced: a foretaste of what to expect?

In the car home, Valerie is so full of praise for my puppy that if I change my mind I think she might be tempted to buy him herself.

Wednesday 26 January

The only way of controlling my excitement about getting Bonzo – still working name only – was to start the preparations. So, progress on my magazine article has been slow. I have decided that the dog's den will be in what Thom used to call the 'outhouse' – the utility room that had been built on to the side of the kitchen. It provides access to the back garden and, via a passageway between the garage and the house, to the road. After a walk, Bonzo and I could enter via the outhouse and avoid muddy paws on my pale carpets. The room houses a washing machine, tumble drier and a second fridge for drinks but has become a general dumping ground.

Almost three years after Thom's death, there are still a box of quarry tiles by the back doorstep (that he had bought when he was thinking of replacing the floor of the outhouse) and a jar of 'slug death' on the fridge (that he used to scatter most nights on the patio). I moved them into the garage and added them to the pile of boxes that he'd brought over from Germany but had never got round to unpacking (and I didn't have the heart to open).

It was only after I'd cleared the outhouse that I spotted a problem: old nails sticking out from the brick walls at puppy height. The previous owners had used them to secure fake pine slats – the seventies Scandic sauna look. (Thom had torn them down because it offended his sense of style, but he had become too ill to finish the job.) I tracked down his tool box from the garage. Although hopeless at DIY, I made a half-hearted attempt at pulling the nails out with a pair of pliers. I needed a Plan B, so I did what I've always done since Thom died, I called round to Michael next door and asked for his advice. To be honest, I hoped he might do the job for me.

However, Michael was too busy replacing fence panels after the Christmas storms for anything beyond a lend of the right tool and a quick demonstration of how to lever rather than pull. With images of a bloodied hound to bolster my resolve, I returned to the outhouse. Amazingly, with the right tool and the right technique, I made light work of what had seemed an impossible job. Perhaps I can hack the single life after all.

I had been planning to buy a new basket but Valerie warned me the puppy would just chew it to pieces. So she let me have one of her doggy cast-offs, which beyond a few teeth marks was as good as new, and a pile of old blankets. Taking the blankets home, I was overcome by a wave of nostalgia. The fifties style with a satin edging was just like my childhood comforter. Like in the *Peanuts* cartoon, I would suck my thumb and drag the blanket behind me. For a few seconds, I was seven years old again and blowing out the candles on my birthday cake.

From the pet shop in the village, I purchased the same puppy food that Mr Foster had been using: Hill's Science Plan. Also, a soft vinyl collar, matching blue lead, a twisted latex two-knot chew (small) and a bouncy toy. The only thing missing was a name identification tag – but what name? Not Bonzo; too stupid for such an intelligent face. Mr Foster had been planning to call him Peanut, which appears on his vet inoculation record. But that did not feel right either.

Years ago, when I hosted a daily radio show, one of my regular guests was a numerologist who claimed to be able to predict my listeners' future by a special number derived from their names. I challenged her: how could our destiny be shaped by the whim of our parents? She replied that our mothers and fathers *think* they choose but really our names are whispered in their ears by some greater force. What utter nonsense, I'd thought.

However, on my way up to the village, the name 'Flash' had popped into my head. I could rationalise the choice by claiming it was inspired by the flash of white fur round his neck or the speed with which I expected him to flash across the fields behind my house, but by the time I reached the shop I *knew* my puppy's name was 'Flash'.

'What name?' the man behind the counter asked.

'Flash.' It sounded good out loud too.

In a mini-christening ceremony, he etched 'Flash' onto one side of a small disc and my telephone number on the other.

Friday 28 January

I had persuaded Valerie to drive me over to Henfield to collect Flash. She must have expected the worst because she had covered the front seat and footwell of her car with old blankets. I was strangely quiet on the journey over there; it might have been last minute jitters but a gorgon of emotions had knotted themselves round my throat. I had waited so many years, but all I could do was stare blankly at the passing fields. It was Valerie who broke the silence:

'What are you going to call him?'

'Flash.'

'Much better name.'

When Valerie had collected her first puppy from Milton Keynes, she had asked the breeder not to feed her before such a long journey. Unfortunately, the breeder had ignored her request and the motion of the car had made the puppy sick all over Valerie. Therefore, we were deliberately picking up Flash – yes, that name feels right – before he had eaten his lunch. I counted off the landmarks: Henfield town centre, Somerfield, turn right at the roundabout past the old converted schoolhouse. I was going to be a dog owner.

There are few days when you know that your life is going to change for ever.

I took a deep breath.

— ❧❧ —

At Mr Foster's bungalow, there seemed less barking than before. When he opened the door, there was just Flash and his mother.

His advert had generated one last call: they'd liked the bitch and he'd decided to be practical and let her go. Flash must have missed his sister because he was delighted to find someone new to play with. He tugged at my sleeve and mouthed my arm with his sharp puppy teeth. I rolled him over on the hall carpet, he struggled away and then flung himself at me with renewed vigour. As a sort of passing out ceremony, I gently fastened his new blue collar round his neck. He gave it a good sniff but seemed unconcerned. The last member of the litter was ready to leave home. I handed over the other £50 and I was given a blue bone toy that Flash liked and the blankets I'd left in his basket.

How had Mr Foster taken his final farewell? I don't know. I was too busy trying to reassure Flash. Later, Valerie told me, he'd whispered in Flash's ear:

'Give him plenty of cuddles, he likes cuddles.'

My puppy training book suggested taking a box – apparently, the confined space provides an illusion of security – and choosing a classical music radio station for the journey home. I had brought a fold-down plastic crate normally used for laundry, but was too self-conscious to suggest Classic FM to Valerie. Thankfully, it was only a short journey, because Flash constantly whined or struggled. When he was up in my arms he wanted to be in the box on the floor, and vice versa.

'We'll soon be there,' cooed Valerie to Flash.

'You're off to start an exciting new life,' I rather self-consciously joined in.

Within two minutes of dog ownership I was talking to an animal and expecting it to understand.

On arrival back home, we entered by the back door – straight into the outhouse. To ensure a warm welcome, I'd brought the convector heater down from my office. The portable radio from the bathroom was playing Classic FM. I was determined not to repeat my mistakes with Tyson. The plan had been for him to sleep in the outhouse and to retire there whenever I went out. However, when his owners had dropped him off, Tyson entered through the front door. He tore round the house, drank from the toilet, and generally caused havoc while I sat quietly in the living room waiting for him to calm down. Eventually, he had, literally, run out of energy and settled by my feet while I watched TV. The only part of the house he had not explored was the outhouse. When I was ready to go off to the cinema and led him into his temporary den, he must have seen it as punishment. On our return, my friend was surprised to find the lights on in the living room. I reassured him they were just security lights on a timer.

'But I can see people sitting on your sofa, watching your TV,' he insisted.

'Impossible.' I locked the car and gingerly crept up the drive. Was I being burgled by someone who never missed an episode of their favourite soap?

I quietly turned the key in the lock and slipped into the living room. Instead of a ransacked living/dining room, I found Michael and Valerie with Tyson stretched out at their feet.

'He was making such a terrible noise, we just couldn't leave him,' explained Valerie.

'We had a call from your other neighbour, who thought a dog had got locked in your garage,' added Michael. Having a spare set of keys, they had let themselves in. I thanked them for their kindness and gave Tyson a filthy look but he just curled into a ball by the radiator and went back to sleep.

From that moment on Tyson only used the outhouse as a shortcut to the garden or to empty his supper bowl.

My training book claimed it takes a puppy an hour to sniff round even a small room and said to allow plenty of time to explore. Flash sniffed the warm air, cocked an ear at the classical music and promptly took a dump in the middle of his carefully prepared new room. Maybe the whimpers in the car had not been caused by leaving home but crossed legs?

Valerie, and Michael, who'd appeared to look at the new arrival, tried not to laugh and tactfully withdrew to let us bond. I cleared up the mess, measured out Flash's midday meal and filled his new shining metal drinking bowl. Eighty ounces seemed a lot of food. Perhaps Mr Foster said eighty grams, but I couldn't remember where I had left his instructions.

Flash took one look at his lunch and backed off.

'But it's your favourite,' I told him.

Perhaps I'd opened the packet in a different way from Mr Foster and confused Flash?

I picked up a handful of the dried pellets and showed him. Flash immediately started eating from my hand and gave my fingers a good licking when he finished. I tried to introduce him to his metal bowl again. I gently pushed his nose down, but he backed off almost immediately. Could he have been spooked by his own reflection or was it a mistake trying to force him?

So Flash ate most of his first meal from my hand or from the floor. I don't think it was nerves, more likely I should have given him eighty grams because after a while he lost interest.

I sat on the back step and fixed his new name tag on to his collar, something I hadn't liked to do at Mr Foster's. I felt guilty enough about taking away his last puppy without admitting to changing his name too.

Next on the puppy training agenda was toilet training. After every meal, I was supposed to take him out to a chosen spot in the garden and tell him to 'get busy'. I put on my wellington boots and marched down to a tree at the bottom of the garden. Flash stood on the steps down from the patio and watched me. Here was our first important Master/Puppy moment. Would he come to his name?

'Flash!' I called in the *delighted* tones recommended in the books.

I had his attention.

'Flash!' I leaned forward encouragingly and miraculously, he came running; lots of praise, hugs and 'good boys'.

In fact, he came so quickly it was like he already knew his name; had always known he was a 'Flash' and perhaps even whispered it in my ear. He was excited not because I'd praised him, but because he'd completed the first bit of dog-to-master training: let them know your name.

After a quick sniff round, especially at the gap which had been closed by appointment to the RSPCA and the path beaten through the grass by the neighbourhood cats, Flash crouched down. Success. Except I'd chosen a tree for him to anoint and he'd preferred the middle of the lawn. Had he given me Master/ Puppy lesson number two? You can train a dog to obey but only up to a certain point.

When my house was extended, the original back doorstep had been incorporated into the outhouse. I decided to return here and invite Flash on to my lap. Being so small, he had trouble making it up but with a helping hand hauled himself up and settled down. If dogs could sigh, that would have been the sound Flash made as he drifted off to puppy nirvana. I opened my newspaper and quietly caught up with the news. Even the disruption caused by turning pages hardly ruffled the surface of his dreams. With Flash's warm body on my knee, and my fingers tracing the individual white hairs that splayed from his neck down into his black coat, a deep contentment seeped into my body too. I had not been aware just how stressed I had been.

— ❧ —

Suddenly Flash woke up. From deep inside his little body came pathetic whimpering noises.

'It's all right, don't worry,' I coaxed him.

He leapt down from my knee and went over to the door we'd entered about two hours beforehand.

'Do you want to go back in the car and back to return to your mummy?' I sympathised. 'But this is your home now.'

I took him back to the doorstep for another cuddle, but he wouldn't settle.

Two seconds later, he was off exploring the outhouse again and before I could stop him had taken another dump in the middle of the room! I chastised myself for not reading the signs and not putting newspaper down by the door to the garden. Puppy-owning was very complicated. Would I ever learn the signs?

His business complete, Flash settled back on to my knee, but I looked at my watch: half past two. I had promised to finish off my article on Divorce Busting by lunchtime. So I carried Flash upstairs and with a sleeping puppy on my knee started typing the final corrections.

Flash proved a slight handicap to efficient office practice as he kept twisting in his sleep and resting his nose on the space bar. Eventually, I finished and logged on to the email to dispatch my copy. The sound of the dial-up modem woke the puppy, so I put him down to wander round the room.

It was difficult to work and be vigilant, but I was determined to nip chewing in the bud. From a visit to my sister's house, I had learned just how much damage puppy teeth could do. I had been amazed that her puppy Shadow (or should that be Saddo?) was allowed to attack the sitting-room rug. He had been rather shocked when I stopped him, but had reluctantly obeyed. Later, Gayle explained that this had become Shadow's rug and that numerous household items had been surrendered to his teething. On the other hand, Shadow was banned from the study – in case he chewed through the computer cables. So a complicated system had emerged of items 'too good' to allow Shadow to destroy and those that were fair game. If I was confused, I'm sure the dog must have been. So when Flash stuck his nose in my wastepaper basket, I put on my firm schoolteacher voice – no guesses where I inherited that from – and told him:

'Flash, no.'

Amazingly, he looked up at me and stopped!

I praised him, made a fuss, and presented the latex chew from the pet shop.

To my untutored eyes this toy looked neither tasty nor fun, but the pet shop owner had recommended it and Flash settled down for a good gnaw.

I finished my emailing.

The author of my dog training book had done a survey with the dog owners at her classes:

'What do you do when your puppy is behaving himself and quietly lying at your feet or playing with his chew?'

The vast majority had replied that they would be grateful for the peace and catch up with their chores.

Wrong answer!

By only noticing a misbehaving puppy, apparently, they were falling into the worst dog training trap: negative attention. Even pushing a puppy away or shouting 'off' gives attention and even a simple glance can reward bad behaviour. Reading this section of the book totally blew my mind.

I am responsible for forming Flash's personality, whether he becomes model hound or terrible tyrant. Every mistake over the next few weeks could take a lifetime to unravel! Panic.

To reinforce Flash's good behaviour, I quickly left the computer and tickled his tummy. His fur was so incredibly silky, the black spots on his white muzzle gave him the air of a naughty schoolboy. All his nails were pink except the right front paw, where one of the black spots had landed and turned the nail black. Flash licked my hands, perhaps he would be a sweetheart after all.

As a first-time puppy owner, I am tempted to swallow my training manual whole. The advice on 'negative attention' seems very sensible – but some of the other advice might be a step too far. 'Stationing' is supposed to show Flash how to behave in each room of the house. My book advises that I should use his lead to tie him to some convenient piece of furniture.

When Flash finished with his chew, he started exploring my office. Of all the rooms in the house, it was most important for him to be well behaved here or I would never get any work done and we'd both be homeless. Would he look adorable at the other end of a piece of string? He certainly had the curly tail worn by all street dogs. I looked on anxiously as he tried to fit himself under the office couch. Should I take the manual's advice and tether him?

However, I needn't have worried. After another short play with his chew, Flash curled up under my desk and fell asleep. He had chosen his own place in the room.

— ❦ —

The first day of Flash's new life proved to be full of intimidating experiences for him. Although he would happily follow me round the first floor of the house, he was frightened of the stairs. Having previously lived in a bungalow, these were beyond his experience. However, with a little coaxing, Flash launched himself up on to the first step. His confidence grew as, with a little bottom wriggling, he hauled himself up. He soon got into a rhythm and made it up on to the landing. Coming down was much worse. He peered down from the top step all the way down to the bottom. Bravely, he started to slide slowly down one whole step, but lost his nerve and tried to scrabble back up again. So I plucked him up from no man's land and carried him down. Going outside was an even bigger challenge for both of us.

As Flash already had all his inoculations, he was ready to face the mean streets of Hurstpierpoint. We burst out of the house with Flash twisting in every direction. Within moments his intricate footwork had turned me into a maypole. I stopped and unwound myself, the lead and the dog. We started again – this time with Flash on my right-hand side – and after about three hundred yards and twenty corrections, he had grasped the central idea.

I relaxed but Flash froze. I followed his line of sight up the pavement. Ahead was a mother and two small children on their way home from school. Flash cowered behind my feet. The kids grabbed fistfuls of their mother's coat. With a little encouragement from me, and a lot more from the kids' mother, we brought the two parties forward to inspect each other.

'It's only a puppy,' the mother told her toddler, who was in tears by now.

His braver elder sister stuck out her hand and Flash gave her face a lick.

We had made our first friend.

Except Flash was overcome by his show of boldness and retreated back behind my feet. I wanted to comfort him – but my book explained this only reinforced nerves – so I stepped aside. It was the right choice because Flash trusted my judgement; with a burst more of curiosity than courage he started scrabbling at the mother's knees. He was rewarded with lots of fuss and we moved on, our heads held a little higher.

The pavements of Hurstpierpoint might be full of intimidating sights – like old-age pensioners who walked strangely or empty plastic bags blowing in the wind – but we could conquer anything. Flash found plenty of treasures. We stopped for him to pick up stones off the pavement, wood chippings from front gardens (apologies to the neighbours who seem to have lost most of their mulch), snails and even some tasty treats (discarded wrappers of individual home-baked cakes with a few crumbs attached were particularly welcome). Cleaning up Hurstpierpoint was a tough job, but Flash accepted his assignment with relish.

Back home, Flash collapsed into his new basket, so I slipped into the kitchen and put the kettle on. He looked so peaceful lying there, five minutes off duty – excellent. I really needed tea and something sweet to boost my energy – wouldn't have minded one of those home-baked cakes. But suddenly, I remembered I had to reinforce good behaviour and nipped across to stroke him. Delighted with the chance to play, Flash immediately put his mouth round my hand and pulled the top off a scab gained removing the nails from the outhouse wall.

What was the old proverb? Let sleeping dogs lie?

I took my tea into the living room, trying not to trip over Flash frolicking at my feet. He leapt straight on to Thom's reproduction Bauhaus sofa. It was a crucial decision: should I let him stay, or would I be hard-hearted Andrew? For a millisecond, I wanted to relent but out of my mouth came:

'Flash, no.'

Back he went to floor level and, exhausted, I collapsed into a chair. Seconds later, Flash tried to leap on to my lap. It might work as a small puppy, I thought, but a full-size Collie/Spaniel would be a problem.

'Flash, no.'

Again, he obeyed. Maybe I'd be able to cope after all.

After I'd drunk my tea, Flash and I found a compromise. I stretched out on the sofa and he laid down on the rug beside it while I stroked his back. I switched on the TV but neither of us saw anything because we were both asleep as soon as I had put down the remote control.

At bedtime, it was hard to convince Flash to leave what had already become his favourite spot by the radiator. He stretched out and fixed me with a mournful look. However, after I started loading the dishwasher, his natural curiosity got the better of him and he wandered into the kitchen. Tempting him into the outhouse was much harder; I turned up the convector heater and switched the radio on. Berlioz flooded out from on top of the tumble drier, over the washing powder, the over-wintering plants and the slightly chewed second-hand dog basket.

'Come on, Flash. This is your new den,' I cooed.

He stood at the edge of the outhouse.

'If it's all right with you, I'll sleep by the fire, thank you,' his body language seemed to say.

'Look, I've put those towels in your basket. Familiar smells.' I showed him the ones I'd loaned Mr Foster.

His look turned to scorn:

'I'm not going to be taken in by such an obvious trick as that!'

My mother had suggested fixing a hot-water bottle. After all, he had been used to sleeping with the warm bodies of his mother and litter mates. I tracked down the hot-water bottle with a furry blue cover I'd bought Thom when poor blood circulation made his feet cold at night. I'd been to half the shops in Burgess Hill and Brighton because nobody stocked them in the summer. It seemed an apt symbol of how much out of kilter our lives were from the rest of the world. So I felt a small surge of satisfaction for finding a use for one of Thom's old possessions. Even though I doubt I will ever need his dumbbells, his weightlifter's belt or his old German textbooks, I cannot bear to throw them away.

Adding Thom's hot-water bottle to the basket finally convinced Flash to climb in. I crouched down and stroked his head. He seemed so small and so trusting. I felt guilty leaving him alone in a strange house listening to the clicks of the central heating switching off and the creaks from the uneven floorboards in my bedroom. The first night Tyson had stayed, I settled him in the outhouse, but he had barked for twenty minutes solid. Finally, I took pity on my neighbours and allowed him to sleep in the bedroom. OK, I might have forced him to sleep on the floor, and beside Thom's side of the bed, but somehow the compromise had all been on my behalf. Not only did Tyson snore badly but on the one occasion that I did manage to entice somebody to spend the night with me, Tyson had burst through the bedroom door at the most embarrassing moment.

I gave Flash a final stroke. He stopped washing himself and started energetically licking my fingers. I weakened slightly.

'You might pretend that it is only for one night,' I told him, 'but what I decide tonight, I'll have to live with for the next fifteen years.'

Put like that, there was no choice. I switched off the lights and tried not to hear his pitiful whines. Climbing the stairs, I offered up a silent prayer:

'Thom, if you did become my guardian angel, like you promised, please look after Flash tonight.' Sleep well, Flash. Good night, Thom.

Saturday 29 January

After a restless night, dreaming of abandoned pups, I finally woke to the sound of distant whines. Six o'clock. Perhaps I should go and check, however the bed felt so deliciously warm another five minutes would not hurt. Downstairs, Flash howled and the sound ripped through me. One hundred per cent awake, I threw on some pants and my dressing gown. When was the last time I'd been up so early?

Downstairs, there was no moaning from Flash's den. Perhaps I could quickly stroke him and slip back to bed. Perhaps puppy-owning would not prove as difficult as everybody claimed. As I opened the door, a hurricane of black and white fur hit me: scrambling feet, abrasive tongue and finally, tiny teeth.

'Hello, Flash.'

Somebody was very pleased to see me. In fact, somebody doubted I would ever return. It would have been easier to calm down a small child at the funfair, but then as far as Flash was concerned, I was his big dipper, ghost train and candy-floss concession rolled into one. I knew then that neither of us was going back to bed. However, there was one bright spot: the newspaper by the back door had been well used (rather than the outhouse floor). In fact, it was impossible to believe that one small puppy could produce so much.

I yawned, cleared up the mess and sat on the back step. Flash launched another broadside. Even fully awake, I could hardly cope with this much excitement. Perhaps he needed to go to the toilet again? At the bottom of the garden, Flash rolled over on to his back and even in darkness his white belly stood out.

'Get busy.' I chanted the suggested code from my book.

Except when I'd taken him out last night, I'd forgotten to give the command. From the bemused look on his face, Flash had decided that 'get busy' was a signal to chase a leaf being blown across the garden. I stood hopefully as he explored the night smells and sounds. No luck. In the velvet remains of the night, the small copse behind my garden seemed almost as busy as Leicester Square on a Saturday night. Strange creatures lurked amongst the brambles, the trees shuddered in the light breeze and I could even hear the dew begin to sink down into the ground. I might have lived here for eleven years, but all this night life was new. I'd flown over the Grand Canyon and dived at the Great Barrier Reef, but had never stood and listened in my own garden. Through Flash's ears, I followed the fascinating predawn noises as the night shift cleared up. He put his nose to the ground and quivering, traced an intruder's process. What was it? A squirrel, a fox or one of the neighbourhood cats? Flash was too excited to return to bed and had no interest in 'getting busy' either. The only option was exercise.

We stumbled round the empty streets of Hurstpierpoint. After a couple of false starts Flash seemed to remember he was supposed to walk on my right-hand side. However, despite inspecting every lamp post and entangling his lead round about half of them, Flash was developing extraordinary bladder control. Back home, I decided some breakfast might help. Flash munched down on a full bowl – at an hour that even truck drivers would still have a queasy stomach – and off we trotted to the bottom of the garden.

'Get busy,' I instructed and right on cue Flash rolled over on his back for a tummy tickle and a run round.

I was beginning to despair and even wondered if I should demonstrate myself, when Flash calmly sniffed the ground, stretched out his body and started to pee. Hoping not to give him a complex, I nipped up behind him and started sotto voce chanting:

'Get busy, get busy. Get busy.'

After extravagant praise for Flash, I felt it safe enough to return indoors. I collapsed on the sofa. Flash collapsed on the rug and I tickled his stomach. It was hard to gauge who needed the catnap the most. I had a strange dream where Kylie Minogue had returned to the charts with an updated version of her first hit called 'I Should Be So Busy – Busy, Busy, Busy'.

I was woken by the thud of my newspaper arriving through the letterbox. Over breakfast, I flicked through the *Express* and studied the profile I'd written of boxer Nigel Benn's kitchen. The picture of his three-year-old twins, Conor and India, peeking out of a cupboard had come out really well. After breakfast, I put aside the section with my article and laid the rest of the paper by the back door ready for Flash's next serving. I wondered if he realised that he was commenting on the way his owner made a living.

So that I could shower without monitoring if Flash was chewing the top off the radiator cap and about to flood the house, I confined him to the outhouse again. The joy of being able to shave and put in my contact lenses in peace. I felt guilty about leaving him, but took a leaf out of my mother's book on child – rearing. Her favourite joke was 'Spanking might not to do them any good, but it makes me feel better'. Right on cue, my mother phoned while Flash and I were having one of our dog and man bonding sessions.

'How are you doing?' she asked.

'He's learned his name and he's not bad on the lead.'

'You've got to make certain you're firm with him, not like Shadow.' (My sister's black Labrador.) 'He pulls terribly.'

Being a new puppy owner means no shortage of good advice, mainly contradictory. On the one hand, you've got to be firm – start as you mean to go on. On the other, he's only young, don't expect too much too soon.

'Thank you for the suggestion of the hot-water bottle. He leapt on it straight away – perhaps it helped him sleep.'

However, it was hard to talk with a restless puppy on my lap, who was trying to wash my face with his tongue. We hung up, but as I already had the 'hands-free', I decided to phone Thom's mother Ursula and tell her about my new arrival.

Ursula speaks no English, so the conversation was entirely in German – amazingly, the German for Collie is Collie and Spaniel is Spaniel too. Instead of wriggling, Flash began to settle down. The more German I spoke, the calmer he became. Next, I caught up with Martina, the nurse who befriended Thom just before he died in Germany. Once again, she speaks no English, and Flash snuggled contentedly further down into my lap.

I remembered how Thom would almost hypnotise our friends' cats by purring German into their ears until even the most independent beast was putty in his arms. For a moment, I was comforted by the fantasy that Thom's spirit had maybe, just maybe, visited small, lonely Flash in his oversized basket last night and soothed away all his fears.

At least I am not the only inhabitant of Planet Weird. The astrologer Jonathan Cainer, interviewed in my morning papers about his transfer from the *Mail* to the *Express*, had explained how he still talks to his wife who died 'after an altercation with a lorry'. I've never had an after-death conversation with Thom, so I was a little jealous. However, when I read that Jonathan Cainer's wife advised on the colour scheme for the bathroom and designed the housing for their bins, I had second thoughts. Thom had always been the interior designer of the household and if he could still talk to me, I know I would have a huge list of chores.

— ❦ —

A proper walk was next on the morning agenda. Flash had not forgotten his lessons on the lead, but every time we met someone on the path, he would freeze and hide behind me. Patiently, I would wait until the stranger joined us and when they were about two feet away, Flash's confidence would return. He'd leap up and cover everybody in muddy footprints. Other dogs were another matter; from Flash's perspective even the village's oldest and most sedate Golden Retriever was really a wolf in a fluffy blonde coat.

When my fears of wolves began, I was probably about five, which – in developmental terms – is probably Flash's age now. I could understand his anxiety. I knew he needed to be soothed rather than challenged, so I crossed over to the other side of the street and put a safe distance between us and the golden wolf. It was almost like there was a second person sitting within my body: watching and measuring. I held the lead and comforted the puppy. The second person leaned over a strange bed, back in Bournemouth, where it first began.

The roads round my house lead nowhere beyond other seventies-style detached homes. As the occasional car came past, Flash would stop to check whether it was about to drive up on to the pavement. So our progress was slow, but he did not panic. I needed to collect the puppy chews I'd ordered from the village pet shop, and buy some meat from the butcher's, so I cut through the twitten (Sussex dialect for a narrow passageway between two buildings). Thom had considered this the spookiest place in Hurstpierpoint and claimed that if we had our own Jack the Ripper he would strike here. As Flash and I inched our way forward, a side gate was flung open and a dustman pushed out a large wheelie bin. The rumbling of the wheels over the uneven path bounced off the high walls. To a small puppy, on his first full day in the outside world, this must have sounded like heavy artillery. Flash cowered; I reassured him and we ventured a couple of steps forward into the High Street. However, the danger was not yet over: the wheelie bin was being attached to the back of a cart. The mechanical lifters thundered into action and the contents of the bin emptied with an almighty crash. Flash's whimpering had turned to howls, so we retreated and waited until the wheelie bin had been returned and the dustman had left whistling for his next stop. Finally, we crept back, through the narrow gorge, into the sunlight of the High Street.

The village is listed in the Doomsday Book and the High Street was laid out in the era of horse and cart. Nobody ever expected lorries would need to make deliveries to the butcher's, greengrocer's, ironmonger's and other small businesses.

At the mouth of the twitten, a lorry was parked on the pavement and all the traffic was backed up in both directions. I had never realised how much noise idling engines could make as they reverberate from one building on to another, but now I was hearing the world through sensitive puppy ears. Flash tried to dig his heels into concrete:

'No way!'

I picked him up in order to carry him to the recreation ground over the other side of the High Street. Up in my arms, he regally inspected this new territory and accepted pats from any passing subjects who were out shopping. He had faced his fears and survived. He licked my face again and decided the village might not be so dangerous after all.

The recreation ground is a rather grand name for a piece of open grassland about the size of one and a half football pitches, with a bowls club and two hard tennis courts attached. Tyson always used to enjoy chasing other dogs here and trying to beat them to the sticks their owners had just thrown. Flash, however, was relieved to find we were alone. So, for the first time, in public, I let him off the lead. To start off with he trotted closely by my side until his confidence grew and he started to explore on his own. I strolled on until I was about fifty yards away, screwed up my courage and tried the 'will he come to his name?' test. My dog training book suggests a firm but excited tone. Apparently, I need to really believe he will obey. I steadied myself and called out:

'Flash.'

Suddenly his nose came up from the patch of interesting grass, he looked at me and bounded towards me with his black Spaniel ears bobbing up and down with excitement. Success! Such a nice change from Tyson – who was sure he had a triple barrel name: Tyson, Tyson, TYSON – rising in intensity until I was almost hoarse.

I attached his lead and we returned to the High Street. The delivery lorry had gone but the road was still busy. Our first stop was the chemist's. Fortunately, the pharmacist made Flash very welcome because I doubt he would have waited outside. Next, we went to the pet shop, where he received so much attention he had to be dragged out. Like all parents, I decided it would be easier to placate Flash rather than be shown up in public, so I carried him the rest of the way down the High Street. The pavement outside the butcher's is broader and the traffic a couple of yards further away. I prayed Flash would not be too alarmed. Rather than going directly to the butcher's, I put Flash down on the pavement and we walked the longer but quieter way round. He stopped being a dead weight on the lead and trotted happily beside me. We reached the butcher's and although churning inside, I tried to be confident. I tied his lead to a hook outside the shop.

'Don't worry, I've got a wonderful treat waiting for you,' I told him.

Flash was not so certain. Whimpering, he followed me right to the end of his lead, and then straining every sinew, managed to poke his nose round the door. While I bought some steak and Chinese-style pork, Flash received his normal chorus from the other shoppers:

'It's a puppy.'

'Isn't he sweet!'

'How old is he?'

In return, Flash almost managed to trip an elderly lady as she came out.

While I waited for my change, I opened the bag of puppy treats and palmed one ready to reward him for not crying too much.

'Here, Flash, good boy.'

He sniffed the treat, took it gingerly and spat it out. I tried it again and this time he broke it into four pieces and pushed it round the pavement. I remembered lunchtime at my infant school and how much I hated macaroni cheese. One of my teachers had tried to encourage me to eat more by mixing the macaroni up with my potatoes and greens and sculpting a giant A for Andrew. We compromised and I managed half of the crossbar of the A. Flash was braver and finally swallowed his 'treat'. I had a sneaking suspicion that my puppy was not going to be bought off with food; he wanted cuddles, strokes, tummy tickles and my undivided attention.

We could have walked home down the side roads, but I decided not to give in to Flash's fear of traffic as this could significantly reduce where I could take him. So we set off down Cuckfield Road but our growing confidence was shattered by a large delivery van screeching past at about sixty miles an hour. My training book delivers lectures on the danger of giving a puppy the wrong attention. If a child is frightened, we can reassure them, but if we make a fuss of a dog in the same circumstances, we just reward them for cowering.

The author might be hard-hearted, but I scooped Flash up and carried him until we left the main road and reached more familiar territory. On the corner of my road we met Dick from number 20 and Polo, his white Bichon. Despite Polo being on the lead and about as savage as, well, a mint with a hole, Flash tried to leap back in my arms again. Perhaps giving into his fears hadn't been such a good idea! So I compromised and put Flash on a low brick garden wall. Now he was three inches taller than Polo, he did not look quite so pathetic.

Dick welcomed me to the dog-owning fraternity and warned about the savage dog that lives at the other end of the road. According to local legend, the owners feed it on raw meat. On Christmas Day, this Dalmatian had satisfied its blood lust by attacking Polo and taking a big chunk out of his left flank. Dick showed us where the wound was only just beginning to heal. Flash and I made a mental note to always pass that house on the other side of the road. Finally, I coaxed Flash down from the wall and introduced him to Polo. They sniffed each other and decided that perhaps they could be friends.

Back home, Flash's courage was coming on in leaps and bounds. Instead of pulling himself up the stairs, rather like Winnie the Pooh, he dashed up in double-quick time. In my office, he tried to chew through first the power and then a telephone cable. In my firmest voice, I told him no. He gave me a disappointed look and curled up in a ball by my feet. Perhaps the sound of typing acted as a lullaby because within two minutes he was fast asleep. I let out a quiet sigh of relief – I had a few minutes off puppy patrol. An hour later, he was still sleeping and I'd broken the back of my article. Normally, by now, I would have found an excuse to leave the keyboard – just get an apple, that plant needs watering – but today I dared not move and wake Flash. Perhaps the new addition to the office team would be good for productivity, after all.

Flash is not the only new arrival in my life. About a month ago, I met someone at my line dancing club. Feeling bruised from my first attempt at a relationship after Thom, I have taken things very slowly. We danced together for two weeks and followed that with an old-fashioned date – where I learned his family used to breed Greyhounds and Labradors. However, I was still nervous about taking it any further. First, his name is also Andrew (and that feels almost incestuous). Second, he's fourteen years younger than me. (When did I cross over into being a father figure?) But there's no harm inviting him over for Saturday night supper, is there?

Andy – I've decided there's got to be some way of telling us apart – was due to arrive at Hassocks station. As it is only ten minutes away, I decided this would be Flash's first car journey with me driving. What's more, if it was a disaster, there would be an experienced dog handler to help with the return journey. Flash eyed my car suspiciously. However, with a little gentle persuasion, he hopped in and sat down in the footwell of the passenger seat. I walked round to my side and got in. Flash immediately tried to climb on to my lap. I pushed him back into the passenger footwell, leaned over and closed his door. We both sat there on the drive, staring at the garage. Was I doing the right thing? Flash obviously thought we were playing a game – and a pretty dull one at that – so he decided to jump up on to the passenger seat and look out of the window. After he'd tried this twice and been pushed firmly down, he got the message. Thank goodness, I hadn't let him on the sofa; thank goodness, I didn't have a puppy who was stronger than me. Thank goodness, I was allowing forty-five minutes for a ten-minute journey.

I switched on the engine. With no negative reaction from Flash, I set off slowly down the road. From time to time, he would try to climb on to the passenger seat to look out of the window. With one hand on the steering wheel, I would use the other to push him down and try to forget about the story of the author Stephen King, who was almost killed while walking along a quiet country road by an out-of-control pick-up truck. The driver had been too busy stopping his dog from opening a coolbox of meat on the back seat to notice how erratically he was driving. I just hoped there were no internationally famous novelists taking a stroll between Hurstpierpoint and Hassocks station. Driving at about twenty miles an hour down the High Street, I was about to switch the radio on when Flash decided to provide his own in-car entertainment and started whimpering.

We arrived at the station unfashionably early, but Flash soon found that eating cigarette ends passes the time. It could be turning into a habit; as every time we walk past a discarded John Player Silk Cut packet outside my house, he picks it up and moves it three yards up the road. Flash had just finished his third tasty treat and spat out the filter when Andy arrived. He smiled at me, played with a puppy on a nicotine high and passed an important test: he thought Flash was the cutest dog ever. The return journey was easier. Andy sat in the front seat and every time Flash whined, he gave him a reassuring stroke.

Back home Flash fretted about our guest, especially when Andy sat down on the sofa with me. He looked up at us with big doleful eyes, unable to understand why there was one rule for Andy and one for him. My dog training books say we humans should be proud of our special status; dogs are the only species that accept us as one of their own. Flattering, but very wearing when Flash felt he had just dropped down the pack order. My other problem was trying to be both gracious host and stopping Flash from chewing the legs of my great-great-grandmother's dining-room table. Why do dogs have an uncanny knack of knowing what we treasure the most?

Just as I was serving up our steak supper, Flash nipped round the back of the dining-room table for his first 'in-house' accident. Andy proved himself the perfect house guest by offering to clear up the mess. Supper was pleasant. Perhaps I am making progress because I felt no temptation to talk about Thom. Once Flash discovered Andy had signed my 'no titbits' pledge, he decided to snooze at my feet.

Settling Flash and Andy down for the night proved easier than I had expected. Flash was exhausted. Fretting must really take it out of a small dog, because he was so ready for bed I almost expected him to arrive in the sitting room changed into his pyjamas and winding his alarm clock. I let the puppy out into the garden, laid out fresh newspaper by the back door and threw two dog biscuits into his bowl. Mr Foster had phoned earlier, worried that he had forgotten to tell me about Flash's bedtime treat. So maybe he was reassured by this familiar routine, for he hopped on to his hot-water bottle without the slightest whine and curled up. Upstairs, I found that Andy was also asleep.

Sunday 30 January

Both Flash and I slept through to seven in the morning. Lying in bed beside the unfamiliar figure of Andy, the bed seemed much smaller than last night. I listened for distressed puppy sounds from downstairs – nothing. Good, another five minutes in bed. Andy snored and turned over. I really should check on that dog. Flash was overjoyed to see me and I was pleased that he was using the newspaper.

In the garden, I was convinced that Flash has aspirations to become a vegetarian. First, he chewed an entrée of evergreen shrub leaf, followed by a main course of clumps of moss (lovingly garnished with early morning dew) and finished off with strands of ivy (preferably pulled up by their roots). Hoping he had a strong stomach, I decided to let him learn from his own mistakes. I cannot bear the idea of becoming the sort of owner who is forever wrenching strange items from their dog's mouth. If I supervised him as closely in the garden as the house, he would begin to wonder if his name was not Flash but Flash NO! I expect I will live to regret it, but on day three I made a pact with Flash: he could forage happily in the garden but in the house the only thing that goes into his mouth (except Hill's Science Plan Puppy Food) is his chew from the pet shop. In fact, this chew has been a great success; not only is it remarkably robust but good for chasing, kitten-style, round the room. My only regret is that I did not purchase more – one for my office, one for in front of the TV and one for the outhouse – now officially renamed Flash's den. I seem to spend half the day hunting under chairs for his chew; still, it's worth it because every time he locks his teeth round anything forbidden, I can produce the alternative.

'Where's your chew?' I chant, as instructed by my dog training manual. Flash always gives me a puzzled look but accepts his multicoloured vinyl toy. So to date the only victim of puppy teething has been three tassels from under a chair in the living room and flattened flower beds. But then I lost all pride in the garden after Thom died. On sunny days, we used to eat outside and I'd notice the flower beds needed weeding or the edges of the lawn trimming. Nowadays, I eat in front of the TV and I've let the ivy, brambles and field horsetail spread from the wilderness behind the house.

Before Flash and I set off on our morning walk, I decided to try teaching him a second command. In the front porch, I authoritatively said:

'Sit.'

With just the slightest touch to his back haunches, Flash sat. Amazing. I praised him, attached his lead and off we trotted. I was so surprised at how well he responded that at the kerb outside my house, I stopped.

'Sit.'

Once again, Flash sat and this time there was no need to encourage with a firm hand. He seemed a little shocked too. Somehow, he had accessed his clever Collie genes. When we crossed over the road, I was sure that Flash held his head a little higher. Except, as my mother would say, pride comes before a fall. At the edge of the estate, Flash started to whimper. We were about to leave his territory. I told him to sit, he complied – which boosted his self-confidence – and we headed towards the Health Centre. Although we were still fifty yards from the twitten, Flash started dancing in fright on his lead. Feeling sorry for him, I relaxed lead discipline and let him sniff round in every direction. The whimpering got worse and I had no choice but to let him leap up into my arms.

I carried him to the village green, but it had seemed grown to immense proportions since yesterday. So I allowed him back into my arms until we had almost reached the entrance to the estate again. Instead of stretching his legs, he cowered behind me. I followed his gaze across the road to a lady in her late sixties rushing to morning service. Her sensible heels clattered machine-gun style against the wet concrete. Oh dear! My puppy might be intelligent but he's also a coward. No, I decided – in the words of one of my school reports he suffers from an 'over-vivid imagination'.

I was feeling guilty for exposing Flash to too many new sights and sounds too soon until, at the end of our road, we met Polo. On familiar territory, Flash was much bolder this time and rushed up to sniff him. Good dog, brave dog! So we showed off to Dick and Polo how well Flash had learned to sit.

Back home, Andy had woken up and I showed him how to use the shower. When he came downstairs, we were the picture of Sunday morning domesticity. I was reading the papers and Flash was asleep. I offered tea, coffee, cereal, toast, but all were refused. Before driving him down to Brighton, Flash and I posed for a set of puppy snaps. When my father took shots for the family album, he always used to complain:

'Take that stupid grin off your face.'

How will I look with a Flash alternately trying to lick my face and nibble my nose? I also took one shot of Andy with Flash to mark the day.

On the way back from returning Andy to his flat in Brighton, I stopped off at Tesco for a few basics. I caught my reflection in the driver's mirror. Covered from head to toe in dog hairs and muddy paw prints, I looked more like a tramp than a writer. So I chucked a few items in my trolley and fled home. In my absence, Flash had not been idle in his room. I'd never clocked that the pipe to the old goldfish pond – which I'd filled in – had been lagged with rubber. I did now because it was in small pieces all over the outhouse floor.

— ❧ —

In the afternoon another friend from dancing dropped round. Brian's partner Michael breeds Shiba Inu – a Japanese hunting dog – so he was keen to inspect my dog. I suspect he was missing having a dog around. Michael is Australian and because of visa problems and his dislike of the English weather returned home with their animals.

Brian rightly declared Flash adorable. However, every time he tried to get Brian's attention by standing on his hind legs and pawing at him, Brian gently kneed him in the stomach.

'Even if you tell puppies "down" and push them to the floor, you're still encouraging them to jump because they've been rewarded by hand contact. A shove and a pat are not that different to an overexcited puppy,' he explained and promptly disappeared upstairs – which I thought a bit rude until he reappeared with a bit of tissue paper attached to his nose.

While jumping up, Flash's sharp puppy teeth had gashed him. I apologised and made a mental note to start the knee trick.

Coming from a tough Tasmanian farm, Michael's approach to animals is very different. One of Brian's favourite ways of winding him up was to discuss the latest edition of the TV show *Pet Rescue*. Michael would get worked up about even the idea of a sanctuary for old donkeys:

'I know where they can go,' he would splutter.

'Where?' Brian would ask innocently – already knowing the answer.

'The knacker's yard!'

Michael had shocked some of their doggy English friends by offering to save them a vets' bill by taking their old and ill dog to the bottom of the garden and shooting it. He has already emailed Brian from Australia to warn me that every decision I make about Flash's behaviour will affect his character for the rest of his life.

Brian and I set off with Flash for a walk – which lasted all of ten minutes. At the end of the estate, Flash started to whine and I turned back.

'You can't let him get away with that,' explained Brian – who had been looking forward to some exercise.

'But he's frightened,' I whined too.

'Do you want to be trapped in just the same few streets for ever?'

So Flash and I compromised. We stayed on the estate but explored side streets we had never ventured down before. Although he acquitted himself well, by mainly walking to heel, Flash did start to pull as we headed home. This behaviour had been a major problem with Tyson. I'd almost strangled him on his choke chain and tried blocking him by holding a stick in front of his nose, but after nine years with his owners allowing pulling, I might as well have danced the hokey cokey for all the good it did me. There was no point asking Valerie because Lily the Dalmatian was almost as bad on the lead – in fact, once when frightened, she had pulled Valerie over and dislocated her arm.

'You've got to learn to think dog,' explained a very patient Brian. 'The advantage of pulling is that he gets somewhere faster. So Michael drags them round and starts walking back in the opposite direction.'

Next time Flash pulled, I turned round and Flash reluctantly followed.

'Now you can turn back and walk in the original direction.'

Amazingly, it worked and Flash walked to heel.

In the evening, Brian and I went line dancing – the first time I'd left Flash alone in the house for more than forty-five minutes. On my return, the newspaper by the back door was clean. I took him out and encouraged him to 'get busy', but with no luck. So I settled down for half an hour of TV before bed and Flash slunk under my great-great-grandmother's dining-room table to take a dump. I wanted to shout, but my puppy training book tells me that just comes across as barking, so I calmly cleared it up. I know he is only a puppy, but I felt violated.

Monday 31 January

When I let Flash into the garden in the morning, the trust and adoration in his eyes made me feel ashamed about being cross last night. As he pranced round and rolled in the wet grass for a tummy tickle, the full enormity of what I'd taken on hit me. Here was a living creature who completely depended on me. I felt a huge tidal wave of longing for Thom. We had always planned to get a dog together.

Much as I have promised myself not to treat Flash like a child, I feel like a single parent. There is nobody to share all the amusing things he has done during the day, nobody to whisper all my fears and nobody to sit with him tonight.

I've been discussing a feature with *She* magazine since before Christmas but it has finally been approved. Great. I have to visit the owners of four very different bedrooms – fetish, minimalist, ordinary and one converted out of a chapel apse – and write how their décor has affected their love life. While I'd thought I had a free week – and plenty of time to spend with my new puppy – I now need to go out at least twice, maybe three times. The state of my finances means I can't turn down work, so I'm torn in two. With no Thom to share the responsibility of being a dog owner, I've had to do something which is becoming increasingly familiar as my long widowerhood progresses: push down my feeling and be practical. So I've asked Valerie if she'll look in on Flash a couple of times this evening (and tomorrow evening too).

Watching Flash eat his breakfast, I felt guilty about prioritising work over his development. Rather than picking at his food, he was really wolfing it down. The reflection off his bowl must no longer be frightening. He must be settling down. So I walked into the kitchen to put on the kettle; immediately Flash left his food and followed. Being with me, or even better the chance of a cuddle, is definitely his top priority. But this afternoon at 5 p.m., I will climb into my car and drive off into the night.

For this morning's walk, we headed for the main road. At the sound of the traffic, Flash tried to leap into my arms, but I made him sit and came down to his level to offer comfort. As I tickled the flash of white fur across his white chest, he calmly watched the cars rush past. So brave, so clever, so how can I leave him tonight?

Polo came around the corner of Cuckfield Road and this time Flash felt secure enough to bound over, sniff noses and even, rather boldly, sniff Polo's bottom. Flash trusts me to do the right thing, but tonight I will betray him by driving off to inspect the bedroom of the managing director of House of Harlot – a high-couture rubber and latex manufacturer.

— ❧ —

I should have been able to concentrate on my work, but my mind kept wandering back home to my lonely puppy. Despite the fake gold fur on the bedroom walls, a print of eight naked women hanging above a waterbed and a large collection of very explicit pornography, Michelle and Robin seemed such an ordinary couple. They had one useful tip for my readers: pet owners should avoid furry walls because animal hairs and dust can set off your asthma. As soon as I'd finished the interview I was straight onto the mobile phone to Valerie; no problems with Flash – thank goodness.

Thursday 3 February

After being out for the past two evenings interviewing couples about their bedrooms, I decided to take Flash with me to Relate in Crawley (where I counsel couples about their relationship problems). Even though the journey is twenty-five minutes, Flash behaved himself in the car and peed on command on the verge outside the offices. I breathed a sigh of relief because the manager is not keen on the idea of me bringing my puppy to work.

'What if everybody wanted to bring their dog in?'

'But everybody doesn't—'

She had made a small impatient noise in the back of her throat.

'He won't be any trouble,' I told her confidently.

There are guide dogs for the blind, hearing dogs and friendly dogs that are taken to meet sick children in hospital. Flash could be the first marriage healing dog. It got me thinking: what else could he do? Having another living breathing being in the house again seems to be loosening the knot of loneliness in my chest. Perhaps Flash could have a positive effect on my relationship with my parents? Certainly, taking Tyson for a visit on the first Christmas after Thom died had filled the awkward silences.

Perhaps Flash could also read minds because he was determined to meet my first clients – positive that a husband and wife united over petting him could never possibly argue. With scarcely a whine, however, he was persuaded to wait in the office during their counselling session – where he was spoiled rotten by one of the other counsellors, who allowed him to jump up at her and mouth her arm.

'Sorry, he isn't supposed to do that,' I apologised afterwards to the bad influence.

'Don't worry, he'll soon learn not to,' she replied. 'Although my Labrador still jumps up and she's two.'

I did not point out the obvious.

Even the manager was mollified:

'I told him to go under the desk and pointed and he obeyed,' she told me.

Sensible dog.

My middle clients had cancelled, so I took Flash to the formal gardens in Crawley. The level of big-town traffic was no problem – perhaps because he was too busy sorting through discarded fast food containers. Outside a hamburger restaurant, there was a gang of fourteen-year-old hard nuts, smoking and trying to impress their girlfriends (who despite being twelve had already discovered hair bleaching). Perhaps it was being a week older or the lure of finding scraps, but Flash rushed up for a stroke. I was more circumspect and tried to pass at a safe distance – difficult as we were joined together by one short blue vinyl lead.

After listening to my final clients' problems and trying to unravel the childhood problems that still colour their lives today, I was relieved to return to the office and resume playing with my puppy.

He is at such an impressionable age; every mistake I make will be etched across his psyche for ever. Am I being a responsible owner? Am I leaving him too much on his own? What problems am I storing up for tomorrow?

Flash just rolled over on to his back for a tummy tickle.

Friday 4 February

Living with Flash, I have gained some understanding of what it must like to be a mouse in a science experiment. Flash is the scientist probing: how far can I go? Our home and the streets of Hurstpierpoint are his laboratory. 'If I whine and pull on the lead, what will he do?' he asks and jots the results down on his clipboard. 'What happens when I chase my tail? Can I gain his undivided attention by jumping up every time he chats on the phone? How far can I go?'

Like my dog training book suggests, I have tried to set down some rules and not slip. I have tried to provide a rhythm to his day: early morning walk and sleeping under my desk until lunchtime, followed by the afternoon walk and another snooze to the sound of typing. At the end of his first week in his new life, Flash is getting bolder with other dogs. I have been walking him in the lane that winds behind the full length of the village – behind the High Street – offering spectacular views of the South Downs. Being a favourite route for dog walkers, it was only a matter of time before we met someone. I did not reckon with it being at the narrowest point, or that it would be two large dogs walking together. Flash froze and tried to climb up into my arms. Looking around quickly, we had two choices: walk forward to face our nemesis or retreat back to the recreation ground. I turned to assess the battlefield, but we had been outflanked. A small white Highland Terrier, straining at its lead, was bearing down on us. Flash's fear was travelling up to me. I was seconds away from taking him into my arms when the lady with the two dogs – a Collie and a Heinz 57 – called out:

'Is he OK?'

I took a deep breath.

'Flash, sit,' I commanded and reached down to comfort him. 'Give us a second and we'll come out to greet you,' I called out to the other owner – all the time the Highland Terrier was closing in.

She took her dogs back to a broader section of the path and I coaxed Flash gently forward, until with a burst of confidence, he rushed onward to meet his foe. Relief. Was this the same dog who had, fifteen minutes earlier, cowered from a cat who was not only fifty yards away but also asleep on the drive of number 24?

Flash and the Collie, which we discovered was called Jasmine, inspected each other.

'I'm keeping back the other dog because he can be snappy,' the other dog walker told me.

When the Highland Terrier arrived, Flash showed no fear but ran up to greet him. I made a special fuss of Flash and we marched off up the lane with our chests puffed out. In fact, I believe a campaign medal would have looked very good pinned to our chests.

He is also learning to cope with traffic in the High Street and strangers are no longer a problem – mainly because half the village is in love with him.

At the Health Centre, the receptionists fling open the window to marvel at his beautiful markings. Elderly ladies stop to pat him and pass on stories about dogs they've owned and loved.

In the afternoon, when I took Flash up to the village convenience store, another customer told me:

'I watch out from my kitchen window for you every day, walking up the hill. He's making wonderful progress on the lead.'

On the way back from our walk, I stopped to allow Flash to greet our next door neighbours, Valerie, Michael and Lily the Dalmatian. They were talking to another neighbour from about seven houses up about a fifty-eight-year-old man, in the next street, who was critically ill in hospital after an aortic aneurysm.

'You have met Andrew, haven't you? And this is Flash.' Valerie introduced us.

'It's nice to meet new neighbours,' the woman told me.

I smiled but did not point out that I'd lived in Hurstpierpoint for twelve years or that I must have walked past her door more or less every day on my way to the post office, the shops or the library.

After we had walked on, Valerie told me:

'There's two ways to enter village life: you either have a child at the village school or you get a dog.'

Saturday 5 February

My best friend and former TV Agony Aunt, Kate, is staying for the weekend. She has been trying to accept that her relationship with her boyfriend is over and has discovered the most unusual twist to retail therapy. She goes into the most expensive stores in Bond Street, tries on a £300 pair of shoes, and pretends to be a Stepford wife:

'My husband is picking me up in a minute, could you put those aside, please. I'll be back to collect them in the morning.'

I have to admire her ingenuity. Like they teach on the playwriting courses I've taken, she has worked out the backstory for this woman: married to someone in the city, the four-wheel drive, money no object. Best of all, there is no damage to her credit card.

I had warned Kate to bring old clothes for the visit as everything will get covered in dog hairs. However, after hearing about her woes, I had an idea. As well as a cuddle with a puppy, she needed a good night out. Every first Saturday of the month is Gay and Lesbian ballroom dancing night at the Rivoli – a genuine thirties ballroom dedicated to glitter balls, gilt and red velour that has somehow remained untouched by changing tastes and London developers. Unfortunately, Kate had nothing suitable to wear so wanted to go shopping in Brighton. As I will have to leave Flash at home tonight, I decided it would be best to take him with us.

Flash was almost overwhelmed by the crowds and all the dropped litter. Our progress was further slowed down by his fascination with pushchairs and everybody else's fascination with him. He had never received so much attention or so much stimulation. Therefore, I should not have been surprised when his normal good behaviour on the lead was replaced by the energy of a child who has been fed nothing but E numbers for a week. When Kate and I stopped for a coffee at a café in North Laine, which had put tables out into the street, I took Flash on to my knee so he would calm down. It proved a bit of a mistake because at this privileged position my home-made chocolate brownie with extra cream smelt even better. Before the waiter had even put it on the table, Flash was trying to dive at my treat. Luckily, I was stronger and quicker, and Flash found himself on the pavement. There must be something deeply addictive about chocolate for dogs. Flash had the look of a crack addict who has just had all his supplies seized by the police. Every one of my mouthfuls was such torture for him, I almost vowed never to touch chocolate again – at least in Flash's presence. Perhaps I have found another use for him – diet dog!

Even window shopping proved difficult with Flash because he kept pulling in every direction. Kate sympathised:

'It's like shopping with a small child – fine if you've got two hours to buy a pint of milk. But otherwise…' She shuddered at the memory. 'Alice was so bad I had to strap her into her pushchair until she was four.'

Fortunately, Flash was on 'reasonable behaviour' inside Ju Ju – a second-hand clothes store – where Kate bought a glittery cocktail dress and I found a Paul Smith shirt (both only twenty quid). Flash turned out to be less acceptable than I had imagined because the owner agreed a discount only on condition that I stopped him crawling under her rails of clothes.

In the next stop, a bead shop, to make up a necklace for Kate, Flash was a nightmare. The stock is arranged into dozens of open boxes so that customers can pick and mix. Unfortunately, lots had been dropped on to the floor.

'Excuse me, your dog is eating our beads,' said the indignant assistant.

Everybody else might have been matching colours and toying with different arrangements but nothing so dainty for Flash, who was systematically hoovering everything up irrespective of size, shape, colour – or even taste. Kate paid for what she had chosen but thankfully, I was not asked to cough up for Flash's selection.

We had a great evening at the Rivoli; Kate looked fabulous and kept all my friends entertained with tales from what she described as Puppy Boot Camp. However, the evening had one cloud: Andy had been due to join us, but despite emailing and calling, I had failed to reach him until late afternoon – at which point he cancelled. Apparently, he had been out on Friday night and only got to bed on Saturday lunchtime and therefore was too tired to come out dancing.

I was calm on the phone, but there's one thing having a puppy has taught me and I expect it works with men too: give an inch and they take a mile. We will have words.

Sunday 6 February

Last night's dancing, getting home late, travelling around the South East to interview couples for my article during the week plus an energetic puppy – who mainly sleeps while I'm working – has left me feeling completely 'monged-out'. (Andy's way of explaining his state of mind after four back-to-back ten-hour night shifts at the supermarket where he works.)

Flash allowed me to sleep in this morning until 9 a.m., but had no patience for breakfast and the Sunday papers. Exasperated and exhausted, I have to confess I understood why teenage mothers leave their babies in baskets in hospital waiting rooms. He's not really half Border Collie and half Brittany Spaniel – more like half angel and half demon. I longed to be able to move from room to room without tripping over the dog; to fold the laundry without first taking a dog's nose out; not to have to watch in case he starts tearing threads off the carpet where the metal edging has come away between the kitchen and the living room. My bed was calling a sweet siren song about crisp linen sheets and lie-ins until lunch; Flash was agitating for a walk. I had no choice: Flash can make more noise.

The fresh air restored a little of my humour and by the time we returned, Kate was up. She offered to take him out in the garden – while she smoked a cigarette and drank her coffee – which would leave me free to catch up on my diary. For the first five minutes, it was bliss. I didn't have to hunt round for his chew or listen out for the different noises made by his teeth against anything else. Heaven! However, my feet began to get cold – Flash normally curls up and sleeps either on them or close by.

'Use the time to concentrate. Think of all the work you'll get done,' I told myself.

I typed out a couple of paragraphs but it was no good. The office seemed so empty without Flash. I wandered into my bedroom, which faces out over the garden, and watched Flash sitting quietly beside Kate on the steps from the patio down to the lawn. His black and white fur seemed to shimmer in the winter sunlight, his head cocked to one side and even from behind I knew he was wearing his quizzical 'tell me more' expression. It was one of the first chances I've had to watch him, unless he's asleep, without worrying. I was filled with a peace I had not felt for so long. A peace I had ached for, almost without knowing it since… well, since I crawled out from under the exhaustion of my first two months without Thom. It was Sunday. Why bother to work?

I joined Kate and Flash on the step. Flash immediately leapt on to my lap, but has grown so quickly over the past week that curling into a ball proved impossible. Eventually, he got comfortable by stretching out lengthways along my knees. As Flash fell asleep, Kate and I shared our fears of never ever finding someone to love us again.

In the evening, Kate went back to Wales and I went line dancing. Outside the hall, I spotted Andy – with a new and rather fetching haircut. Closer up, I realised that he had cuts and gashes on his face.

'What happened?' I enquired.

'Friday night, Brighton seafront. Three men were trying a spot of queer bashing with an elderly man. I stepped in to rescue him and they turned on me.'

Instantly, I felt a heel for being angry about Saturday night.

'You should have seen how they came off.' He swaggered with a bravado which reminded me of Flash's approach to larger dogs. In fact, with his rugby-player body and baby face, Andy is like a puppy whose feet are too big for the rest of its body.

'Weren't you frightened?' I asked anxiously.

'Not until about ten minutes after they'd gone and I started shaking uncontrollably,' he replied.

I decided to put his cancelling our date down to shock rather than rudeness.

After the class, he massaged my back so expertly that I forgave him altogether.

Tuesday 8 February

Although the weather has been quite good, this morning it was raining heavily. The last thing I wanted to do was to tramp out into the garden in my dressing gown and wellies. I opened the back door and tried to persuade Flash to go out. No luck, but he must have needed to pee because the newspapers had not been used.

I'd left my wellington boots outside, in case Flash tried to chew them, and the rain had made them damp inside. Shuddering, I put them on and, head bowed against the wind and rain, struggled across the patio. I looked down, expecting to hear the rattle of dog tag against collar, but Flash was looking out from the warmth of the outhouse.

'Stuff it,' I thought, 'I can't force him.' So I returned to fix his breakfast, hoping that would kick-start his bowels and bladder.

Flash followed me into the kitchen and promptly urinated all over the floor. Furious, I caught him mid-flow and, as the trail towards the back door showed afterwards, picked him up and flung him out.

It was the first time I had outwardly lost my temper with him.

Flash was completely baffled.

— ❧ —

My dog certainly likes his creature comforts. I had to drag him out of the house today for his morning walk. As Flash did not perform on the streets of Hurstpierpoint, I was determined to catch him as he woke from his post-perambulation snooze. It was still raining when I opened the back door again.

Flash looked at me as if to say:

'Are you mad?'

So I put on my damp boots and ran round the garden, waving my hands around and getting thoroughly wet – all in a vain attempt to tempt him out.

Eventually, as gingerly as a Siamese cat, Flash tiptoed across the wet flagstones and took refuge under a bush.

I slogged across the muddy grass to visit all his favourite 'get busy' sites. Pointless.

For first time ever, he left me in the garden and returned to the warmth of the house.

So I gave up and returned inside too.

Back in my office, Flash lay under my desk and groomed himself dry. He is turning out to be a fastidious dog. While Tyson would run through every muddy puddle, Flash steps gingerly round them – even if there is something really exciting on the other side, like a toddler in a pushchair whose face needs licking.

I alternate between worrying that I am pushing Flash too hard, expecting too much from a small puppy, and worrying that he will disgrace me tomorrow in front of my parents, who are making a special trip down to Hurstpierpoint to meet him.

The sun finally returned this afternoon. So our second walk was a pleasure, rather than a chore. The snowdrops have been joined by crocuses. Flash tried to eat both a yellow and a purple one. The village greengrocer has the first cut daffodils of the season in buckets outside his shop.

Spring will soon be here and along with it, the third anniversary of Thom's death.

In the twitten, Flash made friends with an elderly lady, who must have been at least eighty. She made a great fuss of him and confessed:

'I've had dogs all my life. Mine died recently and I do miss him so much. He was fifteen.'

'Are you planning to get another one?'

'No point,' she said wistfully. 'I'm almost blind.'

We both knew that was not what she really meant.

As Flash and I walked away, there was a tear in my eye. I'm glad I finally stopped waiting for the perfect time to have a dog and seized the day.

Today, Flash has passed another milestone in his training by sitting quietly alone in the car while I had my hair cut. As I've graduated from thinning to balding, he did not have to wait very long, but still I was proud of him. Hopefully, we'll both pass muster tomorrow.

Wednesday 9 February

On our way up the village recreation ground, Valerie and Lily, also starting their morning walk, caught us up. I had been discussing taking Flash over the fields, between the High Street and Hurstpierpoint College, for a few days. I'd been waiting until he became more confident – after all, this is where the big dogs hang out. Valerie reported that it was not too muddy, so we decided there was no time like the present.

I had hardly let Flash off the lead before he and Lily were barrelling together down the narrow track beside the new housing development. So when we reached the main field, currently sown with wheat, they were ready for a game of chase and ear tug. As our dogs played, Valerie explained the 'morning slots' system that unofficially operated over the fields. Lily had the 8.00 a.m. slot, which meant that she could avoid Buster – a perfectly nice Irish Wolfhound – but Lily had once become tangled in his lead and they are now mortal enemies.

As we picked our way through the muddy puddles, I could see a woman ahead walking her dog. Valerie confirmed that it was Chloe – an elderly cross between a Collie and a Kelpie (Australian cattle dog). Chloe had been rated by Lily as acceptable, although Lily would sometimes try to intimidate her by crouching down and then charging past. Flash had not met Chloe before, so I was prepared for his whining and trying to scrabble up into my arms. I resisted the urge to pick him up. Instead, I made him sit and comforted him by stroking his chest. Emboldened, he dashed over and happily greeted Chloe. Even a warning bark when he accepted a pat and a fuss from Chloe's mistress did not faze him. His presence emboldened Lily and the three dogs raced together over the field.

With the dogs playing happily, Valerie could fill me in on village politics – far more complex and harder to resolve than dogs' disputes. Hurstpierpoint Age Concern has merged with the neighbouring Hassocks branch and the rota for ferrying elderly ladies over to the day centre is now completely in tatters. Each lady wants to have the prestigious front seat in the best car. Mr Brown with his BMW is, apparently, the driver of choice. While children establish pecking orders by who can run the fastest and climb the highest tree, at the other end of the age scale degrees of infirmity establish top dog status. Some ladies are even suspected of exaggerating their mobility problems to bag the front seat. Today, one of the worst offenders will be asked to practise getting in and out of the back of a two-door saloon in the village car park or risk never having a lift to the centre again.

— ❧❦ —

When Flash and I returned home, I had no problems cleaning the mud off him as we've turned it into a game. Flash retreated to his basket and I threw a towel over his head. While he rolled around playing 'Murder in the Dark', I rubbed him down. Unfortunately, he managed to get his bedding – freshly laundered for my parents' visit today – all dirty again. I had hoped that chasing Lily would have worn him out and made him on his best behaviour for their arrival. However, after a nap under my computer desk, he was invigorated and ready for fresh adventures. As I changed into something a little less dog grimy, Flash tried to climb on to the new chinos I'd bought with my Christmas money.

I had forgotten just how much longer it takes to go anywhere with Flash, so we reached Burgess Hill station just in time – punctuality is important in my family. The 11.28 pulled alongside the platform just as I made Flash sit. My mother and father were not certain whether to greet me or make a fuss of the black and white puppy leaping up at them. I made their mind up for them by giving them both a kiss on the cheek. As my mother petted Flash, my father recited a line from my favourite childhood story:

'We're off to the station to wait for the train…' I had demanded to be read this Little Noddy story so often that over thirty-five years later he can still recite the first few lines.

My family finds it hard to express feelings. Before Thom's death, it was easier to pretend that it didn't matter. However, when my parents *and* my sister could not make his memorial service in England, I could no longer ignore the problem and in a restrained, understated way – typical of my family – I tried to have it out with them all. However, I've since found that dogs are a better bridge than words. When I took Tyson to the Christmas family gathering, my mother showed she was concerned about me by making a big fuss of him. Twelve months later, when I went up to Cheshire to visit my sister and her family, I had longed to give my young niece and nephew a big hug. However, I sensed they would have been embarrassed by such an outward sign of emotion. Instead, they made a great show of wrestling with Shadow – then a six-month-old puppy. I would have loved to get down on the floor too, but instead I asked them about their schools.

When I brought my parents back from the train station, my father took a seat in the living room. I ground beans for Thom's filter coffee machine in the kitchen. My mother took Flash down to the bottom of the garden to play Fetch. Unfortunately, he has still not grasped the concept. He will chase a ball but neither picks it up nor brings it back. After a while, they both got bored and returned to the kitchen and my mother helped carry Thom's coffee set through to the living room.

Even though I have never fed Flash titbits, he tried to beg a piece of my mother's home-baked chocolate cake (which she had brought down from Bedford). Otherwise, he sensed he should be on his best behaviour and we were spared those mad spells where he chases an imaginary puppy round the house.

After coffee, I drove up to Devil's Dyke – a local beauty spot at the top of the Sussex Downs – so we could give Flash a quick run before we had lunch in the pub. The view out across Sussex to the sea was stunning and the wind bracing. Flash was excited by all the new smells and new dogs to meet, so he hung back as we strode off across the springy grassland. As I am trying to establish firm discipline on the lead, I allow Flash plenty of leeway off the lead. So I was a little surprised to find my mother calling him and shooing him away from something tasty in the longer grass.

When my sister and I were children and misbehaved or begged too many sweets off our grandmother, she would threaten us that when we grew up and had children of our own that she would get her revenge by spoiling them until they were sick – leaving us to clean up the mess. As I turned out to be gay, this proved to be an empty threat. However, now I have a puppy, my mother has gone to the opposite extreme and begun disciplining him – without asking me first. Being a Marshall, I did not say anything but did keep Flash closer to us.

Finally, he calmed down enough to 'get busy' and could be safely left in the car. I remember the food my parents had, the fish bake, and I had chicken covered with cheese and bacon – but I have no recollection of what we talked about. Afterwards, we took Flash for a longer run to reward him for being patient. When we got back, I showed my father how he could use the Internet to update the family tree he has been researching. So it was not until we all sat down for a cup of tea and another slice of chocolate cake, before they got back on the train, that I finally asked:

'What do you think of Flash?'

I felt rather ashamed that I was still seeking my parents' approval at forty.

'He's a super dog and I think you're training him very well,' replied my mother.

I reached down and tickled Flash under the chin.

Both of us need praise.

— ❧ —

I have been recommended a dog training class by Valerie Banfield – another of my dog-owning neighbours.

'What should I bring – beyond the dog?' I had asked the trainer.

'Your wife,' Jeff had replied.

I'd meant what kind of training lead, what rewards? But my wife! I had landed back in a seventies sitcom where it was assumed everybody was married; mixed-sex flat shares were the source of endless double entendres and being gay – well – that was off the scandal Richter scale. Perhaps he serves pineapple chunks on sticks with cubes of Cheddar cheese and – on special occasions – they might even be stuck into half a grapefruit.

However, Jeff sounded really pleasant – and unlikely to bark orders at us – so I took down directions.

When I arrived at the Sea Cadet hut in Burgess Hill, I think Flash sensed my nervousness. There must have been a party at the nearby football club because every space in the car park was taken. As soon as he was let out of the car, Flash took a dump, followed by a pee and just to be sure, another dump outside the door of the classroom. I was so pleased that I forgave him for peeing on my hall carpet after we returned from taking my parents to the station.

I gave the door to the hut a good push – a tip from Valerie Banfield, who had almost spent her first class outside because she had been pulling – and timidly entered our first puppy training class. Unlike my sister, who had to be prised off the steering wheel by my mother, finger by finger, on her first day at school, Flash bounded in. We were immediately mugged by a barking Jack Russell called Kerry. Flash was surprised that something so small could be so aggressive, while I was surprised that I was not at Abigail's party and there was no Demis Roussos playing.

A friendly smallish man with a straggly beard and a green quilted jacket strode over and made a fuss of Flash:

'It looks like you have a quiet night for your first time,' he told my dog.

'You must be Jeff,' I said to him.

For the first time he looked at me, rather than the dog. He had kind eyes. It made a nice change from my first day at school, where my first form mistress, Miss Cosgrave, must have been 7 feet 6 tall. In fact, it was Jeff who was slightly intimidated by my notepad and pen.

'Nobody's written down what I've said before.'

The other members of the class were a Cocker Spaniel (Ellie), a large chocolate Labrador with the suitably substantial name of Huxley and a timid Red Setter (Sparkle). I don't know the owners' names because although everybody asked Flash's name, nobody introduced themselves or asked my name.

We were about to start when the door was flung open and in on scrabbling paws came a huge German Shorthaired Pointer. I almost expected Brian Blessed as the Lord of the Underworld to be roaring hell and damnation at the other end of the lead but a thin middle-aged woman with large spectacles was dragged into the class. The dog was called Brian but once again the owner remained nameless.

Flash and I had retreated to the corner with the Calor Gas heater; Flash for the warmth, me to be less conspicuous. It was a mistake. We were the closest to the door, so Brian lunged straight over. Flash did not even come up to his ankles and Brian had to bend down to sniff. However, Flash stood his ground. With many tugs on the choke chain and frantic blasts on a high-pitched whistle, Brian was finally made to sit. I knew that however badly Flash behaved, it was impossible for him to top the class clown.

Finally, we were joined by Sasha, a German Shepherd puppy – whose fluffy coat was remarkably similar to his lady owner's hairstyle – and a Tibetan Terrier called Barley made up the seventh class member.

Flash watched from between my legs while the big dogs were taken in pairs up and down the classroom at their owners' heels. Next came the turn of the smaller dogs to parade up and down; and, as Jeff commented, they put the big dogs to shame. But then anybody could shine next to Brian. Flash and I had yet to meet the Tibetan Terrier, who had performed his turn with prize-winning style, so we went over to introduce ourselves. Although his owner looked like she might follow alternative religions, Barley had none of the Zen calm of his homeland and barked snappily at Flash. Obviously, the star of the class could not possibly mix with a new boy. We retreated to the safety of the Calor Gas heater.

The next exercise was for all the dogs – still on their leads – to be taken into the centre and allowed to socialise. Flash and I stepped into the ring.

'Call your dogs back,' instructed Jeff.

Flash came bounding back straight away.

'Look, the puppy put you all to shame,' remarked Jeff. 'First back!'

Our hearts swelled.

— ❧ —

While the other dogs had their next lesson and we watched, Jeff's assistant judged it a good time to register me and collect the fees.

I was given a card with 'FLASH' in the top left corner and asked for my address and telephone number. I added my name too. Finally, it was time for some individual attention from Jeff.

'Did I ask you to bring any puppy treats?' he asked.

I shook my head but did not add: only my wife.

He went over to his rucksack and produced some broken biscuit.

'I don't like to use food, because you can end up with a dog which will do nothing if you've forgotten the treats, but puppies need a little help.'

We were taken to the top of the classroom and I gave Jeff the lead.

'Hold the biscuit in front of his nose, so he can lick it, and walk forward with his name and the instruction: *close*.'

Flash was mesmerised by the biscuit and followed Jeff for the first quarter of the room, when he suddenly realised I had not moved and he turned back.

'He wants his daddy,' joked Jeff.

Although I don't want Flash to be too dependent, I have to confess I was secretly pleased not to have been abandoned for the sake of a corner of biscuit. My turn to try the exercise and Flash followed the treat, no problem, but he kept nipping at my fingers.

'Flash – close,' I commanded. 'Flash – close.'

'You're holding him back with the lead,' Jeff pointed out. 'Just use the biscuit.'

I tried to follow his instructions but lost my concentration and Flash got his teeth round the biscuit. We tried a second time, but this time I was worse. While I was trying to let the lead go loose, pretend the class was not watching my every mistake and stopping puppy teeth from getting the treat, I kept getting the commands wrong:

'Flash – come' rather than 'Flash – close.'

Tapping my head and rubbing my stomach at the same time, in contrast, would have been child's play.

We retreated from the spotlight and while I watched the other owners for tips, Flash found the chalk from the blackboard and conducted his own experiments into whether it would make a good dietary supplement. As Ellie the Spaniel hung back on her lead, yet again, I learned a valuable lesson: dogs try to wear you down. After all, it is one of the few strategies open to them, and if they repeatedly lunge for an empty crisp packet, it is very tempting to give in. All Ellie was learning was that with enough determination and enough pestering she could eventually win. No wonder Flash has such a fascination for rubbish. I've been unwittingly reinforcing it. Like all wisdom, it was remarkably simple – but if Jeff had told me earlier I would not have fully understood. I needed to witness it myself.

In the final exercise, Brian had a chance to shine. All the experienced dogs were made to 'sit' and then 'stay' in the middle of the room and their owners backed away slowly. Despite being a nightmare on the lead, Brian was happy to wait patiently until his owner called him over.

After class, Brian and Huxley practised their retriever skills and I asked about toilet training. Jeff repeated the mantra of taking them out after every meal, every time they wake up out to the special place in the garden and giving the command.

'I've been doing that but Flash gets distracted by sticks, pruning the honeysuckle or rolling over on to his back.'

'Put him on the lead and take him straight to his spot,' reinforced Jeff.

'When I'm busy on the computer, I can't always spot when he wakes up,' I replied weakly.

Jeff was not accepting any backsliding and repeated his advice.

I hung my head in shame.

'He's a very intelligent dog. I'm sure he will have it learned in two weeks' time.'

I sighed and headed home.

All this talk about his bladder must have had an effect on Flash. As soon as we hit the grass outside, he squatted down.

That night, I followed Jeff's instructions. I put Flash on the lead and took him straight to the spot where the willow tree had been – until its roots started undermining the foundations.

'Get busy,' I told him, and he did.

Perhaps I will eventually gain the upper hand. Perhaps puppy training is not so difficult after all.

Except, I might have spoken too soon. During the night, Flash fought back with his own brand of mind control. In the same way he had used my dreams to worm his way into my life and later tell me his name, he projected an image of himself lying in my arms. Since Thom died, I have been sleeping with a stuffed toy puppy – originally bought to cheer him up when he'd had several days of fever. In the early hours, this cuddly toy seemed to grow into Flash-sized proportions. The notion felt so real, I turned on the bedside light to check Flash had not picked the outhouse lock and sneaked upstairs.

Friday 11 February

Great art doesn't just stay in the gallery or the theatre, it seeps into your life. Visiting the Turner Prize Exhibition at the Tate Gallery, the video installation by Jane and Louise Wilson had been powerful enough to scramble my brain. For *Las Vegas, Graveyard Time*, their cameras had scanned the empty grandiose interiors of the Desert Inn and Caesar's Palace intercut with the corridors of the Hoover Dam pumping station which controls the city's water supply and support system. By projecting the results over four walls of a small room, the sisters achieved an effect like stepping into a kaleidoscope. As I walked out of the Tate, to sit on the steps and answer my mobile, the natural lines of the river, the buildings and the lights strung along the embankment started arranging themselves into similar patterns. The shapes dislodged themselves from their surroundings and danced from the horizon right up close until I could almost touch them. I was high on art.

I had a similar effect after the play *Peggy for You* at the Comedy Theatre in the West End. Maureen Lipman played the literary agent Margaret Ramsay (who is best known for being the agent of Joe Orton and was played by Vanessa Redgrave in the film *Prick Up Your Ears*). Her advice: if in doubt, head for the nearest precipice. Maureen Lipman played her as a woman who was so upfront her emotions arrived ten minutes before she did. Heady stuff for a public schoolboy whose own feelings normally followed ten years behind.

On the journey home after the theatre, the train divided at Three Bridges railway station. Two strangers, one blond and one dark, leapt into my carriage and asked if they were in the right portion for Brighton. When I told them they were, the blond one pulled out his mobile and started speaking quickly in a foreign language.

'My sister,' he explained. 'We're Swedish, although normally we speak English, or everybody thinks we are talking about them.'

Normally, I would have smiled and picked up my copy of *'Tis* by Frank McCourt. Perhaps because the book was disappointing or perhaps because some of Peggy Ramsay's manifesto for living dangerously had seeped into my soul, I replied waspishly:

'They must be extraordinarily self-centred to believe that.'

'The last time I went to Brighton, I had a pie shoved in my face. I was fourteen and this girl told me I didn't understand about true love,' he said changing the subject.

'Was it hot?' I asked. Some of Ramsay's manifesto for writing dangerously had entered my soul too and I was imagining the Swede as a character in a play I might start.

'No,' he replied, puzzled.

'It would have been more interesting if she'd really made you suffer for love.'

He was thinking about enrolling in the Swedish Army for a good general training and doubted there would be another European war:

'If there is, we'll all be in it together,' he smiled and beamed round the carriage.

'I won't have to fight,' I assured him – not being conscripted must be one of the few benefits of being forty. 'I'll be in some warm office typing letters to your mothers to tell them you're DEAD.'

Perhaps I'd taken too much art and crossed over into the loony on the train.

'You'll have to find my mother first,' chipped in the dark English boy who'd got in the carriage with him. 'She disappeared a week ago.'

'What does your father think?'

'They're separated.'

'But he must have an opinion.'

'We don't talk about things like that,' he replied sulkily.

I had overstepped the mark:

'Sorry.'

I returned to my book, hoping it was art rather than dog-owning that had made me so blunt. Please tell me I'm not turning into one of those forthright people who run animal shelters and think they have the right to tell others how to live their lives.

Saturday 12 February

In the early morning spring sunshine, the Downs that stretch out to the south of the village were almost a blue-green. The air was fresh. The village was just waking up to a long peaceful weekend – such a contrast with the bustle of Central London yesterday, especially after locking myself away in the countryside with a small puppy for the past fortnight.

Last summer, I decided to move up to London. I told myself that everything interesting happens in London and Hurstpierpoint is a backwater. If I truly want to make my living as a writer (rather than a journalist), I need to feed myself with adventure and if I wanted to be a playwright, I should immerse myself in the gritty reality of city life. Unfortunately, London's turbo-charged property market ran away from me. Even if I got the full price for my three-bedroom detached house with a garage, I couldn't afford a flat with a second bedroom for an office in Zone Two and I abandoned the idea. However, I have still harboured fantasies of an urban lifestyle – sipping a latte at some trendy street café and shopping for curios off Brick Lane.

Today, as Flash and I extended our walk further along the lane behind the High Street, I began to change my mind. The footpath opens into a large field, where there were plenty of other owners out walking their dogs. I stopped to talk to an imposing man – probably a retired army officer – whose two dogs, a Jack Russell cross and a rather arthritic Labrador, were the scourge of the neighbourhood foxes. He explained where all their different earths were hidden around the village.

Yesterday lunchtime, I had chatted to a secretary walking her boss's dog; she worked at an information technology recruitment business based in the village. I never knew there was anything so twenty-first century in Hurstpierpoint. I might have been invisible before Flash, but I had also been blind to the complexity of village life before I slowed down to dog-walking pace and looked around. And I have enjoyed talking to other people out walking their dogs and discovering the village characters. It seems like I have found my pack.

But what did that make me before? When I used to drive out of the village in the morning to go to work in a nearby town, skulk back after dark and put a chop under the grill, had I been a lone wolf? I could feel the tension rising through my solar plexus, spreading like fever in my chest, catching at my throat and colouring my cheeks the deepest crimson.

— ❧ —

After walking Flash, I went to the gym. On my return, I discovered he had developed a nasty new habit: chewing the door from the outhouse to the kitchen. I caught him at it again and tried one of my dog training book hints: don't scold the dog, scold the object they have been chewing. I felt rather stupid shouting: bad door, naughty door. Still, I think it worked with the spider plant at the bottom of the stairs. It is a descendant of a wedding present given to Thom's parents over fifty years ago. Flash had loved pulling at the baby plants growing down to his level and although I still find small chewed pieces of leaf on the hall carpet, he has not really attacked the plant since it was told off.

In the evening, I had hoped to do something with Andy, but he could not make up his mind whether to honour an existing promise to escort a friend to a London club or not. Either way was fine with me, but I had asked him to decide so I could make alternative arrangements if he wasn't free. Finally, I had an email yesterday informing me he would see how long he slept in and let me know this afternoon. Hopeless. So I told him I would be busy tonight and went to a party in London instead.

Sunday 13 February

The weather was perfect for a walk along the seafront. However, before Flash and I could set off, we had our traditional fight over seating arrangements. I want Flash to sit in the footwell on the passenger side. He wants to be allowed on the seats and preferably on my lap. I will take him round to the passenger side and show him the footwell. He will jump in and I say 'sit'. So far, so good. However, when I close the passenger door and go round to the driver's side, by the time I get there he's sitting patiently waiting on my seat. Pushing him down into his place is getting harder because he's growing stronger and he's learned to brace himself. So I tried a new tactic today. I sat Flash in his rightful place in the passenger footwell and then slid across the passenger seat, over the gear stick and on to the driver's seat. Flash looked surprised, but he stayed in his place all the way down to Brighton.

Hove was so busy I had to drive twice round the war memorial before finding somewhere to park. The esplanade and lawns were equally packed. Fortunately, Flash has kicked his cigarette habit – although a cigar end is still a prized find. Unfortunately, he discovered a new hobby: shredding and eating sea sponges. He would pounce on the largest piece possible and run behind me with it in his mouth. He tried to keep up as I strode towards the 'Meeting Place' for coffee and cake reward but the temptation to stop to rip up his latest sponge would be too great. Before too long, I would put twenty-five or even fifty yards between us. On the village green this would not have been a problem – because there is normally only one pair of legs to chase after. However, with half of southern England enjoying the early spring sunshine, Flash had to run up to pair of jeans after pair of jeans before I put him out of his misery and called his name. His ears pricked up, and his short legs raced in my direction: outsized ears and white chest frantically bobbing up and down. Occasionally, I slowed down and he ran straight past without recognising me.

Hiding amongst the crowd is probably the urban equivalent of the tip my sister was given when Shadow was a puppy. They walk him in the woods near their house, but he would keep disappearing into the undergrowth after rabbits and not reappearing for ages. Instead of standing on the path calling his name, their dog training instructor suggested hiding behind a tree – that way he could no longer assume they would wait for him and he would learn to keep an eye on their progress.

At the café, I put Flash on the lead and order filter coffee and a doughnut. Balancing both on a tray and not being pulled off balance by Flash proved tricky. Especially when the sea breeze blew the milk sachet out of the saucer and Flash tried to give chase. I found a free table, put down the tray and slipped the end of Flash's lead under a chair leg. I sat down just in time to stop the chair being dragged behind Flash, who wanted to investigate a seagull that had landed nearby. Despite the coffee being slopped into the saucer, it tasted good – almost as good as it did when Thom and I would make our Sunday afternoon walks along Hove seafront.

Andy failed to show for line dancing, so the Valentine I had carefully chosen to be funny rather than romantic remained in the car.

Monday 14 February

Valentine's Day and no card. Not even the electronic one that Andy hinted he might send. The feelings of rejection were compounded by a phone call from the *Sunday Times*. I had suggested a profile for their 'Life in the Day' feature on Dee Forman, a fifty-nine-year-old mother of four and grandmother of five, who owns and runs Britain's longest-running gay sauna. The magazine editor had been worried how it would read in a 'family newspaper' but I wanted to add the *Sunday Times* to my stable of papers and – for the first time in years – agreed to write the profile speculatively.

The interview with Dee had been fun. Although broad-minded about what her customers got up to in the 'rest' cabins, she preferred to be euphemistic about the details. 'I ask my clients to treat the place as if it is my home – which I suppose, in a way, it is. To avoid any nasty surprises when cleaning up, I have signs saying: "PLEASE PUT THE SWEETIE PAPERS IN THE BIN". Most people understand what I'm referring to – without me having to use "the word". However, I did have some people asking for a complimentary mint. I told them to use their imagination.' With Dee sounding like she had stepped out of a Carry On film, I doubted even *Sunday Times* readers could object.

However, half an hour after emailing the copy, the editor phoned back to inform me first, I had not followed the format properly – which could have been fixed – and second, it was too seedy. I kicked myself for not studying the other 'Life in the Day' features and for messing up this opportunity. Overconfidence or sabotage? Perhaps I'm fed up with knocking out formulaic articles, but lack the courage to dedicate myself to writing something more creative.

Needing to feel wanted, I gave Flash a cuddle on the outhouse step. However, I made the mistake of switching on the radio that I leave on for Flash when I'm out. Classic FM was full of Valentine's Day requests, which did not help my depression. So I picked up my morning newspaper and read an article about how Valentine's Day sentimentality stops us experiencing real love – not a good move either. I started thinking back to past Valentine's Days. Thom and I had not really gone overboard but normally exchanged small presents rather than flowers. What had we done on our final Valentine's Day together, back in 1997? I went upstairs to look at my appointments diary. It had one entry: Gemeinschaftskrankenhaus Herdecke. I had checked Thom into his German hospital, for the last time. Within a month, he was dead. Last year, I had taken Brandon – my ex who had an allergy to dog hair – to a Valentine's party thrown by Richard O'Brien, who created *The Rocky Horror Show*. (I had interviewed him for a feature for the *Daily Express* and the invite was O'Brien's way of saying thank you.) I'd thought, after losing Thom, that I would never love again. However, twelve months ago tonight, I had spoken those 'three little words'. Confessing my feelings had set me free and I remember floating through the streets of Soho, looking for somewhere open for snacks on a Sunday night. A couple of weeks later, he told me that he loved me too. Six months later, it was all over.

Too blue to work, I took a pile of washing upstairs to the bedroom and started folding and putting it away. Flash, naturally, followed me in. It was the first time he'd been in my bedroom for more than a few moments. I watched his reaction to a large mirror leaning up against the wall. (It had been on Thom's bathroom wall in his German flat and when he moved over to England, five years ago, he'd left it temporarily in our bedroom and I hadn't moved it.) Flash was studying the small Border Collie/Brittany Spaniel cross mix which was staring back at him. Being a clever dog, he had worked out there was some connection between him and his reflection. It was fascinating to watch him move slightly to the right and the matching response in the mirror. I could almost see his brain storing away the information and then trying something else. He sat down, cocked his head to the right and was amazed when the second dog matched him. It was almost like the classic pantomime sketch where somebody breaks the Dame's mirror and has to pretend to be the reflection. However, the Dame smells a rat and tries more and more outlandish tricks to catch them out. I stopped matching up pairs of socks and sat on the bed watching Flash wonder at the world around him.

For the first time in months, I laughed.

Tuesday 15 February

I was woken this morning at 6.40 a.m. by barks to be let out. Flash had been so tired last night, he had taken his late-night snack – biscuit by biscuit – into his basket. As he'd been out into the garden about an hour earlier, I didn't have the heart to take him out into the rain. Although I was paying for it this morning, I was pleased that he had alerted me. For the first time in almost a week, I did not need to put him on the lead as he sprinted to his spot. The early mornings are slowly becoming less grey and, for the first time, I didn't shiver under my dressing gown or jump from foot to foot in my wellington boots. Flash started searching in last autumn's leaves and I tried to revive the hyacinth shoots that he had flattened by rolling over for a tummy tickle, then inspected the daffodils planted in Thom's memory. They should be in flower for his third anniversary on 9 March.

We joined Valerie and Lily for the 8.00 a.m. slot across the fields. On some wet mornings the sound of the traffic from the A23 London to Brighton road carries across a dozen or so fields as a dull drone. This morning, the only sound was a woodpecker tapping against a tree. Squinting into the low spring sunshine through the copse, I spotted the bird and Valerie identified it as a spotted woodpecker. Latest news from the Age Concern battle for the front seat: the old lady in question has refused point-blank to try climbing into the back of the four-door car. Her claustrophobia makes it unthinkable. Her main rival claims it would be impossible for her without flashing a stocking top, which modesty, of course, forbids.

I had a lunch meeting in a Fleet Street pub with Austen, a former colleague from Radio Mercury (where I worked between 1984 and 1996), who has given up journalism and become a screenwriter for American made-for-TV movies. I had hoped for some contacts, but his agent has been left a paraplegic after a car accident and he has lost the contract. Austen alternated between memories of the golden days of Fleet Street, when all the daily papers had their offices and printing presses here, and trying to persuade me to return to radio management. He was worried that after Thom's death I had locked myself away in Hurstpierpoint. However, the more he talked about the challenges, the more I knew locking myself away in a corporate office would be a slow form of suicide. On the train back to Sussex, I could not decide whether sticking to my resolve was a positive sign of my commitment to my own writing or the curse of bereavement's long shadow.

Flash had not been idle in my absence. His project to strip all the rubber lagging off the pipes that run through the outhouse has almost been completed. He has also excavated the concrete which failed to set properly when the washing machine was plumbed in. It is hard to believe that only three weeks ago I thought the room puppy-proof. On a more positive note: the back door was not more noticeably chewed.

I am profiling the kitchen of the hypnotist Paul McKenna for the *Daily Express* tomorrow. He has an accelerated learning video to promote, so I put it on and settled down on the sofa and Flash curled up at my feet. However, after an early start and a busy day for both of us, we were both exhausted. I woke half an hour later to a blank screen and a snoring puppy. I'd been so deeply asleep that balancing on one foot to slip on my wellington boots, to take Flash out, needed my full concentration. No wonder the tape sternly warns not to operate any heavy machinery after watching. Still, if it had such a dramatic impact on me, what effect will it have on Flash?

Wednesday 16 February

I have been visiting famous people and listing the contents of their fridge for just over a year. It used to feel terribly intrusive but

I'm so used to it now that on one occasion I forgot to ask before opening the door and whipping out my pad and pen. Amongst the standard questions I have to ask is: who do you live with? As Paul McKenna is single, I tried to introduce the topic in an offhand sort of way. Why this should seem intrusive when I already know what brand of low-fat spread he uses is beyond me – but it does. So, first a couple of compliments about the kitchen – all in pale wood – to soften him up. Throw in a diversionary tactic like: how long have you lived here? Finally, the killer question:

'No, I live alone,' he replied.

'Any cats or dogs?' I asked hopefully. The house suddenly felt terribly empty.

'No.'

'Is there anybody special in your life at the moment?' Not something my editor insists on knowing, but I just could not bear the idea of him being so alone.

I've profiled everything from happily married with loads of kids, through to single mums and celebrities living with some variation of the extended family – their mother or even their brother – but this was the first time I'd come across anyone totally alone. First, I was struck by an overwhelming sense of sadness and then by the realisation that one month ago that was me too. Despite Paul McKenna's two terraced gardens with views over Kensington, the second flat in New York and the fact that celebrities like Leonardo DiCaprio, Hugh Grant, Liz Hurley and Christina Ricci come to his shows, I did not feel even a shadow of envy.

The contents of Paul McKenna's fridge were very revealing:

'It seems to have been filled by the girls I've dated. Perhaps that's why I have such an eclectic mix of ingredients. No need for a photograph album, I can open the door and remember. I don't know what the lemon juice is for, so it was certainly bought by a former girlfriend – same with the salsa. There's even a mystery bottle with no label – hopefully it's not a revenge time bomb!'

Over the past few months, Paul has reassessed his life and started cooking again:

'Pretty much all my career ambitions have come true in the last ten years. However, I still feel vulnerable in relationships; cautious about letting myself go. My heart has been broken three times, but I've chosen to move on. My new goals include a wife and a family. I think I'm ready. I've enjoyed the single life, but I'd like to be in a relationship and for the contents of my fridge to finally settle down too!'

I left his home feeling glad that with Flash I'm no longer alone, but wishing I had McKenna's confidence about the future.

Dog classes included all the usual suspects, with the exception of Barley – the Tibetan Terrier – which Flash considered to be no great hardship. One face we had not met before was another Collie called Sniffy. His owner was a pretty girl in her late twenties/early thirties with an educated Scottish accent, a nice laugh and a laid-back approach to the class. In fact, Sniffy seemed to watch with the same detachment and the closest a Collie can come to a wry smile. Flash and I also proved the axiom that owners become like their dogs, or vice versa, by both trying too hard to please. We started well. The small dogs were lined up one side of the Sea Cadet hut and the big dogs on the other. Jeff instructed us to walk across to them, turn and call our dogs back. Under the cover of a group exercise Flash and I were relaxed: perfectly at heel, perfect recall.

'You'll have trouble keeping up with them.' Jeff praised the small dogs and wound up the big dog owners.

Unfortunately, Sasha, the Alsatian puppy, was determined to be a bad influence. Considering that Flash had spent a large portion of the day on his own, this was not hard. Sasha pulling on the lead towards Flash and barking to play seemed remarkably similar to when I was caught at school flashing a secret code – using playing cards – to my best friend Richard Groves during our French lesson. After I had completed the punishment of moving benches round the playing fields, my headmaster surveyed the red detention slip detailing my crimes and signed by the French master:

'Distracting Groves in class,' he read out sternly and then paused. 'Next time, try something a little more ambitious.'

For the next exercise, Flash and I had to wait while three other pairs of dogs walked up the room at heel, turned, walked back, executed a second turn and sat down. We had been practising the turn – so no problems there – and although I had not expected the second turn or the sit, we were quietly confident. Brian, the unruly German Shorthaired Pointer, seemed to perform better than last week, but neither his owner nor Jeff seemed to think so. He was made to repeat the exercise again.

By the time it was finally Flash and Sniffy's turn, Flash was bored and I was anxious. To make certain he had a proper incentive I produced a puppy training treat; normally, they remain hidden in my pocket until Flash has stayed 'close'. However, the temptation of an easily accessible treat proved too strong for him. We executed the first turn perfectly but on the second one, he kept jumping up and I kept telling him 'no'.

'Can I show you where you were going wrong,' said Jeff and sent us promptly back to basics: holding the treat at Flash's level and allowing him to lick it as he walked to heel.

'But he's fine at home,' I found myself using the same lame excuse that everybody else had trotted out.

Jeff looked at me sternly.

I bit back the temptation to blurt out: 'But it's true!'.

The next exercise involved taking the younger dogs over to the older dogs, one by one, and getting them to sit for a few seconds before calling them back to us. However, Jeff singled out two dogs – Sasha (the Alsatian puppy) and Flash – for an easier version, where they were excused waiting in a sit. I had been a little miffed that we had been put in the same category as Sasha and suggested Flash and I would walk and sit.

Jeff agreed that we could try the full exercise. However, Flash became confused and I had to raise my voice above the din to shout: 'SIT!'

He ignored me and I was told off for being too firm too quickly. Really, I must relax and stop trying to be the perfect pupil.

Flash and I hung back after class to ask for a task for the next two weeks. I am off to *Sing-a-Long-a Sound of Music* next Wednesday. Jeff explained that after 'sit' comes 'stay' – apparently, I should eventually be able to walk right round Flash without him budging from the 'sit' position.

Thursday 17 February

I have been invited to another party on Saturday in London. Last weekend, I'd dropped in for an hour or two and rushed back to let Flash out for a pee. This weekend, I want the option of having a drink and staying over and who knows what else…

On one of Flash's first walks around the village, I met Emma and her dog Jasmine – as usual with a second dog that she was exercising for its owner. She also does boarding but only if the dog gets on with her cats. So today, I took Flash round to her flat at the bottom end of the village.

I had not realised that when she referred to cats she meant nine! Or that she lived in a one-bedroom flat with her mother, who has badly damaged her back, and Jasmine the Collie too. While Flash and Jasmine wrestled on the four-square feet of available floor space, Emma and I discussed terms for a sleepover, and his bedtime routine. Fortunately, Flash ignored the cats who walked haughtily along the top of the sofa and Emma's mother's armchair. However, his behaviour towards Jasmine was not so impeccable. Their play had become even more intense and suddenly – watched by Emma, her mother and nine cats – Flash started humping her. His knowledge of anatomy was a little hazy, but his technique was perfect.

'I don't think Jasmine is coming into her first season, none of the other dogs have spotted it,' explained Emma.

'I'm sorry, he's getting the chop as soon as he's old enough. Does this mean he can't stay?' I worried.

'Never seen anything like it. He's not even four months old. I've been in the dog-sitting business for years, bred dogs all my life,' Emma mused, 'but he seems very…' and she paused before finding the right word 'advanced.'

That's the last time Flash is watching my Paul McKenna accelerated learning tape!

'Still, we're thinking of breeding from Jasmine, so if he does manage it, the puppies would be three-quarters Collie.' Emma was resigned. 'I know of at least one home who would want one.' She brightened up.

— ➳◦❦ —

In the afternoon, I was interviewing Lucinda Lambton – famous for her TV tours of architectural oddities – and her husband Sir Peregrine Worsthorne, the former editor of the *Sunday Telegraph*. From the clippings of their previous interviews, I knew they were great dog lovers and decided to take Flash along with me. Perhaps I could train him as an interview dog? He could frolic innocently at their feet while I stuck a difficult question into an exposed flank.

The hour and a half journey to south Buckinghamshire passed totally uneventfully, and I was very proud of how well Flash settled down in the car. Shortly before arriving at our destination,

I turned off the main road and parked in a farm gateway. Flash was rather startled to find his bowl and lunch being produced from the boot, but voted alfresco eating a big hit. I arrived in the village where Lambton/Worsthorne lived with enough time to give Flash a runaround. We found a delightful old pub with a dog bowl full of water outside. Guessing that Flash would be welcome here, I took my notes into the public bar. The barmaid was delighted to see him and wanted to offer him a dog biscuit; as he had just eaten I refused on his behalf. To prove he really could manage a morsel, Flash strained on his lead to search in their open fireplace for a cinder instead.

The clientele was a strange mixture of businessmen and pensioners, and I spent a happy half hour explaining his breed and agreeing he was a) handsome and b) well behaved. Flash had just lain down by the fire when the barmaid came over to make a fuss of him and he started jumping up over her and mouthing at her bare arms.

'He's so good,' she cooed in his ears.

'I'm sorry, he's not supposed to do that,' I apologised.

'Such a nice temperament; unlike my Jack Russell, who can be evil. Do you know he bit me yesterday?'

'What did you do?' I asked.

'Waited and then bit him back…'

Experienced dog owners are strange, I thought.

'But he just bit me back again,' she finished, sadly.

Just before my interview, scheduled for two o'clock, I returned Flash to the car and rang what I thought was the Old Rectory's front door. It was answered by an elderly man with no trousers who looked very startled when I told him I'd arrived from *Woman & Home* for the interview. Wrong house! I had hoped that Flash would be invited in to play with the Lambton/Worsthorne dogs, but at the right house as soon as I crossed into their gothic hallway with the flagstone floors, ornate trimmings and a midnight blue ceiling festooned with golden stars I knew this was a house in mourning.

'Flint, our Lurcher, died about a week ago in a terrible accident,' explained Lucinda. 'I'm seldom depressed but sat in my office like Ray Milland in *The Lost Weekend* – not moving for two days. It was Perry who cheered me up by talking about Flint in ennobling terms and his glorious death. Perry had tears pouring down his face – it's a nice feature of him – I adore his sentimentality. He really loved Flint because, as a little boy, he had had a dog like him. Life had come a full circle. This huge Lurcher – the size of a horse – would come and sit in his lap every night, so he misses him terribly. When Perry's down I'll try and cheer him up too. We're having a monument built to Flint in the garden and have found some wonderful old stone.'

It sounded like a glorious marriage, but a few questions soon revealed something more complicated:

'Marriage has taught me how to sit on the edge of a volcano and still enjoy myself,' explained Sir Peregrine Worsthorne (aka Perry). 'I used to be rather hysterical but in comparison with my wife I'm a calming influence. She'll often throw things: cameras, saucepans, bottles of chutney. In fact, there's very little she hasn't – even knives. Last night she chose the carving knife; it really escalated because I came running through the hall with a log above my head, screaming abuse, and then threw it at her head. Lucy claims to aim at the floor near me, but I do fear for my life because in that sort of mood she is uncontrollable.'

The next stop, for Flash and me, was Relate in Crawley, where he had his supper in the car park. To reach his 'get busy' grass verge, we had to walk past the entrance to the offices and I was amazed that despite this being only his third visit he tried to anticipate our route and head for the front door. He performed as required on the verge and my expertise with a plastic bag has improved dramatically.

Friday 18 February

When I moved to Hurstpierpoint, in the late eighties, the nearest large supermarket was a half-hour drive away and I would buy everything for the weekend at the small shops which line the High Street. Saturday morning shopping had a touch of Mapp and Lucia – comic novels by E F Benson written in the twenties and thirties, where two upper-middle-class women vie for social dominance – as everyone bustled from queue to queue buying provisions and catching up on gossip.

When Thom finally moved over to England, he opened an account at Clive Miller Butchers at the top of Cuckfield Road. Clive knew my full name – from my Christmas order – and Thom's first name so somehow our account became Thom and Andrew Marshall. Although Thom was against the idea of gay marriage, becoming Thom Marshall at the butcher's appealed to his sense of humour. After he died Valerie asked if there was anything she could do, so I asked her to inform the butcher and all the other shopkeepers Thom knew. So the account was changed to just Andrew Marshall and a couple of weeks later, I settled up and closed it down. By this time a supermarket had opened five minutes away in the neighbouring town of Burgess Hill; I did most of my shopping there and it seemed pointless having an account for an occasional chicken breast and three sausages.

Since Flash's arrival, I have been using the village shops a great deal more. I walk past them twice a day. It is much more convenient than driving to a town centre and with the exception of Alldays convenience store, the butcher's and the library, I can bring Flash inside – perhaps because dog walkers are the most loyal customers.

This morning, Mr Hilton at the electrical shop told me he was retiring. I will have to find somewhere else to order the strange light bulbs that Thom's German lamps need. The ironmonger's are trying to get out of their lease but despite six months of trying, nobody will buy it off them. I don't expect anybody to make a living out of the batteries and ant powder I buy there – but still it seems extraordinarily sad.

Flash had his first visit to the vet this afternoon – just a quick check-up and to enquire about neutering. I had expected the waiting room to be full of sick parrots and lame dogs, but when he raced into the small modern reception area – behind the new post office/newsagent's in the neighbouring village of Hassocks – it was completely empty. We were led into a small room with a large table covered in blue plastic. Flash gave the vet a good licking and was weighed – eight kilos at four months. I left with one worming tablet and a packet of anti-flea treatments but forgot to ask about neutering.

When I got home, I discovered the packet for the worming tablet was marked Flash Marshall – which I found unexpectedly touching. Flash was not so keen. Despite eating stones and mud, he turned his nose up at the small white pill in his food bowl. When I presented it to him on the palm of my hand, he was prepared to try, but realising he had been duped, politely spat it out behind the washing machine. It was third time lucky after I hid the worming tablet in a corner of bread crust.

It had been a long day and we both slept soundly through Friday night TV.

Saturday 19 February

The day started well. We went for an extra-long walk across the fields and Flash had a good play with Chloe the Collie/Kelpie cross. I felt good. I'd been warned dog-owning would change my life, but all the changes have been for the better. Early morning walks listening to the skylark, great lungs full of fresh air, having to tighten my belt another notch, I was at peace with the world. For once, I was not worrying about my career or the house being repossessed or whether I'd ever find love again. Why doesn't everybody get a dog?

—— ❧❧ ——

The naughtiness began with Flash refusing to come when it was time to head home. Although he was only a few feet away, I had to go over to him to clip on his lead. On the way back, it was like he was testing me: pulling just a little but not quite enough to have to stop and check him. After a while, I thought he'd stopped complaining about being back on the lead but he was saving his worst defiance for a witness.

A middle-aged woman returning with a full basket from the High Street called out:

'You've got your hands full.'

I could understand the shame of mothers whose children perform spectacular tantrums in the middle of Tesco. I smiled through gritted teeth:

'He's not normally this bad.'

When a dog pulls on the lead, the instruction is to turn and walk in the opposite direction. It does the trick with Flash. Except today, I'd set off in the new direction and straight away he would be excitedly rushing ahead again and I'd have to turn back round again. My patience was so sorely tried that I yanked Flash round so quickly, he was nearly the first dog in space. I told him 'close' but with no treats in my pocket to reinforce, it had no effect. I even tried stopping, making him sit and reasoning with him – totally pointless. I might as well have acted out the section from the movie *All About Eve*:

'Fasten your leads, it's going to be a bumpy walk.'

My temper was heading towards Lucinda Lambton proportions and throwing around carving knives was beginning to look attractive. I tried to calm myself down but I just seethed inwardly.

'No more long exciting walks off the lead for Flash; at least until he can learn how to behave again.'

I sounded like a punishing father, confining their teenage son to his bedroom, and felt deeply ashamed. It might be a bit late but I decided to look up both Brittany Spaniels and Border Collies and find out more about Flash's parentage.

'Adolescent Border Collies often go through a phase where they challenge their master's authority.'

The website also warned about boundless energy and a need for constant stimulation.

Apparently, the Brittany Spaniel is a comparative newcomer to the British Isles – having arrived in the 1980s, they love exercise and have great stamina:

'They like to have a job but, without the proper guidance, they will often choose something you don't approve of…'

The guide identified Brittany Spaniels as a 'hunt, point and retrieve' breed. It made sense of Flash's emerging personality. I'd already recognised when he went into the classic Sheepdog crouch but not why he would raise a front paw as if pointing at something in the undergrowth.

I wondered what would happen if Flash could look up my genetic inheritance and the impact of my upbringing. Would he understand my need to get things right as a desire to please my mother? Like many women in the fifties, she gave up her career to focus on bringing up first me and then my sister. Although she has never complained and only once talked about what she'd liked to have done – if she hadn't been a mother – I seem compelled to prove her sacrifices were worth it.

— ෯෯ —

Next on my agenda for Saturday morning was a Body Pump class at the local gym, where everybody regaled me with their own stories of disobedient dogs. I was a little anxious about what I would find on my return home. Flash seems to believe that leaving him alone in the morning is an affront to his routine of sleeping under my computer desk. He had scattered all the newspaper I had left by the back door, but my mild irritation soon turned to concern. He had dragged a particularly large chunk of broadsheet into his basket and had been sick. He seemed perky enough, even though he passed on lunch, so I decided not to alter our plans and head on down to Brighton. I was meeting my friend Brian, and Flash was getting another module of his training: walking on the lead in a busy urban environment.

He settled into the car without any problems but when we pulled up outside Brian's flat I discovered that Flash had been sick again – fortunately in an empty cassette case which had fallen on the floor. Perhaps the worming tablet had been too strong? Amazingly, he was not all perturbed and set off confidently to explore the litter of Brighton with Brian and me.

After his performance on the lead this morning, I was surprised to find him quite manageable, with a 50 per cent improvement since two weeks ago and our last walk through the Laines. He must have lost some of his puppy charm, because about 50 per cent fewer people rushed up to stroke him. At lunch, at a pavement café, I tied him to my chair and although he still found countless ways to wind his lead around the table, he did settle down eventually and watch the passing parade.

However we both decided not to notice the Boxer who – despite being off the lead – marched past perfectly at his master's heel. He didn't even look from side to side until, without breaking his stride, he turned and gave a quick glance in our direction. The dog equivalent of sticking his tongue out?

Getting up early to let Flash out, lots of long walks and this morning's Body Pump had taken their toll and I was completely exhausted. I needed a nap before going out tonight and decided I would sleep better if Flash was safely deposited at Emma's house for his sleepover. So I decided to take him round slightly early. He watched in fascination as I loaded his basket, food bowl and hot-water bottle into the car.

Unfortunately, Emma was not back from feeding her horses, and surprisingly, her mother was not in either, so I decided to take Flash round the block instead. We had hardly set off when he started playing up and pulling ahead on the lead. I reversed and walked back the other way until he stopped pulling. Fine. Off we set again. Two steps later, Flash exploded towards something on the verge and my right arm was almost ripped out of its socket. Angrily, I repeated the whole process and turned around, but Flash tried to garrotte himself.

Furious, I shouted at him.

No effect.

While I seethed, Flash looked at me innocently.

I took a deep breath. There were two choices: lose my temper again – tempting, especially when suffering from sleep deprivation – or let him have his own way. Fortunately, I decided on a third option. I calmly followed my dog trainer's instruction and took him in the opposite direction; again and again and again. But with no sharp tugs and no shouting, Flash followed my example and calmed down too. Hallelujah! I had not been disciplining him, I had been frightening him.

We were now able to enjoy our walk around the maze of Hurstpierpoint's local authority housing. I was amazed to find a fish and chip van parked on the verge – according to the bright lettering on the back it also sold American-style doughnuts and hot dogs. I would have bought something but there was a long queue. The van's appearance was obviously part of the Saturday teatime routine, because more residents magically appeared from the surrounding flats. For some reason, it never visits my part of the village. By the time I'd found the way back to Emma's flat, both she and her mother were climbing out of the car. Flash was thrilled to see Jasmine again, I let him off the lead and they wrestled endlessly across the communal lawns.

'I'm afraid that he has been very difficult today.' I was pleased to have someone to share my doggy parenting problems. 'Is four months their equivalent of teenage tantrums?'

'More like the terrible twos,' joked Emma.

'Or perhaps he knew you were planning to leave him,' added her mother.

'But it started this morning, before there were any clues we'd be spending time apart,' I protested.

'They can sense it,' she insisted.

'But I didn't feel guilty, I knew he'd have a wonderful time,' I protested.

Flash streaked past us with Jasmine in hot pursuit.

'Give us an emergency contact number and the name of your vet,' Emma asked.

And then I did feel guilty.

Sunday 20 February

It had been such a good party that it was almost seven in the morning before I made it back home. I did miss Flash, but there was something very refreshing about being able to grab a couple of hours in bed, tidy my bedroom and read the Sunday newspaper without having to worry what mischief my puppy might be up to. However, by lunchtime, the novelty had definitely worn off and I was almost counting down to when I was scheduled to collect him. I'd also been slightly worried that Flash might have had such a wonderful time with Jasmine that he would not want to come home.

Emma answered the door and Flash, as always full of curiosity, stuck his head around the door. Suddenly, he recognised me and bursting with delight started leaping about – for once I did not complain when he started mouthing me and trying to pull at my clothes.

Flash had been a model house guest. Although he hadn't tried to climb on to the furniture or molest the cats, some of them had taken exception to his boisterousness and the pregnant cat had left the house in a huff and was still to return.

Back home, I sat on the stone steps from the terrace down on to the grass with Flash nestling on my lap and opened the Culture section of the paper. The sun had not disappeared behind the house; the combination of birdsong, reading and a warm puppy melted away the edges of my hangover. I sighed and wondered why I'd even bothered to go to the party. By the time I'd reached the Business section, Flash was getting restless so we played ball in the garden and practised 'sit'. Unfortunately, every time I hold out my hand for 'stay' – like I'm a policeman on points duty stopping the traffic – Flash gets overexcited and starts jumping around. Jeff will not be pleased.

I had been hoping to spend the afternoon with Andy. He'd half accepted an invitation for a late Sunday lunch before going to line dancing together. However, he'd asked me to phone at midday to double-check. I'd bitten back my automatic response that such indecision makes shopping almost impossible. Before leaving to collect Flash, I had phoned him and what a surprise: answering machine. I'd left a message and when he'd not called back by two, started to fix lunch for one. I was still hoping to see him at line dancing, but he had not arrived at the start of the class. I kept checking the door – which made it hard to remember the new dance steps – but I had to admit the truth: double no show and no message.

However, I did receive a long-distance dog training tip from Michael (my Australian dog training guru) via his partner Brian:

'Don't push Flash too hard, too soon, or he'll become bored.'

I decided it was just as good advice for dealing with potential boyfriends.

Tuesday 22 February

I dragged myself out of bed early enough to join Valerie and Lily on the 8 a.m. dog-walking slot. I wanted to exhaust Flash – because I would be out for most of the day – and double-check that Valerie could give Flash his lunch and supper. Being half-term, my sister Gayle, my nephew James and niece Nicola were in Bedford, where my family is based, visiting their grandparents. My mother had booked tickets for the Millennium Dome and I was going up to join them for a family day out.

When we met up at London Bridge, the first thing the children wanted to know was whether I'd brought any pictures of Flash. They managed to contain themselves until we reached the Jubilee Line but as soon as the train arrived they demanded that I pass round the puppy snaps. While James and Nicola tried to decide whether Flash took after his mother (Collie) or his father (Spaniel), my mother began sorting through and deciding which ones she'd like copies of:

'That's a nice one of Flash's face,' she held it up for my inspection, 'you can really see his white belly in that one.'

'Is he frightened of the traffic? We had to carry Shadow when he was a puppy,' said Nicola.

I explained how I'd coaxed him up the High Street but felt a bit guilty betraying his secrets.

'I can see you have the Marshall family smirk in that picture,' my mother said and then as an afterthought: 'That's quite a nice photo of you.'

She held up a photo of me looking radiantly happy with Flash in my arms.

'Have as many as you wish. I ordered a second set so the children can have the rest,' I told her.

Nobody asked who had taken the shots of Flash and me together or commented on the one picture of Andy with Flash.

Having watched the Dome being built from Canary Wharf, where I used to work as an Agony Uncle on the cable station Live TV, I was excited to finally be able to visit. Sadly, the contents of the Dome were nowhere near as interesting as the architecture. The main arena acrobatic show, which I'd been particularly looking forward to, broke down halfway through and had to be abandoned. In the play zone, we showed our true colours in a game to test the speed of our reactions. We stood on opposite sides of a large sheet of clear perspex and every time a light flashed we had to press it. The quicker the reflex, the further through the sequence the game could progress in thirty seconds. Adults and children alike were equally determined to score the highest and we were all slightly surprised when each of us knocked off twenty-four lights.

In the play zone, we also sampled a game tailor-made for our family: dogs versus cats. My mother used to, and probably still does, throw a scrubbing brush at any cat who has the temerity to cross our garden. The object of the game was to stop a computer-generated dog from gobbling up the cats on a screen at the front of the auditorium. Even for a pro-dog family this seemed a little bit gory, but nobody said anything. The audience were divided into two teams and by turning batons either to the front or the back could control a wall to protect their cats from the mad dog. The quicker everybody in the team reacted, the quicker the wall rose and the dog would bounce off towards the opposition dogs. The effect was rather like the first generation of Atari tennis computer games. We tried not to groan when our team lost or at the government-approved message the game show host grinned at us as we filed out:

'This just shows what we can achieve if we all just work together.'

Tired but happy, the Marshall family declared the Dome a wasted opportunity and even the children seemed to gain as much pleasure from listing its faults as from its attractions.

Wednesday 23 February

I thought that Flash had coped well with my absence yesterday; after all, Valerie had popped in at regular intervals and he'd been invited into Lily's garden to play. However, today he was remarkably fretful and as soon as he woke up from his post-morning-walk nap, he wanted my undivided attention. I threw his latex chew around to encourage him to play with that instead, but he was not so easily diverted. Every two minutes, he would stick his nose between my legs – his favourite ploy for diverting me from work. Having taken yesterday off, I had to finish my articles on Lucinda Lambton's marriage and Paul McKenna's kitchen so I used the tried-and-tested strategy for all harassed parents: bribery. Brian had given me some treats – left behind after Michael and his dogs returned to Australia. I produced a large chew – made from what looks like cowhide and knotted at both ends. Flash fell on it with relish. Beyond the sound of gnawing, I spent a quiet morning. However, the effect was rather like plonking the kids in front of trashy American cartoons – keeps them quiet in the short term but leaves them hyped up in the long term.

I took Flash for an extra-long walk after lunch to wear him out, but after flopping down for half an hour, he was up and pacing my office again. Out came the hide chew again, and Flash fell on it like a demented demon. Half an hour later, the chewing stopped. The silence sounded ominous. I stopped typing up details of Paul McKenna's favourite restaurants. I was just in time to stop Flash from swallowing and choking on the knotted head of the chew.

Having narrowly averted a disaster, I remembered the warning I'd been given about getting a puppy: you don't know what you're letting yourself in for.

Now I do: constant vigilance.

— ❧ —

After Flash's almost neurotic behaviour today, I had terrible guilt attacks about leaving him this evening. However, I had already booked tickets for *Sing-a-Long-a Sound of Music* in Brighton. I had arranged to meet a group of my ballroom dancing friends in the bar next to the Theatre Royal, but it was hard to spot them amongst the throng of nuns, men in lederhosen and people dressed as 'brown paper packages tied up with strings'. Watching the film, we were instructed to boo the Nazis, hiss the Baroness and singalong with the words that appeared across the bottom of the screen.

The last time I'd seen *The Sound of Music*, in a cinema, I'd been about seven and our family had travelled all the way to Cambridge to watch the wide screen. It was against my school's rules to visit the cinema during term time, so I spent most of the movie worried that I might be spotted by a prefect and given a detention. This time, I worried whether I'd remembered to leave newspaper down for Flash.

Friday 25 February

From time to time, I play a little game with myself. Have I gone a whole day without thinking about Thom? I can be engrossed in something and suddenly the thought pops into my head:

Did you think about about him yesterday?

It's almost like the painting by William Frederick Yeames (1835–1918) *And When Did You Last See Your Father?* The son of a royalist is being questioned by Parliamentarians during the English Civil War for clues to where his father might be hiding. (There was a waxwork tableau recreation of the painting at Madame Tussauds, which made a great impression on me when I was a boy.) Except in my version, I'm trying to work out how my recovery from bereavement is going and I'm both the young boy in blue and the panel of interrogators. Somehow, I think if I can manage twenty-four hours without thinking of Thom that will be some kind of milestone.

I tried the game this morning, hoping that Flash and his training had crowded out Thom, but I quickly identified three moments. I put my car keys down on the kitchen worktop and guiltily scooped them up because Thom believed they would spread germs on to a surface where we prepared food. When I walked past Hurstpierpoint Health Centre I remembered a patronising and homophobic remark one of the doctors had made to Thom during his illness. Finally, I'd been looking for something to read from the bookcases that line my office walls and I picked up *The Naked Civil Servant* by Quentin Crisp. Beside my signed version (he'd been a guest on my radio programme) there was Thom's copy, where he'd translated the most difficult English words into German in blue biro. He'd stopped after the first three pages, but I ran my fingers over the slight indentation he'd made on the reverse side – almost as if I could recapture some of his life force.

I don't know why I torture myself like this.

Instead of playing stupid games with myself, I went into the garden to play with Flash. He had a great time chasing his ball under the bushes and skidding across the grass. After I'd taken the edge off his boundless energy, I decided to practise 'sit' and 'stay'.

Normally, he gets overexcited and starts jumping up. Jeff's goal of him sitting while I walk round him seems a long way away and I've begun to have sympathy for my mother, who told me that I was always the last baby at the clinic to sit up, to crawl or to walk.

However, this time, as I asked Flash to sit, I knew it would be different. He cocked his head to the right with the same penetrating expression from five weeks ago in Mr Foster's kitchen – the look that lured me into his life.

'Stay,' I told him and made the stop sign with my right hand. Slowly, I took one step back, all the time maintaining eye contact.

Flash stayed.

At seventeen weeks old, the correct software package had been downloaded into his brain.

I gave him a treat and made a big fuss of him.

Saturday 26 February

Flash had coped so well with his overnight stay last Saturday and I have still heard nothing from Andy, so I decided to accept a date with someone I'd met at last week's party. I sensed that as Emma's cat had failed to return for twenty-four hours, Flash would not be especially welcome there. Valerie and Michael are attending a dinner dance at the Grand Hotel in Brighton. Although Valerie is too English to say anything directly, she has dropped hints that I spend too much time away from Flash. Fortunately, I still have one other option.

On one of our trips to Brighton, Flash and I had bumped into Lel, another of my dancing friends. She made a special fuss of him and begged to be allowed to look after him the next time I went away. Little did she know how soon her dreams would come true.

This afternoon I arrived at Lel's flat with a mountain of Flash possessions and a long list of instructions. In a homage to *Paddington Bear* – one of my favourite childhood books – I headed the note:

Please look after this dog

Do not feed me titbits.

Don't let me jump up.

Don't let me on the furniture.

Please make me sit before crossing the road.

Please feed me three time a day – approximately 7 a.m., 12.30 p.m. and 5.30 p.m.

Night time, I like two dog biscuits and my hot-water bottle filled.

I can only be trusted for two hours before being told to 'get busy'.

If you sit on the floor, I like to climb on your lap.

If you let me chew my brush, I will let you wipe my paws.

Signed: Flash.

My cousin Wendy signs Christmas cards on behalf of all her dogs and it seems I'm turning into that sort of person too.

— ❧ —

Lel was really pleased to see Flash and he returned the favour by curling up by her feet and promptly falling asleep. I suppressed a twinge of jealousy by noting her chair was nearer the radiator and therefore a far better choice. Lel is thinking of getting a dog too, so Flash will be the 'dry run' Tyson was for me. Although how 'dry' Flash will be is debatable.

After a cup of coffee, we took him up to the park opposite the Booth Museum. Lel took the lead and he was quite well behaved. She gave him a treat so he would know she was somebody to whom it was worth listening. While Flash started to explore, I tried to hide so we could test if he would come when Lel called. It was not easy because he always keeps one eye on me. Eventually, he found an interesting scent and disappeared under a bush. I hid and Lel called. After a little hesitation, Flash romped off to her, his tail wagging furiously. I was not certain if I should be proud for raising an obedient puppy or annoyed at how easily his affections could be bought.

Sunday 27 February

It was early evening by the time I collected Flash because I had been to a writers' group in Hampstead. The woman who runs it makes us take our shoes off in her house, so I doubted she would have welcomed a dog.

Flash had never been so thrilled to see me and almost launched himself into space with excitement. Lel reported he had been good as gold. He had come when he was called and travelled safely in her car. They had taken a long walk along the seafront and been caught up in a fun run – where Flash was very much the centre of attention. The waves crashing on to the pebbled beach still remained a little bit of a worry.

Lel's verdict on dog-owning? She would wait until she had a flat with a garden. I could understand why having to take off warm slippers and put on cold wellingtons, first thing in the morning, could take the shine off having a puppy. Worse still, Flash had twice come back from a walk and performed on her carpet.

I had expected him to be clinging when we returned home. He certainly enjoyed a cuddle while I caught up with *Coronation*

Street but after five minutes leapt up to explore the house again. It was only when I had put him to bed and had gone into the bathroom, to clean my teeth and take out my contact lenses, that I discovered a large pile of steaming turds on the carpet. He had already been fifteen minutes earlier, on the journey from Lel's front door to my car.

Monday 28 February

I have been thinking what it must have been like for my mother taking me home from the hospital in Northampton and the huge responsibility of not just caring for a baby but knowing that how she raised me would affect my character for ever.

With this in mind, I worry about the damage I have done to Flash by going away so much. Although I gave him a long walk, in the hope of settling him down, he has been fretful all morning and keeps jumping up every time the telephone rings. Over the weekend, he has perfected his melting eyes 'don't abandon me' look, which he turns on me even if I disappear for thirty seconds to the loo.

Fortunately, he was going through one of his quieter half hours when I was interviewed, on the phone, for BBC Radio 5 live's Nicky Campbell show about whether or not men should feel able to cry. The topic was prompted by the Chancellor, Gordon Brown, who has admitted to bursting into tears of frustration after a fight with Number 10's spin doctor. I was pitted against a man who claimed not to have cried for seventeen years – even at the birth of his children.

Halfway through the phone-in, we were interrupted for a report on the ending of quarantine for dogs arriving from Europe. The historic arrival of Helen de Borchgrave and her dog Frodo Baggins, the first dog not to have to go into quarantine, changed the tone of the whole debate. Previously, I'd been in a minority of tearful men, the radio host even wondering if he would cry at his parents' funerals, but now caller after caller spoke movingly of their love for their dog and the misery of pet bereavement. Next time I was asked for my opinion, I gave Flash, who was curled up at my feet, a quick name check so he would not feel left out.

However, master and hound bonding would soon take another setback. At lunchtime I had a phone call while halfway through feeding him. An email I'd sent had gone to the wrong person – could I resend immediately? I chucked a second handful of dog food into his bowl and headed upstairs. I was only at my computer for about three minutes, but it was long enough for Flash to pee on the landing carpet.

My patience finally snapped in the early evening when he took a dump in the living room – just fifteen minutes after I had fruitlessly taken him into the garden. Previously, I have praised him when he performs in the right place and cleared up calmly on the other occasions, but this time, something snapped. I forced Flash to look at what he'd done, tapped his nose, scolded, grabbed him by the scruff of his neck and took him back to his 'get busy' spot at the bottom of the garden. While I cleaned up, he slunk back into the house and watched me sorrowfully. I instantly forgave him. He had obviously thought he had been abandoned at Lel's and the shock had made him regress further back into puppyhood. It serves me right for putting my pleasure first.

Tuesday 29 February

The rain sluiced down and the wind blew harshly in our faces on the 8 a.m. walk. Halfway round the field, not only were Valerie and I wet and miserable but so too were the dogs, so we turned back. Sloshing through the mud, I finally confided my problems with house training but had to pretend it was caused by breaking Flash's routine. I'd originally told her we were both going away for the weekend together – a harmless white lie – but I was too ashamed of traumatising Flash to tell the truth. Completely out of character, as I've always prided myself on being honest.

One small advantage of continually clearing up after Flash is that I've become a lot less squeamish. So when my foul water drain blocked this afternoon, I tried to solve the problem myself.

Four years ago, Thom and I had had one of our few major rows over the drains. He'd tried to resolve the problem by carrying bucketloads of sewage from one drain to another. We had also purchased special rods and spent ages trying to feed them through the drains.

Thom believed I should be helping, while I pleaded pressure of work – although looking back to my 1996 diary I can't imagine what it could have been. He had a friend staying from Germany and had co-opted her instead. It was a miserable time as neither of us was very good at arguing. Eventually, he agreed to let me phone the professionals.

So, in a sort of homage to Thom, I found a bucket and his rods and set to work. I soon understood his frustrations, but this time I could not retreat to my office. Flash found all the bucket carrying and assembling of rods very entertaining, but even climbing down I could not get the right angle to feed the rods into the drains and shift the blockage. I worked until it became dark before going inside to get out the *Yellow Pages* and to have a bath.

Wednesday 1 March

Thought for the day: 'The dog has seldom been successful in pulling man up to its level of sagacity, but man has frequently dragged the dog down to his' – American cartoonist James Thurber (1894–1961).

The best antidote for worrying about Flash's behaviour is to hear horror tales from other owners. I spoke to my newish neighbours – four doors up – for the first time today. Their Labrador, Harvey, watches Flash pass every day with great interest, his nose pressed up against their living-room window. Harvey has chewed remote controls, slippers, and a whole other catalogue of missing or destroyed items. By contrast, Flash has only eaten a couple of tassels from under a chair, pulled up a couple of shoots from a spider plant and chewed the back door. When the drain men finally arrived in the late afternoon, one of them told a sad story about an earlier visit. They had not closed a field gate properly and a German Shepherd dog had sneaked into their van and stolen his sandwiches. If his mate had not taken pity and lent him some money, he would have starved. I reassured them that Flash was very well behaved, but he rather let me down by stealing one of their rubber gloves. Despite the advice from my training manual not to chase after a dog as it makes the prize more precious, I finally caught him under the Christmas tree, which the previous owners had planted out. After all the effort, I was slightly peeved to be told the drain men discarded the gloves after every job. They followed this up with the news that my drains had probably collapsed and they would need to send a camera down.

In the evening, the dog training class had nine other excited dogs. Flash particularly enjoyed greeting Sniffy the Collie; in fact, they started mounting and humping each other. His owner is also thinking of giving him the chop, but her dog books recommend waiting until one year old; apparently, this gives the dog's personality time to form. If the operation is undertaken too early, they can be left frozen in puppyhood – heaven forbid! We had a newcomer – a Golden Retriever who had to be almost dragged across the floor and the floor mopped after him every five minutes. (Flash, I'm pleased to report, asked to go outside towards the end of the class.) Although we tried to hide in the corner, we were allocated the space next to the worst influence: Sasha the Alsatian puppy. However, Flash spent more of the class sitting or lying quietly and less trying to scrabble on the linoleum floor over in Sasha's direction.

I was much less nervous this week, but Flash found the long waits for his turn left him overexcited. After a couple of false starts, he did 'sit' and 'stay' but I was told off for backing away with a treat in my hand. In future I should stand beside him and then walk off. In comparison with reprobates like Brian who totally refused to sit for his owner even with her full weight pressed down on his haunches, Flash is a star pupil and therefore we receive little attention. Our dog guru, Michael, is returning from Australia at the end of the month. Perhaps we should opt for one-to-one training.

Thursday 2 March

We met a dark golden Labrador on the walk today. Apparently, Winston is the breed's original colour, until fashion bred them lighter and lighter. He slightly startled Flash, who initially ran away with his tail between his legs, but was soon streaking across the field with his new playmate. There are few sights that make my soul soar more than watching Flash run – partly because I know he will sleep and I'll get plenty of work done – but mainly at his pure uncomplicated joy. I wish I could follow his example and live in the moment rather than worrying about the next magazine commission and whether I'm going to be trapped for ever writing about celebrities' fridges. I stood with Winston's owner under the hedge, which offered some shelter from the rain. Apparently, Flash and I should have been honoured because

Winston is a relative of the Queen's favourite dog, Bracken. Even though there are ten generations between them, there is enough Sandringham blood coursing through his veins to merit at least a tug to the forelock.

We also bumped into Lily's nemesis, Buster. Maybe she told Flash just how she feels because he was very wary and kept his distance.

It was certainly our day for meeting new dogs. Diagonally opposite from my house lives Kit, an electrical engineer, his wife and their new black Labrador puppy. Knowing he must be close to twelve weeks old and started on his inoculation programme, Flash and I went over to make his acquaintance. Kit made a fuss of Flash and called his wife. He shared stories about the perils of puppy-owning and his wife showed me her wrists. She was so covered in scratches and teeth marks that if I hadn't owned a puppy I would have thought she was deliberately harming herself. Their puppy, Jasper, had been madly tearing about for the last two hours and was currently in the flop stage. However, they called him out to the front gate. A velvety black bundle of paws and ears trotted out of the kitchen. Jasper pushed his nose through the wooden gate and sniffed Flash and I couldn't help but be amused at the similarity between master and hound. Kit is a round barrel of a man and his new puppy was the thickest-set Labrador I have ever seen. Hopefully, Flash is not too much like me because my school report would often complain, 'does not respond well to authority'.

In the afternoon, we met a Golden Retriever called Holly, who had been attacked by the ferocious Dalmatian that lives at the opposite end of my road. Her owner had been badly scratched and had bled.

'What makes it worse is that when I went back they denied it altogether,' she said angrily. 'I've heard some terrible things about that family. It's a rented house, you know.'

'Somebody ought to report that dog before it does some serious harm, like attack a child,' I replied – but I'm afraid I was more concerned that it might be Flash.

'I reported him to the dog warden and it wasn't the first complaint. It bit the milkman too and it would have been very nasty if he hadn't been wearing thick trousers.'

'Surely if he phoned the police…'

'I tried to persuade him, but he doesn't want to upset a customer,' she replied.

Are doorstep deliveries really that finely balanced?

'It's how they just brazened it out, not even coming out of their house to check I was all right that makes me fume,' continued Holly's owner.

'It seems the dog has inherited their antisocial habits,' I commented.

'I hope I don't take after Holly – at least I'm not as muddy,' she said as looked down at her dog's hair matted from a run across the fields. I looked at her mud-splattered jacket, caked boots and strands of fair hair escaping from under her hat.

First, I laughed and then she laughed, and then something magical happened. We had been standing outside one of my neighbours' houses, where a row of dwarf conifers had been planted in the front flower bed. Flash had been sitting quietly, waiting for us to finish talking, but suddenly he stood up and for the first time ever cocked his leg over a tree – just like an adult dog. I knelt down to double-check: yes, there was a damp patch. Hurrah! I felt as proud as a parent whose child has taken his first steps.

Friday 3 March

Will I ever house train Flash? By keeping an eye on him and taking him out regularly there have been no accidents in the house again. However, in his den, the outhouse, he has stopped being dry overnight. This morning I came down to three dumps and three pees! Where does it all come from? He had done both when I put him out before bedtime. Worn down, I slowly cleared up all the mess and sprayed the outhouse floor with a cleaning product called 'Flash Spray with Bleach'. I thought it was a great joke when I put it in my supermarket trolley but now it is wearing a little thin.

When we walked across the fields, Flash was forever squatting down to take a dump but could produce nothing but a small trickle. He had obviously eaten some rubbish that disagreed with him and I felt ashamed that I'd been annoyed with him.

I'm going off to London for a meeting today. After being with Flash almost constantly for the last forty-eight hours, I must admit I'm looking forward to escaping parenting duties for a while. On the telephone yesterday, Brandon (with whom I had a brief affair last year) teased me over a newspaper article about a gay man who replaced his lover with a dog. I'm getting used to the idea of Flash being a surrogate child but surrogate partner?

Perhaps Flash understood what I'd been typing. When I decided to pop downstairs for an apple he woke – from his usual place – curled over my feet. Instead of following me downstairs, for the first time ever he crept off to my spare room and went back to sleep there.

According to researchers at Budapest University dogs really can read our minds. They put fifty-one dogs into a 'strange situation test' which had originally been devised to study the bond between mother and baby. Just like small children, the dogs were keen to play and explore unfamiliar rooms – just as long as their owners were there. The article quoted an animal psychologist:

'Dogs can pick up on their owner's behaviour patterns. Some breeds are better at this than others. Collies are great people watchers and are much more tuned in to their owner's moods.'

It shouldn't really be a surprise because scientists agree that dogs and humans have evolved together. Canine remains at our burial sites suggest that we started to domesticate them 14 000 years ago – which is long before we acquired goats, cattle and sheep. But researchers at the University of California now date the split with wolves another 120 000 years back. To be honest, the extra years feel like a relief because I still haven't got my head round the idea that I've invited a former wolf into my home. But I'm full of contradictory feelings because, by these calculations, pet ownership could have started earlier than such cultural pillars as art and burying the dead. No wonder I am comforted by Flash's presence and no wonder he understands my moods. Our coexistence has been preprogrammed.

— ❦ —

It was wonderful to wear non-muddy-paw-printed clothes and stroll through the streets of Soho without a dog straining at the lead. I had lunch with the director of the short video I had written last year. He was amused to discover just how much of the storyline – a young man who decides to adopt a dog to combat his fear of wolves – has actually come true. The rough cut will soon be ready to watch. The director had some constructive suggestions for the full-length film script that I'm currently working on.

Back home Flash was as delighted to throw himself against my legs as I was to stroke his back and tickle his belly. I spent most of the evening on the floor cradling a contented puppy in my arms, trying to decide the shape of the second half of my life: should I lock myself away in Hurstpierpoint or re-engage with the outside world?

Saturday 4 March

I've spent a lot of time thinking about Thom recently – perhaps because the third anniversary of his death falls next week. The daffodils I planted in his memory are finally in bloom – the yellow crowns and the orange trumpets emerging after the bleak winter to herald the arrival of spring.

Flash and I set off over the fields for our morning walk. While we walk with Valerie and Lily from Monday to Friday, at the weekends we go at times to suit ourselves. I always hope we'll meet another dog to exhaust Flash and provide someone for me to chat with. After following the edge of the cornfield behind the house, the public footpath joins a single-track lane and it was here that Flash spotted a large Golden Retriever. Unable to decide if it was friend or foe, he alternated between whining and his Sheepdog crouch ready to play. The owner, an elderly gentleman in his seventies, slowly ambled up, calling out that there was nothing to worry about. Eventually, Flash edged his way close enough for his last-minute streak of courage and they started to tussle.

'Clint loves to play.'

The name and the dog were both familiar, but I could not place the gentleman in the country tweeds and cap. Had we met them before?

'Do you normally walk him?' I tried to clarify.

'My wife used to take him out, but she died last year.'

'With a tennis racket to stop him knocking her down!' Finally, I remembered, the summer I had looked after Tyson and how his wife would often join Valerie and me on our morning walk.

'That's right,' he confirmed.

I instantly had a picture of a woman who still retained the grace of a dancer even sloshing through the mud in wellington boots. I was about to share my memories of Barbie – yes, that was her name and now I remember Valerie telling me about the unexpected heart attack – but decided that might upset him. So instead we chatted about the local gyms and he asked advice on which one to join.

I get annoyed when people pretend Thom never existed. However, instead of sharing my memories of his wife, I reviewed the facilities of the new Triangle Sports Centre in Burgess Hill. What stopped me? English reserve?

Clint was now rolling on his back with Flash on top. Unlike his owner, he was certainly not hanging back:

'Gently, Clint,' called out Mr Buck. I'd remembered his surname.

'Don't worry, Flash needs to know when he's overstepped the mark and get gently slapped back,' I replied, and the possibility of any deeper connection was lost.

The dogs had brought us together, revealed our shared bond but also, sadly, provided a distraction from true intimacy. I walked back up the lane with Mr Buck and Clint in silence. At the gap in the fence, I said goodbye and started off home along the top end of the field. Flash could not understand why we were leaving and tacked back through the hedge for a final farewell.

Three years later, I still miss Thom terribly so what must it be like for Mr Buck, just starting out on the same journey? Rather than going back and breaking the silence, I called Flash and we each went to our respective homes alone.

When I looked in the mirror, I discovered a corner of lavatory paper still stuck on my chin from a shaving nick. That's the ultimate problem with living alone: nobody to tell you when you look or act foolishly.

Sunday 5 March

I had sent the first section of my diary to the writers' group made up of graduates from a course I'd taken at the London New Play Festival.

'But not everybody likes dogs,' exclaimed Maria, who was hosting the event and first to comment on my writing, 'or wants one jumping all over them.'

'I stop Flash from making a nuisance of himself, honestly…' I said and trickled into silence.

Maria had kindly allowed me to bring him to her house and he had rewarded her with taking a leak on her carpet. I had, of course, cleared up, but the damage had, so to speak, been done.

In fact, catching him crouching down beside the sofa had provoked me so much, I had clipped him round the backside with Maria's short film script. It was the first time I had hit him well, not so much hit, more firmly tapped. Immediately I can hear the tutor on my Relate domestic violence course:

'The perpetrator always seeks to play down the extent of the abuse. They must be made to acknowledge what has happened.'

I feel mortified, but in my head, I start justifying: he let me down; he made me do it.

'The perpetrator always blames the victim,' continues my tutor's voice. 'They must take responsibility for their temper.'

Double mortification. I'd just brought him back from a walk, I argue back, he had plenty of opportunity.

'There are no excuses.'

If I had a tail, it would be between my legs.

After Flash had disgraced himself, I had sharply deposited him in the garden and grabbed a roll of kitchen paper. I had expected him to cower when I let him back in the house but I still got the same enthusiastic welcome – as if we'd been apart for hours, not minutes – and the same adoring eyes. What makes the bond between master and dog so strong that even hitting him does not destroy it? Everybody always draws on the parallels between a puppy and a baby, but a smacked child would never have responded like Flash. What's more, a good parent brings their son or daughter up to leave home while a dog grows closer and closer.

If Flash is not a surrogate child, could Brandon be right and could he be a surrogate lover? I certainly felt possessive when Liz, a forty-plus American, encouraged him up on her knee.

'He's not allowed to do that,' I told her.

'He's doing no harm, are you, Flash?' She fondled his Spaniel ears.

'It just encourages him to jump up at people.'

'He'll learn that it's only allowed with his Auntie Liz.'

Flash gave me his 'look what I'm getting away with and you can't do anything about it' eyes and settled into her warm lap.

Over tea and toasted hot cross buns with home-made jam, we discussed our love lives. Maria reported on her latest beau and Liz confessed a complete zero. She tickled Flash under the chin:

'Since I arrived in England nobody has even asked me out. I'm not only resigned to living the rest of my life alone, I'm enjoying it. For the first time, I feel really focused on my work.'

She has taken on a commission to write a screenplay.

Flash was almost purring with contentment. What was I the most annoyed about: her disregard for my puppy training rules, jealousy at her success with my dog, or maybe her career advancement?

I excused myself and nipped upstairs to the loo.

As I expected, Flash leapt off Liz's knee and came charging after me. I take him places so he is well socialised and not too dependent on me, but I hate it when he makes his own connections.

When it was time to leave and I had gathered up Flash's bowls and food, Maria kissed me on the cheek:

'I think you're doing very well with that dog.'

It was sweeter praise than if she'd told me I'll write a Pulitzer Prize-winning novel.

Wednesday 8 March

I have been commissioned to write an article on celebrity dreams for the *Daily Express* and it seems I was not the only child to have nightmares about animals.

'I don't like horses. They're too big and they have no brakes,' said *GMTV* Weather Girl, Andrea McClean. 'In my dream, Mum's cooking tea in the kitchen but I'm sitting on a horse – a huge and very handsome brown one. It rears up and starts bucking.'

Even more bizarre is the dream from Caroline Barnes of the pop group Scooch: 'I dive down into a swimming pool to pull out a plug from the bottom. No water drains away instead goldfish swim in. When I get closer, they're not goldfish but tinned sliced peaches, which start nibbling at my skin and swimming costume. I start bleeding and slowly, the sliced peaches eat me up.'

I decided to take a break from pestering minor celebrities about the dark corners of their psyches and take Flash back to meet his mother. Mr Foster had phoned a couple of days ago for a progress report and I'd suggested a walk together.

Any questions about whether Flash would recognise his old home were immediately dispelled. One bark from Jessie, his mother, and he bounded into their garden with no sign of his usual reticence around strange dogs. A joyful tussle was immediately followed by a tug of war using one of Mr Foster's slippers. Round the corner of the bungalow came the true owner of the slipper and Flash broke away and launched himself at Mr Foster for a mad frenzy of jumping up and arm chewing, two habits which are strictly discouraged at the Marshall household. I smiled weakly.

In the kitchen, Mr Foster's grown-up son was eating his lunch. Flash sailed straight into his lap for another bout of frantic horseplay, something I normally avoid because, to use my mother's words, there will be tears before bedtime.

'Are you pleased you got him?' Mr Foster's son asked.

'Of course,' I replied, strangely reticent.

Meanwhile, Flash had torn back into the garden to chase round Jessie again. Amazingly, he has grown to only an inch or so shorter than his mother.

'Has he settled down with you?' Mr Foster enquired.

Flash raced from his mother to Mr Foster, back to his mother and on to Mr Foster's son. I smiled politely from the sidelines – like a distant relative at Flash's family wedding.

'Come here, Peanut.' Mr Foster's son called out his old name.

No response.

'He's called Flash now,' his father corrected before I had a chance.

'Flash,' he called out, and immediately Flash came trotting over.

I was feeling less a stranger.

While his son finished his lunch, Mr Foster, Jessie, Flash and myself set off for a walk across the fields behind their house. After a few more games of chase and ear pull, Jessie became bored with Flash and decided to head off on her own walk. Flash stayed close to me.

'He's unlike his mother. Sometimes I scarcely see her,' noted Mr Foster and I began to relax.

Returning to his birthplace, a lot of information about Flash started to make sense. During our forty-five-minute walk, we spotted not a single human being and therefore no other dogs. The traffic was not even a murmur in the distance. No wonder Flash had been frightened of strangers and cars in Hurstpierpoint.

At the bottom of a field of cabbages, both dogs disappeared into the undergrowth. I'd finished telling Mr Foster how Flash walks round puddles when he re-emerged soaking wet from following Jessie into the pond. Just as I'd thought I was beginning to understand him, Flash pushed a wet nose into my hand as if to say: look at me, look what I've achieved.

Back at the bungalow, the Fosters made a special fuss of Flash before he left. Watching the open affection from the sidelines, I felt a strange connection to my mother. Her best friends – the ones given the honorary title of aunts to my sister and I – were more exuberant and more open-hearted than her. My mother had been brought up in a family where difficult subjects were not discussed and therefore she had no language for emotions. Did she long to match her friends' 'moreness' but her natural or learned reserve meant that she would always end up holding back? I'd expected to learn about Flash's family, but I'd uncovered something about my own.

I'd hoped that a tired Flash would be an easy-to-control Flash for puppy training class. However, he was either overtired or had regressed to six weeks old. Walking to heel was a disaster. He kept wandering off in the direction of other dogs. When it was our turn for 'sit' and 'stay', he rolled on to his back and waved his legs in the air. Although later, when the spotlight was switched off, and the whole class repeated all together, he was fine. Afterwards Jeff came over to praise Flash and offer some advice to me:

'If only you didn't get so anxious on solo exercises,' he wagged his finger at me, 'it transmits to your dog.'

Why do they always blame the parents?

As my mother would say: 'I was only doing my best.'

Thursday 9 March

Three years ago today, my partner Thom Hartwig died at the Gemeinschafts krankenhaus Herdecke. Emotionally, I have travelled a long way but the past still weighs me down. His weights rust in the corner of the bedroom, the fourth coffee set is still boxed in the garage, the pile of bricks he planned to block up a window with remain by the back door and the German exercise books for the language school in Brighton still clutter the office.

On the first anniversary of Thom's death, I gave a dinner party for our friends. Although a great success, I instinctively knew making it an annual event would be considered mawkish.

On the second anniversary, I thought I was at a crossroads. I'd fallen in love again. To prove to myself I was ready to move on, I performed a small cleansing ritual: throwing away Thom's old dressing gown. I had started wearing it the day after he died in hospital in Germany. It was practical – I was away from home and had only packed a small overnight bag. It made me feel closer to him. If I really screwed up my imagination, I could still smell him in the folds of fabric. I also hoped daily exposure to this symbol of his illness would rob his final five weeks of the power to wound me. My new boyfriend, Brandon, would pretend that Thom's multicoloured robe was so garish that he needed sunglasses and even a hoarder like me had to accept that the belt had been tied and untied so often it had become badly frayed. So, on the morning of the second anniversary, I bundled the old dressing gown into a black plastic bin bag, put it outside the back door and felt virtuous. OK, I'd given away Thom's possessions, even sold off his old vinyl collection, but this was the first time I'd thrown any of his relics away.

Later in the day, Brandon joined me for the annual pilgrimage to Beachy Head, where Thom had requested his ashes were scattered. I'd thought the invitation was further proof that I was finally opening myself up again. However, in the car back from Beachy Head, Brandon announced he'd chosen that night to confess our affair to his partner. So what should have been a day to support me turned into a day to support him. Worse still, I was forced to admit that I was doing something that went against all my values. I'd convinced myself that Brandon's actions were on his conscience but, faced with the consequences of hurting someone else, I had to accept that I had been deluding myself. Although Brandon did eventually leave his partner, it was not the start of our new relationship but the beginning of a slow goodbye drawn out over five months.

—— ❧ ——

Having made such a hash of the second anniversary, I was keen to find a better formula for this year. I decided to invite Maureen, a close friend of both Thom and mine. She had helped organise his memorial service, but ill health had prevented her from attending the scattering of his ashes. However, Maureen had forgotten about the anniversary, and my invitation, and had arranged for a Tesco home delivery. So Flash and I will make the journey alone.

After the morning walk, I doubled back through the village and bought eleven bunches of daffodils; some to scatter at Beachy Head and some to brighten the house. Next in my annual Service of Remembrance, I made a phone call to Thom's parents. Erwin, Thom's father, answered because Ursula, his mother, was back in hospital again. From my limited German, I reckon that she was having her knee replaced, but I could have been wrong. Maybe it was talking to Erwin who is less emotional, but for the first time I didn't cry after putting the phone down. Instead I brought out the 'Thom and Andrew' official photograph album, with all the approved shots of our life together. (Thom would tear up any photos which did not meet his high standards.) Our whole life together is chronicled from meeting on holiday in Sitges in 1989 through to his last public appearance at the Relate New Year's party in 1997. Thom is laughing as he loses his balance and falls off a log; Thom is trying to conquer his vertigo on a swinging rope bridge; Thom is in fancy dress; Thom is showing off his muscle-sculpted chest. But none of these familiar pictures retained the power to move me, even the one I'd taken of Thom kissing me. I closed my eyes and tried to recapture the sweetness of brushed lips, his sensual touch in the small of my back guiding me to where he'd parked the car. But I got scared. I couldn't remember on which shoulder he had the eagle tattoo. What did he sound like? How did he move? Thom seemed to be slowly fading away until I wondered whether he ever existed. Perhaps I just made him up? From the back of the cupboard, I found piles of old discarded photographs and selected every half-decent shot to add to the album. The range of Thom's expressions was immediately expanded: frowns at having his picture taken, pretending to wince when I hit him over the head with a toy baton, sticking his tongue out. It felt good, but I knew I was chasing a chimera.

The weather started fine, but just like the day we scattered Thom's ashes, the mist rolled in off the sea. With only the occasional stunted tree for protection, the wind cut across the grassland and through Thom's old puffer jacket, which I wear for walking the dog. Flash bowed his head and set off behind me, the gusts splaying out his fur coat – which I'm sure is growing longer. Perhaps it was the cold, perhaps I was numbed by hunger, but as I tossed my daffodils into the air I was just going through the motions. No connection with Thom's memory, no connection with the undulating beauty. I felt flat. The task completed, I took Flash for a run, but the wind had become so strong I was frightened he'd be blown over the cliff. So I fed him and drove down to the hotel at Birling Gap to feed myself ham, egg and chips.

I had saved a final bunch of daffodils to cast into the sea, at what had been one of our favourite Sunday afternoon destinations. The chalk cliffs were such a stunning white that even my depressed senses were stirred. Flash took a little persuading to follow me down the wooden steps to the shore – the open slats must have been quite off-putting for a puppy. While he ate as many sea sponges as possible, I delighted in the sound of the sea pounding stones and the hiss of retreating waves. The yellow daffodils looked almost jubilant as they waved their crowns over the incoming foam. I looked at my watch: ten past two. Although I wanted to stay longer, I needed to return inland, where I could get a mobile phone signal and pick up the call I was expecting from Kaye Adams, host of an afternoon ITV chat show, with more information on her childhood nightmares. I told Flash to leave the sea sponges alone and headed back for the car.

Five minutes later, Kaye called to tell me her dream of being pursued by a large shaggy gorilla until she reached a large canyon and had to decide whether to stay and fight or try to leap to safety. I understood her dilemma: I've been chased by Thom's memory and I cannot decide whether to stay and honour it, or escape and forget. With a couple of hours before my copy deadline and Flash still needing his afternoon walk, I stopped at a small copse which I'd driven past a hundred times before. High and Over car park is at the top of a steep hill just outside the village of Alfriston. From the road, it looked nothing special but within moments Flash and I emerged from the muted sunlight of the wood into the most dazzling views. Down in the valley, the River Cuckmere had carved a snake across the rich pastures as it repeatedly doubled back on itself. Across to the left, a red tractor was ploughing the almost white fields, a flock of birds shadowing the furrows. Further down the path was a large plinth and a plaque: 'IT WAS THE WISH OF WILLIAM REES JEFFREY 1872 TO 1954 THAT OTHERS SHOULD SHARE HIS ENJOYMENT OF THIS VIEW'. A large wooden bench had been provided by another benefactor and on the backrest was another dedication. The picnic benches had similar inscriptions. Surrounded by so many memorials, I felt inspired to do something I'd never normally consider and offered up a prayer of thanks to William Rees Jeffrey. He had obviously left a legacy because the pebble path was well maintained, the grass clipped and litter removed. I also thanked Flash for prompting me to stop here and for the first time today felt truly at peace.

A National Trust information board explained we were at Frog Firle Farm: firle is Saxon for 'oak covered land' and frog most probably because they were plentiful in the lazy bends of the river below. However, the most interesting nugget was that this hilltop had been a prehistoric burial mound, with remains dating back to 1000 years before Christ. Three thousand years of memories, no wonder I no longer felt alone. My reawakening – emotions, kick-started by the cliffs at Birling Gap, were now stretching wider and wider, embracing the Sussex countryside all around me. I felt alive.

When I returned home, the postman had been. I was extremely touched to discover that my parents had remembered today and sent a card.

— ❧ —

In the evening, I had clients at Relate. However, there have been lengthy negotiations between me and the manager about the wisdom of bringing Flash. Eventually, he was given special permission but there are two provisos. First, only in the evening, when everything is quieter. Second, he must be trained not to follow me down the corridor to the counselling rooms. Up to now, he's been staying with the receptionist but the shut door – which has kept Flash under control – has aggravated her claustrophobia.

My plan was to use 'sit', 'stay' and 'reward' to make it past the door frame of the office without Flash following me and over the next few weeks to build up the distance. However, he was having none of it, and however firmly I spoke to him, he took no notice. So I tethered him to a chair and walked across the corridor to greet my new clients. Unfortunately, they had to pass by the open office door and could not miss a crying puppy, who was trying to drag a heavy chair behind him. Naturally, they stopped to stare while I naturally tried to ignore the puppy I'd blithely promised would be on best behaviour. When I opened the door to the counselling room to usher in my clients, they were still standing open-mouthed down the other end of the corridor. What I meant to politely say was: 'If you'd like to walk this way, please' but in my dog training voice I found myself telling them: 'Come on.' To complete my mortification, I was being observed by a student counsellor.

Sunday 12 March

Flash was on his best behaviour today. Even walking along Hove seafront, with a million distractions, he did not stray too far or jump up at strangers. When I stopped to buy an ice cream at a kiosk, he was about to run into their shop so I told him to 'Sit.' Miraculously, he complied and remained sitting while I chose, paid and put my change away.

I bumped into friends from line dancing who were very amused when, from time to time, I shouted at a crowd of strangers:

'Flash.'

'I hope nobody takes your command literally,' Graham joked.

I had never realised the double entendre of his name.

'Don't walk him in a dirty mac,' added Leon.

In Hurstpierpoint, everybody would assume I was talking to a dog. In Brighton, who knows?

— ঔৎ৶ —

I had been expecting to see Andy at line dancing. He had phoned during the week to check I was going. I'd thought I'd given up all hope of a relationship, but my heart beat a little faster. So I was rather disappointed when he failed to show, yet again.

(If only men were as easy to train as dogs!) I would have liked to think we could have been friends, but what made him a disaster as a potential lover rules him out as a potential friend – both relationships need nurturing and constancy.

Tuesday 14 March

The crops in the field behind the house have been sprayed. The white foamy residue looked particularly poisonous, so we took an alternative route through the village and out towards the South Downs. Lily, who is normally thrown off balance by the High Street, followed Flash's calm example.

In every light, the chalk uplands look different and the early morning sunshine had turned Wolstonbury Hill almost blue. With new smells to explore, the dogs were not chasing each other and anyway, Flash needed all his concentration to solve puzzles like how to climb a stile and wind himself through a kissing gate. Each time I pointed the way, he would immediately understand the instructions.

'He really is a very clever, and a very good dog,' said Valerie.

She's allowed to say it. I wouldn't want to boast.

At the first farm, after leaving the village, a dog shot out of the stables. Flash recognised her as Jasmine and even Lily, who normally avoids strange dogs, decided to accept his recommendation. He really is making her bolder.

Emma – who looked after Flash the first time I went up to London – emerged next, holding a pitchfork.

'He's certainly grown and his coat is getting much longer,' she remarked. 'You'll be pleased to know our cat returned, so after she's had her kittens, Flash will be welcome back.'

The topic of procreation had obviously inspired Flash because he started humping Jasmine. Emma was quick to react.

'She really is in season now,' she explained.

'If you do want a litter of puppies, I'm sure Flash would be only too happy to co-operate.' For someone who has been considering getting my dog castrated, I was acting very strangely. A basket of mini-Flashes had taken such a firm grip on my imagination that I was already looking forward to playing with them. Either Flash is practising mind control again or the human desire to breed is lodged somewhere beyond rational thinking.

'I don't think he's mature enough for that,' Emma laughed.

Flash and I tried not to let her scorn dent our male pride.

The primroses had come through in the woods and the first tree buds were breaking out. Perhaps it was the excitement of spring or perhaps my new Flash-found connection to my surroundings because I found myself suggesting to Valerie that we organise a Millennium Street Party. She was a bit doubtful about whether the older residents would be keen, but we decided I would make up a flyer to invite everyone to a planning meeting.

Thom and I often used to take a late-night circuit down our street and back along a neighbouring one. On clear nights, he used to enjoy gazing up at the stars in the clear skies over Hurstpierpoint – a sharp contrast with the industrial Ruhr city where he had lived before. It had been part of our ritual of connecting and unwinding at the end of the day; part of the glue of our relationship. So I've walked the street where I live many times before. However, I've never really seen it; neighbourly etiquette prevents staring through windows and the generous front gardens make it difficult anyway. So this evening, when I walked up the drives with Flash to deliver invitations to join the Millennium Street Party Planning Committee, I had a clearer view of replacement windows and doors, new driveways and for some reason hedgehog-shaped brushes for cleaning boots. I only bumped into one resident, who was wearing rubber gloves after washing some cans and bottles for the blue recycling box.

However, I was beginning to have second thoughts about the invitation. Not only did I live in a house which barely comes up to the 'house beautiful' standards set by the rest of the road, but in the words of the Anglican Church, I am a 'practising homosexual', a lifestyle that many residents of my village would approach with rubber gloves. Not only was I putting my head above the parapet but inviting them round – even the residents with the notorious Dalmatian at the other end of the road. I had considered 'forgetting' to post a slip through their door, but first, there was no sign of the dog; second, the letterbox was already open for an electric cord to charge their car's battery; third, their reputation – like mine – is probably highly exaggerated.

Flash and I returned home in time for a documentary on Animal Planet called *Wolves at the Door*. Normally, I would rather have poked red-hot needles into my eyes, but I thought I might glean some greater understanding about Flash. The programme was about a pack of wolves that had been created by scientists to explode the myths. Apparently, since European man arrived in North America, two million wolves have been shot but not one human has been killed by a wild wolf. I was amazed at how familiar the games of the wolves were from watching Flash and the neighbourhood hounds. Normally, Flash ignores the TV – with the exception of the theme to *Coronation Street*, often a lunchtime signal for feeding time. However, he was transfixed by all the yelps and snarls and kept padding round the box, hoping to join in.

I already knew the importance of status in a pack, and how the alpha male fed first, but not how fluid that order could be. As the wolves feasted on their kill, the omega, bottom of the pile, would forever try to sneak an early snack. Each insurrection was fought off with snarls and bared teeth. No wonder Flash is forever testing me, trying to bend the rules, and that visitors disrupt our relationship so much.

The scientists needed to move their pack into a protected reserve and had gained the co-operation of a tribe of Native Americans to use their homelands. For the Indians, the wolves were an important symbol. Their ancestors had learned a lot by mimicking how wolves work together on a hunt and how wolf pups are nurtured by the whole pack. Perhaps we did not domesticate wolves, they domesticated us! For the first time, I wondered what my childhood nightmares were trying to tell me.

Contrary to my expectations, I had no bad dreams. In fact, I slept deeper and woke more refreshed than I had in ages. I phoned my parents and made plans for Flash and me to visit over Easter.

Wednesday 15 March

Just when I think I'm finally winning in one area of puppy raising – like house training – Flash develops new antisocial activities. I'd been reading through my latest screenplay in the garden, when the phone rang and I rushed inside. Five minutes later, I returned to find a crater had been dug in the middle of the lawn. Although it had never had the clipped smooth sheen of my neighbour's, I had achieved some minimum standard of suburban respectability. Flash was rather proud of the new flower bed he had created and started joyfully making it larger. 'No,' I told him sharply, but as my mother would say: why waste your breath? So I put a laundry basket over the hole and hoped this would give the grass a chance to grow back. I'm still trying to decide which looks worse, a crater or a black and orange crate in the middle of the lawn.

As my confidence as a dog owner has grown, I've stopped consulting my training manual, but I decided to look up Flash's two biggest issues: mouthing and leaping up. Apparently, mouthing is an attention-seeking ploy. Certainly, Flash is most likely to try it when I come down in the morning, and it should not be allowed after fourteen weeks. Oh dear! Apparently, my mistake is to pull my hand away; this is interpreted by puppies as an invitation to play. The advice in the book is to make an 'ah, ah' noise. When I tried it, Flash took my reprimand for wild encouragement and settled in for a really good mouthing session.

'That's the problem with books,' Jeff explained when I told him at this evening's dog training class. 'They assume every dog has the same personality. I bet they didn't give an alternative.'

'No, but it is very good.' I felt I needed to protect the author.

'Keep with the "no" strategy,' he finished.

However, I will take the book's advice on jumping up: a short snap on the lead is suggested. (Apparently, pulling encourages play.) It seems I've been too ready to let Flash off the lead at places like Relate and then don't have any means of control, beyond helplessly shouting 'no'.

It was another full class. Benji, the Golden Retriever who joined two weeks ago, has been transformed into a different dog. The vet has put him on the doggy equivalent of Prozac, which has made him less anxious and removed the dark rings round his owner's eyes. After Benji almost destroyed the house, she became a virtual prisoner for fear of what he might do during her absence.

I had innocently suggested confining him somewhere:

'I tried that, but he broke down the door.'

The vet proposed having Benji destroyed. His owner consulted a behavioural expert, joined the class and the results have been really impressive. In marked contrast, Brian, the unruly German Shorthaired Pointer, still takes very little notice of his mistress, yet is as meek as a lamb with Jeff. The more I watch him with his mistress, the more I believe his naughtiness has nothing to do with how she handles him. It is something far deeper. Although his mistress adores him, it is a one-way relationship. Brian has no bond back.

With Flash reaching the five-month mark, and the end of the winter dog training term, I thought it would be a good time to take stock of his progress:

Flash's School Report

Temperament: Intelligent and willing to please.

House training: Generally good. However, still needs newspaper overnight.

Lead work: In familiar village surroundings very good; however, walking in busy unknown streets needs attention.

Recall: First class, even other dogs do not faze this pupil. However, tasty treats hidden in the undergrowth still hold a strong fascination.

Chewing: Top of the class. This dog has learned both not to chew household items and not to bring permitted items – like sticks – from the garden inside.

Mouthing: Sadly, Flash lets himself down badly. He likes nothing better than to wrap his fangs round a tasty hand. Although not painful, his teeth are becoming sharper and this behaviour should not be encouraged.

Strangers: This pupil is to be praised for his happy outgoing nature, but still has to learn that a friendly greeting is not an invitation to leap up.

Barking: Flash is generally a quiet dog. When alone in his den, he barks at people who come to the house. Good guard dog potential. He is also to be congratulated for not barking at his owner when he is in his den, but has not yet been released.

Bedtime: Understands when to retire to his basket and is happy to sleep alone.

Vocabulary: This dog understands: his name, 'no', 'basket', 'sit', 'stay', 'get busy', 'close', 'come on'. The 'lie down' command is partially understood.

Special comments: A loyal and intelligent hound who is eager to learn. However, sometimes his enthusiasm overwhelms his sense of what is allowed; this comment is made with respect to leaping up and mouthing.

If scientists are right and wolves/dogs were important in domesticating humans, it is only fair that Flash should have a chance to assess my progress:

Andrew's School Report

Temperament: He is finally beginning to calm down. Instead of cramming every evening with outside activity, this owner is recognising the pleasures of a night in with a dog on his lap.

Walking on the lead: Must learn to accept that I am only a puppy and therefore not to expect too much too soon.

Recall: When will he learn that interesting smells and a quick snack are more important than charging after him? Some owners are just too egocentric.

Vocabulary: Is finally beginning to understand my repertoire of whines and looks. Finally, he has realised when to stop the car and allow me to use the grass verge.

Observational skills: No longer walks around with his eyes closed. This owner now knows important local information like where the local foxes have their lairs and which of his neighbours are having an affair.

Affection: Although Andrew cares for me deeply, he is still not very good at showing it. However much I jump up and show him my love, he still hangs back.

Special comments: Although I accept Andrew as my pack leader and trust his judgement, he must remember to follow my advice and live in the moment. Still has a tendency to alternate between an unhealthy obsession with the past and an unhelpful fear of the future.

Friday 17 March

I met up with a group of friends from when I worked in radio – except 'worked' does not even begin to describe the depth of my obsession. At school I'd joined the local hospital radio; I chose my university not on the quality of the course but the campus radio station; from graduation until the age of thirty-five, I'd progressed from journalist and DJ to programme controller and general manager. With responsibility for a product that operated twenty-four hours a day, seven days a week, three hundred and sixty-five days a year, I was never off duty.

Originally, my friends and I were going out for supper. However, after a last-minute change of plans, we decided to eat at Mark's house. If I'd known earlier, I would have brought Flash. It turned out to be a very 'Bridget Jones' evening with four late thirty-something and early forty-something gay men moaning about the impossibility of finding a boyfriend.

We must all be at a broody age, because my stories about Flash were greeted with envy. Mark and his flatmates had planned to adopt a rescue cat but the Cat Protection League demanded more structural changes to the house than when he remortgaged. After sausages, cauliflower and mash, we opted for an early night rather than going out clubbing and so it seems we are all destined to remain single.

Although I enjoyed seeing my old friends, not even the spiciest gossip about radio tempted me to return to that world. The combination of Thom's illness and general boredom has allowed me to walk away. So why do I find it so difficult to stop C-list celebrity journalism? The rates have been cut; more work is undertaken in-house and it no longer challenges me – yet still I hang on.

Saturday 18 March

My article on the hypnotist Paul McKenna and his kitchen was in the *Daily Express* this morning. The headline quote from the interview seemed to sum up my life: 'I FELT INSIGNIFICANT, SO I SAT DOWN AND DESIGNED THE SORT OF LIFE I WANTED'. Ten years ago, his career as a radio DJ was making him increasingly paranoid so he closed his eyes and visualised what he'd rather be doing. With these goals securely in place, according to McKenna, working out how to achieve them was easy. It certainly sounded better than where I am: wallowing in a general sense of dissatisfaction.

Flash was curled up at my feet as I ate breakfast and read the paper. There was something very peaceful about his warm muzzle lying across my slippers. I reached down and ticked his tummy, but couldn't decide if he is the first step away from my old life with Thom or a new way of chaining myself to the house. Certainly, it would be difficult to find a better place to keep a dog: nice-sized garden, helpful neighbours, while my current career, and being self-employed, provides the flexibility needed for a contented pet.

My social life with Thom had revolved around dinner parties. He was not only an incredible cook but also the owner of hundreds of crystal glasses and mountains of fine porcelain plates, sauce boats and vegetable tureens. It took me a long time before I had the courage to fly solo, but so far I've only invited new friends – those whom I've met since Thom died. I've also had pot luck suppers with individual old friends, but I've not had the 'gang' round together. However, tonight, I've invited the core of our mutual friends – Maureen, Elaine and Thelma – round for full dinner party treatment.

Planning the meal turned out to be great fun. I decided on chilli prawns with coriander, lime and mango as a starter, sauté d'agneau au citron (lamb with lemon, cinnamon and saffron – served on a bed of rice) for the main course and finishing off with rhubarb crumble and cream, then cheese and biscuits. While I chopped, marinated and simmered, Flash played happily in the garden. From the kitchen window, I watched while he tracked down the plastic plant pot specially hidden for him behind the shed. They provide hours of entertainment: somewhere interesting to stick your nose; next, you can tear round the garden with them in your mouth; followed by ripping apart and finally, settling down for a good chew.

All the preparations for the meal went smoothly, except I ran out of cornflour to thicken off the lamb sauce and had to nip up the village, and there was even enough time to give Flash a quick brush down before the guests arrived.

I'd been worried about entertaining alone but when the doorbell rang, I discovered I had help after all. Flash elected himself the official greeter and provided the entertainment while I took coats and offered drinks. Even Maureen, who could not cope with a force of nature like Tyson, was charmed by Flash. Thelma offered to look after him while I'm away. Elaine tickled him behind his ears.

Of course I missed Thom beaming from the top of the table, but it was a manageable regret rather than overpowering sadness. Flash sensed it was a 'best behaviour' evening: not too much jumping up, no begging for food and quickly settling down under the table while we ate. He also found a new role after I spilled rice on the kitchen floor and became official 'clearer upper'.

By the end of the evening, both Flash and I were exhausted. I was slumped on the sofa and he was curled up over my feet, a perfect excuse for contented laziness:

'Could you bring me another cup of coffee. I don't want to disturb the dog.'

Sunday 19 March

Walking over the fields, Flash was busy playing a boisterous game with some other puppies – so we did not spot the arrival of Lily's mortal enemy, Buster. Flash and Buster sniffed each other politely and I began to feel his reputation was rather undeserved. So while the other dog owners turned back, Flash and I walked on with Buster and his owner – a woman in her early sixties. The dogs were happily chasing each other around but when we reached St George's Lane, she became very unsettled:

'I'll have to catch Buster, there's a patch of grass where he goes mad.' She ran after him.

We found him with his head down a drain.

'A fox must have been through there,' she said.

Buster was growling and pawing the ground.

She dragged him away and then rather than calming him down, started what could only be described as confrontational play. He would bare his teeth and she would pounce forward:

'Who's attacking you,' she lunged, 'who's attacking you', and she tensed her body and made a strange jerk forward.

Flash and I looked on, bemused at this teasing. It was becoming increasingly clear that the source of Buster's madness was not a patch of grass. By now he was running up and down in the most demented fashion.

I took a step back. Flash, who was not yet a good judge of dog body language, mistook the noise for an invitation to play and started running around Buster. I could sense the tension climbing and Buster snapped at the black and white fur whizzing past. There was an explosion of snarling and whimpering. With his tail between his legs, Flash retreated back down the lane.

The madness was spent. Buster's owner calmly leaned down to pet and comfort him.

'I think it would be better if we walked on.' I was still shocked by what I had witnessed.

Buster's owner did not apologise. But I felt compelled to turn in the lane and add:

'It's OK, but he has to learn that not every dog wants to play.'

It was only writing up my diary that I realised the real lesson wasn't for Flash but me: not all dog owners can be trusted.

As Jeff would say, but is too polite: I've never met a problem dog, only problem owners.

Monday 20 March

I went up to London for a meeting of the New Producers Alliance – an organisation for budding film makers. It was in a hip East End venue and most of the members were ten or even fifteen years younger than me. While I listened to the introductory talk, I realised I still had Flash hairs on my trousers.

I had hoped that the event would be good for networking – and there was an opportunity to socialise in the bar afterwards – but I decided to leave early. Although I can work a room, if needs be, it was not the right place for me. They were mostly one-man companies who not only produced and directed but also wrote their own scripts too.

On the train home, I started thinking that I might be tackling this the wrong way round. Instead of finding someone who needed a script and writing something to their specifications,

I should write what I want and what I know about. In the new writing journal that I subscribe to, there had been an advert from a rural theatre company who wanted a one-act, one-actor play to tour villages in the South East. While I've no idea how to appeal to East End hipsters, I do know what people in villages are interested in: other people in villages.

I had a brainstorm. What if I wrote about a dog walker? They see everything that happens and know all the gossip. My character could be in her late fifties or early sixties – like most of the people I meet. Maybe I could turn my morning walks with Flash into research for a play…

Tuesday 21 March

Every morning at 8 a.m. Lily the Dalmatian is waiting for Flash on the front drive. The barking starts as he emerges and reaches a crescendo while he creeps down the passageway beside the garage. Flash's natural bounce and enthusiasm for his walk has rather dwindled by the time he is pounced on. To show he accepts Lily as top dog, he usually rolls on to his back and exposes his belly. Rather than accepting her homage, Cruel Queen Lily barks in his ear – just in case Flash has somehow forgotten his position during the night. Lily as leader of the pack is a rather bizarre idea; far from being a motorcycle and chains sort of dog, she is about as frightening as a gang of 'My Little Ponies'. However, Flash has accepted his role and they happily coexist.

I wonder what my relationship will be like with my neighbours after tonight's Millennium Party meeting. There are about thirty-five houses in the road and my RSVP slip was returned by two-thirds; two houses were not interested; twelve wanted to participate but were busy, and I'd set out ten of my second-best glasses for tonight's meeting. When Jackie from number

26 popped over to explain that she had double-booked herself, Flash had hurled himself at her.

'I'm sorry, I'm trying to break that habit,' I explained as she tried to stop him from pulling on her jumper. 'Flash, NO.'

'It would be a pity if you had to shut him out,' replied Jackie – rather pointedly, I thought.

I resolved to put Flash on his lead, which would allow me to check him sharply before he launched himself at my guests. He certainly had to attend the meeting because without him, I would never have suggested it in the first place. His Sheepdog curiosity was on full alert as I rearranged the furniture and pushed my great-great-grandmother's dining-room table against the wall. By the time Valerie and Michael arrived with some extra folding chairs, Flash was getting frenzied. Perhaps it was the familiar faces who often arrive to feed him, or being on the lead indoors, but he started barking. When the same pattern happened with the next ring on the doorbell, I slipped his lead off and left him to his own devices. I was too busy taking coats and orders for white or red wine – which I promptly forgot – to keep an eye on Flash. However, he had stopped barking and in between making introductions, I would catch glimpses of black and white fur between people's legs. Once again, Flash was making certain that everybody was properly greeted and had a topic of conversation: namely how gorgeous he was. So I left him to his own devices. By 8.35 p.m. everybody had arrived and was seated with a glass of wine.

I discovered that my road is full of natural organisers. Brian, at number 43, produced the village Millennium guide so we could check if our proposed party would clash with the Horticultural Show or the Tennis Club open day. Veronica, at number 8, volunteered to speak to the parish clerk and discover whether permission would be needed. A consensus was quickly emerging around a marquee, which would be erected on a large expanse of grass outside number 13. A date was set, catering discussed and who exactly would be invited; meanwhile Flash stretched out contentedly in the middle of the room. I too was beginning to feel part of a larger pack. I found that my neighbours were looking to me to summarise the mood, hand out tasks and stop the meeting becoming obsessed with trivialities. I had become chairman and everybody else was slotting into their roles. Sam, an elderly man with a face like a northern music hall comedian, elected himself committee joker and kept making strange noises. The first time, I thought the dog had broken wind or that the central heating was playing up. Flash, who had previously been happy to explore all these strange feet and even sleep by some, was particularly startled. Like a small child, he immediately returned to me for reassurance.

When the meeting finally broke up, Sam left with a final click and a whirr and a twinkle in his eye. Everybody else left full of excitement. Joan from number 19 said:

'My last street party was in 1945.'

Wednesday 22 March

In the lane behind Hurstpierpoint's Anglican church, we met an elderly Old English Sheepdog and an equally frail owner. Flash bounded up to sniff hello – normally, with older dogs this is enough. However, the owner started waving her walking stick at him, which translated into Flash speak must have been an invitation to play because he mounted the Old English.

'Haven't you taken your dog to training classes?' thundered the elderly owner.

Normally, I receive only compliments on his behaviour to which I modestly reply: he does have his moments.

'Flash, NO.' I pulled him off. Sometimes, I worry that he thinks NO is part of his name.

'You'll need to do something about his manners.' She was firm.

'He's only young.'

'You need to get him fixed.'

Although I am considering getting Flash neutered, her suggestion made my hackles rise.

Last night, a documentary on Channel 4 called *Puppy Love*, had featured psychologist Dr Aric Sigman, who claimed the fashion for castrating dogs had arrived hand in hand, if that's not an indelicate metaphor, with the women's movement. To paraphrase the doctor: women can't bear dogs behaving naturally because it reminds them of the base instincts of men.

I had never realised that the future of Flash's testicles would be so political.

Saturday 25 March

Flash and I went across the fields on our own this morning, so we did not witness Lily's fall from grace. While Valerie and Michael were distracted, she disappeared into the hedgerow and discovered something she considered fragrant to roll in. Rather than a dab behind each ear, Lily did such a thorough job that even her collar was caked with indescribable horribleness. Back home, she had to be sponged down with washing-up liquid and rinsed off with water from the rain butt – apparently, it's not as cold as from the tap.

In the morning papers, the Queen had visited a 'living museum' at Ballarat, Australia, which recreated an 1850s goldrush village. At the grocer's store, Her Majesty had purchased a bar of dog soap for the royal Corgis. Tilley's Timid Joe Dog Soap was used by the prospectors to wash the dogs they kept to protect themselves from rival miners. According to the label: 'TIMID JOE DOG SOAP RENDERS THE SKIN HEALTHY AND SOFT AND THE COAT SMOOTH AND GLOSSY'. It should also be used for 'MANGE AND OTHER SKIN DISEASES' and 'INSTANTLY KILLS FLEAS AND OTHER VERMIN'.

My paper failed to mention how much the bar of soap cost or how the Queen, who famously never carries money, paid, but I am sure it was cheap at twice the price. For Lily the worst indignity was not forgoing dog soap, by royal appointment, but losing her precious collar. Pacing up and down the kitchen waiting for it to be washed, Valerie reported, it was like Lily was complaining she felt naked. But for a rescue dog, who arrived at their home without a collar, it must be her badge of belonging.

I still enjoy reading the column advertising puppies for sale in the *Friday Ad*, so I picked up a copy while waiting for my Body Pump class to start. One advertisement was so bizarre, I had to read it out aloud:

'Non smoker required to rescue cute 6 year old small bitch'.

The dog welfare charities seem to be getting pickier and pickier.

'It must be some sort of code,' declared one of my classmates.

'Russian Grand Spy Masters are placing advertisements in the Crawley, Haywards Heath, Burgess Hill, Horsham and East Grinstead edition of the *Friday Ad*? It's certainly a possibility.' I scanned the column. 'What about this one? "Rottweiler Bitch 4.5 months reared with children/cats, adorable temperament". 4.5 months, it's very precise?'

'Send reinforcements. We're going to advance into Chechnya,' replied my lycra-clad classmate.

Wednesday 29 March

Our Millennium Street Party has hit an implacable barrier. Two sets of the residents, who live very close to the small green at the centre of the crescent, are totally against the idea. I could understand, but only just, them not wanting to join in. I could understand if it was a late party, but we're finishing at 11 p.m. If the sound of everybody else enjoying themselves outside will be annoying, why not go out for the evening? Even Veronica's gentle diplomacy with half a lifetime of being their neighbour, and the enthusiasm of everybody else in the road, cannot budge them. Is there a strange pay-off to being obstinate?

The weather has taken a turn for the worse and Flash returns home from our morning walk coated in mud. Previously, he has agreed to have his paws wiped if I put the towel over his head and give him the brush to chew on. Now he gets wildly overexcited and wants to hurl himself at me and rip the towel apart. He seems to think we're having some sort of play fight. Except, I am feeling increasingly uncomfortable. It brings back too many memories of wolves in my childhood nightmares. What big mature teeth you have, Flash!

On the afternoon walk, Church Pastures turned out to be wetter than expected and my left wellington sprung a leak. I have simply worn through the cheap and cheerful boots that I'd bought for gardening. So I took Flash to a shop on the High Street that I've never visited before: Harper and Eades' Country Store.

We walked through a courtyard full of ploughs and tractors to the shop with a wide range of waterproof clothes, over twenty types of boots, heavy-duty string and strange implements whose use I could only guess. I bought a pair of green heavy-duty boots and matching waterproof jacket and trousers. I have the badges of a true countryman, but it will take a little longer and much more work to acquire the soul.

Friday 31 March

I went up to London to conduct another celebrity interview and arranged to meet up with my former boyfriend for lunch at our old meeting place: Costa Coffee in Old Compton Street.

Eighteen months ago, the last time I sat waiting for Brandon on the same sofa with the dodgy springs, we were in love. Today, we are 'just friends'. Like in the past, I arrived ten minutes early and flicked through proofs of the autobiography of the magician Paul Daniels, whose marriage I was profiling later. From my sofa, I instantly recognised Brandon's well-muscled legs at the top of the staircase. Finishing a story about Prince William ruining a magic trick, I reached up for a friendly kiss on the lips. Perhaps men truly can't do two things at the same time, certainly I should not be trusted to simultaneously read and greet. Brandon pulled me closer for a hug and feelings I considered buried began to stir.

We exchanged news and then Brandon kept our table while I returned upstairs to order his hummus and salad sandwich – no butter, he's allergic to dairy products – and a tuna melt on tomato bread for me. Brandon was particularly keen for news of Flash, which seems ironic as his allergy to pet hairs means they will never meet. Eighteen months ago, I had thought that Brandon would help unravel Thom from my life but looking back, all our short affair had achieved was to stop me from becoming a dog owner.

Brandon's gym-sculpted thigh was pressing against my leg. It felt warm.

I asked if he was dating anybody else; he's not.

He asked if I am seeing anybody; I shook my head.

I decided to run my hands over his head. It must have been a couple of days since the last time he'd shaved it; small dark hairs teased my fingertips. We had another kiss on the lips; the merest brush past.

'I've been thinking a lot about you lately,' I confessed.

'Have you?' he replied archly.

'I've decided to write a novel inspired by our relationship,' I said quickly.

'What kind of novel?'

I should have teased him and said a comedy, or perhaps nearer the truth: a tragedy.

'Thriller,' I explained and brushed the back of my hand across the bony lump at the top of his spine. If Brandon had been a panther he would have purred. He settled deeper into the sofa. I knew he would have agreed to sex, for old times' sake, but I also knew closed chapters are best left that way.

All I wanted, perhaps all I ever wanted, was to touch him and be touched; to stroke and be stroked back.

'What else are you writing?' he asked.

I was annoyed by his lack of curiosity about the plot of my dark and twisted thriller, but I didn't want him to know that.

'I'm keeping a diary about Flash.'

'How on earth are you finding enough material?'

'It's not just about dogs, because raising a puppy brings back all the memories from my own childhood.' Suddenly, I had some inspiration. 'You've studied dreams, haven't you, as part of your counselling training?'

'Yes?'

'Can you make any sense of my childhood dreams of wolves?'

Brandon looked at me blankly.

'It's all tied in with my childhood desire for a puppy.'

'All I know is that we are every part of our dreams.'

'So, I'm both the small boy running and hiding under the bedclothes and the wolf with long spindly arms and big teeth chasing him?'

'Exactly. It's strange that you should be frightened by wolves – I've always rather liked them.'

I shuddered.

He went on:

'In fact, my spirit guide is a wolf.'

'How did you find that out?' I asked. We were heading for Planet Weird.

'Meditation. He's my protector.'

I was not certain whether to laugh or wonder if this could explain my strong attraction to Brandon.

— ❧ —

Later, when I interviewed Paul Daniels and his former assistant, Debbie McGee, I discovered not only does she not want children, but her allergies rule out conventional substitutes like cats and dogs. Even a rabbit, used for a magic trick, caused her problems. At one point, during our interview at the Grosvenor Hotel in Park Lane, she sneezed and joked she was probably allergic to me. I did not tell her about Flash.

Back home, Flash was overjoyed to see me and leapt all over me and added more hairs to bother unsuspecting magician's assistants. I noticed a strange green speck at the corner of his right eye. At first, it seemed a piece of grass was trapped there. However, as I tried to remove it, I realised he had a slight eye infection.

This is where the diary turns strange: three days ago when I was rubbing down a damp dog, small green specks had danced across my eyes – like some strange acid-type trip. Today, I am wondering if I had a premonition.

Are Flash and I so linked I can predict his health problems?

If so, maybe Brandon can indeed have a wolf spirit guide.

Saturday 1 April

I had a lie-in this morning, partly because the weather was horrible and partly because of a late night. Two friends, Richard and James, had taken me to see *The Talented Mr. Ripley* at Brighton Marina Cinema, followed by supper. I had good company, great food and the twists and turns of the movie had provided some inspiration for my thriller, but I was jealous of my next-door neighbours, Valerie and Michael, who had invited Flash round for a quiet night in. Sometimes my overwhelming need for him is frightening.

Today is my nephew James's twelfth birthday; I phoned to wish him many happy returns, but he was out playing tennis. My sister and I would normally have nothing to say to each other, but this time we traded sick dog stories. Shadow, their Labrador, had been unable to settle after a long walk. Eventually, he collapsed but was in too much pain to make it to his supper bowl; he had to be hand fed and finally carried to his bed.

I shared Flash's eye infection and his tummy upset, which after three days has still not cleared up. It was not until after putting down the phone that I realised I'd not asked after the children. I had no idea what James had for his birthday (beyond the desk lamp I sent) and discovered nothing about Nicola's latest triumphs at school.

Sunday 2 April

I saw a TV programme which claimed that sheep's (and any other herbivore) droppings provide the bacteria needed to sort out a dog's upset stomach. Previously, I have avoided fields with sheep but this morning I decided to take Flash over to Little Washbrook Farm for his first 'upfront and personal' encounter.

With Flash safely on the lead, I allowed him and a large black-faced sheep to stare at each other: his ears quivered with interest and she calmly sniffed the air. Something in his Collie genetic inheritance was clicking into place. The sheep blinked first, turned heel and flouncing her dread-locked wool, sauntered back to the flock. Flash looked up at me expectantly; these sheep were far more interesting than the ball he sometimes fetches to humour me.

With reports of hill farmers abandoning sheep in telephone boxes, unable to afford transporting them to market, where they fetch only the price of a packet of crisps, I almost wish I could buy him a couple. For the cost of a latex chew, I could probably get half a dozen sheep.

Unlike the last time we'd walked these fields, when I'd spent half the time shouting 'no', Flash was allowed to feast on the droppings of sheep, rabbit and even horses – which must have been baffling for a young dog. It would be wonderful if an ancient natural remedy could cure his stomach problems rather than modern antibiotics.

The distant downs were a brooding dark green, above us the sky whitened by almost transparently wispy clouds. Perhaps I should reconnect with the earth too; forget cyberspace, virtual reality, commuting up to London and the placeless future.

It strikes me before discovering who I am without Thom, maybe first I need to understand where I am.

Monday 3 April

Flash was not waiting on the step the other side of the kitchen door when I came down this morning. He did not jump up – which would normally be a cause for celebration – and his coat had lost its shine. He almost looked smaller, as if his sickness had reduced the space he took up in the house. I bathed his eye with salt water as Valerie had suggested. ('One teaspoon of salt to a pint of water from the kettle,' she explained. 'Sterilised water is what they suggest for babies and I use the same rule with dogs.' Not having had children I have missed out on all this vital information.)

The eye was not getting any worse, but then it wasn't getting any better. He managed only half his breakfast and retired to his basket. I went upstairs to phone the vet, but their answering machine told me they would not be open until 8.30 a.m. I turned around and discovered Flash's natural curiosity had brought him out of his basket and up into my office.

I was caught between two immovable instincts. What I'd inherited from my mother: doctors should only be consulted as the last resort and that the body is best left to repair itself. What I'd learned from Thom: the fragility of life. I am longer cocooned by a belief – which I'd never consciously articulated before – that nothing too terrible will happen to me. No wonder I'm fitter at forty than I was at any time since I was eighteen. Body Pump twice a week, dancing at least once and two long walks a day.

The vet took Flash's temperature by inserting the thermometer up his bottom. Flash yelped, but worse was to come:

'The best cure is to starve him for twenty-four hours,' explained the vet.

Our appointment was at 5 p.m. and Flash had been agitating for food for the last hour.

'Tomorrow lunchtime, he can have something bland like chicken and rice.'

We left the torture chamber with a bottle of kaolin and morphine (liquid concrete as my mother used to call it) and eye drops for his conjunctivitis.

I had been expecting a terrible evening, with Flash demanding to be fed every five minutes, but once suppertime had passed he seemed to accept his fate.

At bedtime I weakened and let him have a dog biscuit, but was given such a mournful look that I caved in completely and provided the usual ration of two.

I might like to pretend I'm firm, but Flash knows it is just an illusion.

Tuesday 4 April

I sat on the kitchen floor and tempted Flash over for a cuddle. Just as he got settled, I whipped out his eye drops and squeezed the white gooey medicine into his eye. He wriggled away from me, but it was too late.

I was irresistibly reminded of my childhood garden and my mother sunning herself in a deckchair. We still lived in Northampton so I must have been under seven. I'd rushed home from school to tell her about a story I'd written and she'd listened encouragingly. I'd gone off to play – possibly with my toy wooden dachshund on wheels. The faster I ran, the faster its ears and paws would rotate. But my mother called me back to her stripy deckchair:

'Tell me again about the story.'

I have no recollection of the plot, but I remember my excitement that she wanted to hear it again, but then the pain as she reached over and ripped a plaster off my knee. Not so much the physical pain but the pain of betrayal:

'That hurt.'

'I couldn't resist it,' she laughed.

If I am in Flash's bad books for squirting medicine down his throat and into his eyes, Valerie is definitely in his good books. She brought round a casserole of cooked chicken for him and a bag of boiled rice. For the first time ever, while I was preparing his supper, Flash stood on his hind legs and put his paws on my work surface for a closer look.

— ✌ —

In the evening, we had a meeting of the Millennium Street Party Committee at my house. With the grassy patch ruled out for pitching a marquee, we have decided to rent Hurstpierpoint

Scout Headquarters instead. It has solved the problems of dissenting neighbours and provided a dance floor, toilets and cover from the rain.

Jackie from number 26 was rather disappointed that it would not be like a traditional street party with shrimp and fish paste sandwiches, Union Jack buntings and something called welfare orange squash. Joan and Sam, who must be eighty or beyond, have offered to print tickets, bring their industrial-sized coffee machine and use their cash and carry card to buy plastic plates and knives and forks.

Wednesday 5 April

This morning Flash was back to his usual joyful self, chasing and being chased by Lily across the field behind our houses. The weather has turned bitter. In other parts of West Sussex there has been snow. Valerie blames Michael for planting his early potatoes over the weekend. He must have got carried away because Sunday, being the first Sunday of the month, he was also allowed to have a bonfire on his allotment.

— ❧ —

Ever since Thom's death, I have been searching for answers to questions I cannot even begin to form. I've been hoping to find love again but maybe I need spiritual sustenance instead – or perhaps they are one and the same. The British novelist and playwright Charles Langbridge Morgan (1894–1958) claimed: 'There is no surprise more magical than the surprise of being loved. It is God's finger on man's shoulder.'

Many of the self-help books that I've been reading, from the spiritual (*Tibetan Book of Loving and Dying*) to the worldly (*How to*

Get What You Want and Want What You Get), have recommended meditation. The trouble is every time I close my eyes and try to empty my mind, I remember the lint needs cleaning out of the tumble dryer or I should buy more teabags. However, Brandon has sent details of courses at a Buddhist centre in Brighton with a note attached:

'Take what you need and leave the rest behind.'

There was a guided meditation described as an ideal introduction for beginners on Wednesdays at 12.30, followed by a vegetarian lunch for a donation of £1.50.

The idea of walking up the driveway to the centre – which used to be a retreat for Catholic nuns – felt intimidating. So I decided to take my security blanket: Flash. Of course, I will have to leave him in the car, but the knowledge that he's waiting outside will provide a sense of normality. Hove Lawns and St Anne's Well Gardens are only a few minutes' walk, so he can have a run when I've finished.

When I entered the Bodhisattva Kadampa Meditation Centre, I had expected to find everybody sitting on the floor chanting, but instead there was a large lounge with comfy sofas and low coffee tables. The impression of a slightly rundown café was reinforced by the offer of a cup of coffee. OK, the woman handing out the mugs was wearing orange and red flowing robes and had clipped her hair back to a number one or possibly number two, but otherwise it all appeared rather, well, conventional. I stood and drank my coffee, torn between hanging around awkwardly on my own and worrying that if I spoke to someone they would try to convert me to Buddhism.

Just after half past twelve, we were ushered towards the meditation room and I followed everybody else's lead and took off my shoes. Inside, there was a large Buddha. Thom would probably have made some remark about the combination of bright blue carpets and the orange curtains:

'Thank goodness we will soon have our eyes closed.'

I found the prayers difficult to follow but the words were strangely hypnotising. Surrounded by other people with the same goal, it was comparatively easy to slip into a deep meditation. I pictured myself swimming through deep green stagnant ponds, which, slightly worryingly, I have used as a symbol in the thriller I'm writing, to suggest schizophrenia and madness. Towards the end of the meditation, the group leader asked us to focus on the feeling of inner peace and file it away, ready to access whenever it was needed.

Afterwards, over a lunch of baked potatoes with cheese, baked beans and salad, I joked with the other participants that I would be experiencing both ends of the peace scale today: afternoon meditation and evening puppy training classes (with eight dogs barking in a small room).

Flash was overjoyed to see me again, especially as it was finally his lunchtime. We walked towards the seafront with a fellow seeker after inner peace – who claimed her cat and dog had lived so long together that the cat had learned to sit on command and come for walks.

The sea was as calm and unruffled as I felt inside.

— ❧❦ —

The dog training class was smaller this week but Sasha (the Alsatian) has grown to be twice Flash's size over the past three weeks and Brian (the badly behaved German Shorthaired Pointer) is back. His owners live on a farm and, despite being walked through sheep since a puppy, he wants to chase the newborn lambs:

'I'll have to come round and sort him out,' said Jeff.

'You better make it quick, or he might not still be there,' threatened Brian's owner as he struggled to greet his classmates. 'Leave,' she shouted, but as usual, he paid no attention to her.

Jeff took control and walked Brian up and down the hall and tried to make him sit. He refused so Jeff took the end of his lead and gave him sharp clip round his backside. Brian dutifully sat. I felt a little less guilty about hitting Flash for peeing in my friend's house.

With fewer dogs in the class, we had to take it in turns to parade up and down with our dogs at our heels. Unfortunately, I have not been reinforcing the 'close' command as often as I should have. In other words, I had not done my homework and was hoping to busk it. We were last to go – so I had plenty of time to be anxious and, as Jeff keeps telling me, anxiety travels down the lead. So I remembered my meditation class and retrieved the calm feelings I had filed away.

Confidently, Flash and I stepped into the ring. Amazingly, Flash kept his face close to my thigh, his intelligent brown eyes looking up. If we had been competing at Crufts in Dog Obedience, I could not have asked for anything more.

'Drop the lead, but keep walking,' commanded Jeff.

It took me a while to unravel the lead – my relaxed frame of mind was slightly undermined by how tightly I had wrapped it round my hand. The pause broke Flash's concentration but only for a second. Even with the lead trailing behind him, he still kept to heel and cornered beautifully.

'Give him lots of praise,' said Jeff.

'He's not this well behaved at home,' I said, amazed.

'That's the first time I've heard it that way round,' joked Jeff. But then I doubt that few of his pupils have come on from Buddhist meditation classes.

Flash was so well behaved, sitting quietly between exercises, that I wanted to give him a big hug. Sadly, I didn't – I just ruffled his tummy, patted his head and whispered in a slightly strangled tone:

'I'm so proud of you.'

Sunday 9 April

A group of my friends go on a monthly ramble and this time they have chosen Hampstead Heath. So for the first time ever, I took Flash on a train. With a small amount of persuading, he leapt on to the Thameslink train to London and we settled down at the far end of the carriage. He needed, of course, to check under the seats for any discarded food, but eventually settled down to his chew while I settled down to *The Sunday Times* (and an interesting article about a medieval zoo at the Tower of London, where visitors were exempt from the entrance fee if they brought a cat or a dog along to feed to the lions!).

Closer to London, I discovered the advantages of travelling with a dog. The Thameslink seats are so close together that you are in danger of rubbing knees with the passenger opposite (seldom a pleasant experience). As the train filled up, everybody decided with Flash at my feet they would choose another seat. So while the rest of the carriage huddled up together, we enjoyed splendid isolation. Between London Bridge and King's Cross, a beggar joined the train and while she systematically asked everybody else for money, she turned her large plaintive eyes on me and said:

'Can I stroke your doggie?'

After Flash had licked her face she moved on, satisfied, without asking for 'the price of a cup of tea'. Either, as I was in my dog-walking clothes, she thought I was a fellow beggar, or had decided that some things are more precious than money.

Flash coped well with the Underground and soon became accustomed to the rocking motions – swaying with the carriage as the train took sharp corners. Some of my fellow passengers even smiled. When we changed trains, at Camden, a thirty-something man was crouching on his haunches on the platform, staring into the middle distance. His hands were at Flash level, so he was rewarded with a friendly passing lick. It was such a shock to the man that he almost went into orbit.

The weather was glorious and Flash enjoyed exploring the Heath, although before I could stop him, he had found a used condom in the undergrowth and swallowed it. After running for two hours solid, Flash was still going strong, but Mike, Graham, Robin and I were ready for lunch and returned to Hampstead High Street and a gay pub called the King William.

While we had to pay for our food and drinks, Flash was given a slice of roast beef and a bowl of water. I think the landlord had taken a shine to him. Graham rather fancied the landlord. The boys all agreed that a dog was a very good way of meeting men and offered to take Flash out more often.

Monday 10 April

For the first time ever the camellia which Thom planted in our front garden has exploded into white blooms. On the morning walk with Valerie and Lily, even the buds on the oak trees are about to detonate and the flowering cherries are a riot of colour. How could I ever have imagined living in London or why, come to think of it, have I applied for the post of head of communication at Relate? Not only is it full-time, and based in Rugby, but I can picture the hours of being locked in stuffy meeting rooms.

The interview is on Thursday and I have to prepare a ten-minute presentation, write a press release and bring two pieces of work of which I am particularly proud. Unfortunately, I haven't written a newspaper article that arouses my passion for at least eighteen months – proof that I need to stop the freelance journalism. Why can't I believe in the thriller I'm working on and believe that it's possible to make a living from books or screenplays?

Strangely, I am not worried about Flash, who is adaptable enough to come to work with me, but would Relate be flexible enough to accommodate us?

Wednesday 12 April

My fourth birthday without Thom. His parents sent a card from Germany and I also received one from Martina, the nurse who had befriended him in hospital and witnessed his death with me. My parents have sent a cheque and my sister, Gayle, bought a new collar for Flash and a lead. Unfortunately, she seems under the impression that I own a pit pony as the collar would have fitted his waist. I called her to say thank you and we had a nice long telephone conversation about our respective dogs' growing patterns. While Flash still has plenty of slack on his first puppy collar, they went through four before Shadow reached adulthood. Next, we tried to outgross each other out about our dogs' respective nasty habits and I reported Flash's latest wickedness: chewing the ends of my leather rucksack straps. Finally, Gayle and I have a common bond.

Later, I met Kate at Patisserie Valerie in Old Compton Street in London. Rather than a traditional birthday cake and candles, we improvised with a rum baba covered with fresh fruit and cream. Slicing into the sponge and watching the rum trickle out, I wondered if Flash was proof of the power of all those childhood birthday cake wishes. I certainly couldn't have asked for a more faithful companion. As Valerie said this morning:

'It's like he's permanently asking, "What would you like me to do next?"'

If there had been candles on the cake to blow out, what would I have wished for this year? A lover? A better job? Certainly, head of communication at Relate would not have featured in my fantasies. However, the more I thought about it, I realised

I was content to be sharing this moment with Kate. A perfect cup of Earl Grey. A corner table and hot gossip. Her previous boyfriend had been a respectable lawyer trainee shipping lawyer who preferred to comb her hair than make love. She is currently dating a builder and visits all the lowlife pubs of Cardiff (because he's been thrown out of the rest) and is woken in the night for gymnastic sex. He loves her so much that last night he phoned her from a karaoke bar to pledge eternal love with 'Me and Mrs Jones'. (This weekend Kate will be part of the chorus for a sell-out performance of Verdi's Requiem at St David's Hall.)

We took a short walk through Soho. These days I find it hard to be cooped up inside for too long, but the rain started again and we took refuge in the lobby of the Berners Hotel. I always enjoy the riot of plaster mouldings on the ceilings and the comfortable sofas. By a strange coincidence, I bumped into Joanna, the producer of a short film I wrote, inspired by my childhood fear of wolves. She was having a meeting about editing the footage we shot last October. I told her about getting Flash and she was so convinced life has been imitating art that she wants my next project to be about film makers who become fabulously wealthy.

Kate treated me to a meal in Chinatown and we saw Maggie Smith in *Lady in the Van* at the Queen's Theatre. The play is based on Alan Bennett's real-life experiences of a tramp who parked her van on his driveway for three months but stayed for fifteen years. Although greatly entertained, we were both uncomfortable about being encouraged to laugh at a woman who was obviously mentally ill.

Meanwhile, Flash had enjoyed his day at Valerie and Lily's. I hope he has not picked up too many bad habits. He is turning into a copycat of Lily, right down to cocking his head on one side when she does. Unfortunately, this means he also receives a slice of carrot when Valerie is preparing their evening meal and a small portion when it is served up. Flash might be a well-brought-up young dog, but now he's venturing out more and more into the outside world, who knows what bad company he might fall in with.

Thursday 13 April

The journey up to Rugby for my job interview at Relate was terrible. A strike by Connex South Central drivers meant I was dumped at Watford Junction with for ever to wait for a connection. Instead of arriving with an hour to spare, I had five minutes. So there was little time to reacquaint myself with Rugby, which I used to visit for training weekends about ten years ago.

It was impossible to judge whether I impressed the panel or not – Equal Opportunities legislation meant that each candidate was asked the same general questions. I much prefer the cut and thrust of a genuine interview. When given the opportunity to ask any questions, I stifled my desire to find out the policy for bringing dogs to work. I did accept the tour of the college and discovered, if successful, I would be sharing an office. Was there room for a dog basket in the corner? The grounds of Herbert Gray College would allow Flash to have a scamper round at lunchtime and Rugby must have parks. However, the job would mean relocating and I could not decide whether my reticence is concern for Flash's welfare or my own.

Three years of locking myself away after Thom's death should be more than enough. I feel ready to return to full-time work but is this the right job?

Saturday 15 April

Michael, the friend who has been providing long-distance dog training advice, has returned from Australia and taken delivery of what he reckons must be hundreth dog. Driving down to Hove to meet up with him and his partner Brian, I was feeling rather nervous. The new residents' parking restrictions mean that finding a space is fraught and I was worried what Michael would make of Flash and whether we would graduate with honours.

Michael's new dog is an Akita Inu – a Japanese dog which he specialises in breeding and showing. My concerns that Flash might overwhelm this three-month-old puppy were immediately dispelled. As soon as the door to their apartment was opened, a large furry blond teddy bear threw himself at Flash. The wrestling contest was pretty evenly matched. Flash had speed and good cornering, Max had weight and the home advantage. There was a brief intermission while they followed us into the kitchen. It took Flash about a hundredth of a second to discover that Max was a fussy eater and turned his nose up at both the dried and the tinned dog food, which lay unloved on the floor. But not for long! Flash attacked both of them with relish.

Ever since I stopped giving him lunch, he has had to rely on finding his own midday snack – the bench on the recreation ground, by the public conveniences, normally provides the most tasty morsels of discarded or dropped food.

Michael had hoped that Max might follow Flash's example, but his puppy was instead following my mother's instructions for when guests came round: FHB – family hold back. On the stove was a pot of chicken that Michael was cooking in a final bid to tempt Max's more discerning taste buds. I'd thought he would refuse to cater to his dog's whims but obviously I was wrong.

I had two main discipline problems with which I wanted Michael's help. Flash is still mouthing (putting his jaws round my arms but not strongly enough to break the skin) and still jumping up.

'Try kneeing him in the chest,' counselled Michael.

'But I've tried that, it just seems to make him more excited,' I said.

'Then try it harder. I've almost winded dogs. They might get up and try again and perhaps a third time – but they soon get the message.' His deep brown eyes gleamed.

The idea of Flash sprawled across the kitchen floor, most probably hitting his head on a kitchen cabinet, was not very appealing. However, something needs to be done about the jumping up because Flash can now jump high enough and with enough force to catch me somewhere very tender. I don't think Michael's more brutal approach is the answer, though. He didn't have any suggestions for mouthing beyond exaggerating the hurt from his teeth, but I've tried that without any success.

We took the dogs for a walk along the seafront and Max was immediately the centre of attention. With everybody wanting to stroke his coat, which has the consistency of a luxury bath mat, Flash was overlooked. He's going through an ungainly teenage stage – his head seems too small for his body and his legs too long.

When we'd been stopped on the sixth or seventh occasion by someone wanting to pet Max, Michael whispered angrily to me:

'Can't they get their own puppies?'

At Hove Lawns, I was surprised that Michael did not let Max off the lead. Apparently, he hasn't learned to come when called. Meanwhile, Michael was impressed when I stopped Flash from wandering on to the beach with just a 'no' command and how swiftly and reliably he came back. Two skills that I taught him without recourse to my dog training book or classes.

Although I'd seen Michael as my training guru and waited months for his return, he had little to offer. Except, perhaps, for one valuable lesson: the answers for what is best for me and my dog are all within me. When Flash ran eagerly up to me on Brighton seafront and showed off by sitting on command, I knew there was no standard dog training package.

Michael's requirements for Max, who will ultimately be a show dog, and mine for Flash are totally different. It's a bit like my experiences of recovering from Thom's death. Ultimately, there is no right or wrong way of mourning and there is no right or wrong way of training a dog. Everybody must search for their own way – if that doesn't sound too 'Zen and the Art of Dog-Walking'.

Tuesday 18 April

I remember not only where the wolves arrived in my life (via a dressing gown hung on the back of a bedroom door of a family friend's house in Bournemouth) but where they left too. Up to this point, the wolves had followed me from bedroom to bedroom by clinging to the roof rack of our Ford Zephyr family saloon. It must have been hard for them to hold on with such pointed claws, but I suppose in those days there weren't many motorways so traffic moved slower. Anyway, as these wolves – I never knew how many were in the pack – had the power to make themselves invisible during the day, I expect they possessed other special skills too.

However, in the summer of 1966, when I had turned seven, the senior partner at my father's accountancy firm lent us his holiday cottage at Thorpeness in Suffolk. As usual, the wolves travelled with us from Bedford on the top of the car, but unlike previous holidays, they did not return home with us.

It must be something about being forty-one and at what is, hopefully, the midpoint of my life: I need to understand the first half before I can find any shape for the second. While my childhood is one long blur of suburban niceness, the wolves have stood out as the defining motif. But what do they mean? And what have they got to teach me? So I have decided to face my fears of wolves and return to Thorpeness.

Most of my memories of that pivotal summer are centred round the Meare – a boating lake where I had learned to punt and enjoyed the adventure of finding the forts, houses and a crocodile that had been hidden on its many small islands. I'm sure that my maternal grandmother came down to visit for a few days. The only photograph of the two of us together was taken on the steps outside the cottage. I am holding a small multicoloured plastic windmill on a stick and probably she is holding one too; which is how my father stole the snapshot. (She hated having her photograph taken, so would normally grab something to shield her face.) The picture of her with a basket over her head was presumably taken on a beach nearby. Those are the sum total of all of my recollections from Thorpeness and to be honest, most of them could have come from the family photograph album.

However, I am absolutely convinced that when we packed our cases and returned to Bedford, the wolves stayed in the holiday cottage. Why? I have no idea. While my father loaded up the car, my sister and I watched the swallows gathering on the telegraph wires to migrate back to Africa. It must have been an omen because when we got home and I checked under my bed – no wolves. Maybe something seminal happened in Thorpeness that allowed me to move on and literally leave my nightmares behind? Perhaps returning to Suffolk and retracing my steps will dislodge more memories? I wonder if the wolves are still living there?

Although it would be possible to make the round trip in one day, I have decided to take a mini-break and on the spur of the moment I invited along a friend. By a strange coincidence, it's the friend whose house I'd been staying in when I had the dream of Flash in my garden and decided he was the right puppy for me. Steve Leder's employers have gone into liquidation and he readily agreed to take a few days off job-hunting. Instead of driving straight to Thorpeness, I suggested it would be easier to find a hotel in nearby Aldeburgh.

— ❧ —

Time has stood still in Aldeburgh. Creosoted sheds sell locally caught crab and lobster and the fishermen's ropes and pots (much-mended, with a green, black and white netting) are strewn all over the stony beach. Flash enjoyed hunting for discarded fish heads amongst the rusting machinery, discarded floats and iron washing pails. He was slightly startled when an ancient petrol engine was fired up to winch a boat out of the sea over lumps of wood and metal railway sleepers up above high tide.

At the centre of the town there is a small raised boating lake, where two small boys, probably about seven, had launched their sail boats and were delightedly running round to stop them crashing into the sides. It could easily have been a scene from my own sixties visit to Suffolk.

While we were searching for a hotel or a B&B, I was approached by a married couple in their late fifties. They complimented me on my dog and the husband claimed he could guess his name.

'Hello… Flash.' He started tickling his chest.

'Did you hear me calling him?' I didn't think he had. Flash always keeps an eye on where I am.

'No.'

'So how?'

'I just looked at him and I knew,' explained the dog mind reader.

I look startled.

'My husband can also guess friends' Internet passwords,' chipped in his proud wife.

As Steve had once been a hotel manager, I sent him into the beach-front hotels to negotiate a good rate and plead Flash's case.

Dogs proved to be no problem and we chose the White Lion Hotel – even though they charged Flash a £2 supplement. He was happy to stay in the room while we had supper in the restaurant, but I could not persuade him to sleep in the bathroom.

I spent a restless night, not disturbed by nightmares about wolves, but by the sound of Flash roaming around the bedroom and by him licking my face at three-thirty in the morning.

Wednesday 19 April

Thorpeness was the inspiration of Glencairn Stuart Ogilvie, who inherited an estate just after the turn of the last century. Between 1911 and 1937, he built the core of his holiday village around the Meare – a lake which was dug by local fishermen at the rate of eight old pence an hour. The homes have a whimsical feel and range from small cottages to relatively grand houses – apparently, they needed to be large enough for the middle classes to bring staff to manage the self-catering aspect of a holiday at Thorpeness. With ornamental arched gateways, a fake medieval tower with ecclesiastical windows, and a Dutch-style tulip cottage, the village is a forerunner of today's Disney-style theme parks. The most stunning building is the 'House in the Clouds'. Ogilvie's sense of style and his fertile imagination could not allow a water tower to spoil his vision, so the steel box frame was clad with black weatherboarding and a traditional house built at the top.

On returning to childhood haunts, the surprise is always how small everything seems through adult eyes. What I had remembered as a tiny holiday cottage, however, could most probably sleep eight and the Meare, which I had expected to be only a little larger than a municipal boating lake stretched over sixty-four acres.

I decided to start Thorpeness Revisited by hiring out a punt, but our journey was delayed because while I was talking to the boatman, Flash either fell or jumped in the Meare and Steve refused to sit with a damp dog. After he'd been towelled down we set off with a copy of the original map to uncover hidden treasures. There were no problems remembering how to punt – although as an adult I decided to be brave and stand on the back. It was a sobering thought to realise I am now older than my father had been when he originally taught me to place the pole close to the side of the boat, walk my hands up to it and finally, to twist to stop the hook from getting stuck in the mud.

Flash settled down quickly – even though Steve had to stop him from leaning over the side to inspect the passing wildfowl. Although we rediscovered the crocodile, the dragon's lair (half a metal boat with a freshly painted fire-eating monster on the top), Peggotty's House (another boat on the roof), the Pirate's Lair and Wendy's House, I could bring back no memories to explain the wolves' disappearance.

After lunch, while Steve read his book, I decided to return to the cottage where we'd stayed in 1966 and really focus. Across the road a medlar tree had been planted – on 29 July 1981 to commemorate the marriage of the Prince and Princess of Wales – and a bench seat had been built round it. While I sat under the low-hanging branches, and tried to recall the wolves, their distant descendant chewed lumps of discarded bark. The cottage, with its black weatherboard exterior and eves so low the bedroom windows jutted out, certainly could have been Grandma's house from the *Little Red Riding Hood* myth. Except, even tracing the wolves back to the last place I'd seen them brought me no closer to solving their disappearance. Disappointed, I almost called Flash and returned to Steve.

Instead, I tried to conjure up the photograph I remembered with my own grandmother on the steps outside the cottage. Next,

I placed myself, aged seven, in the picture and tried to take my imagination through the front door. Short trousers, thick glasses – it was certainly me. In my imagination, I started walking up the garden path, but I never reached the door. I crouched down at the window and peered inside. The wolves were still living in the cottage. No wonder I couldn't enter. They were laying the table for tea with a red-and-white checked tablecloth. I counted them. Four wolves: daddy wolf, mummy wolf and their two cubs – one male and one female. How did I know? Since I'd last seen them, they had learned to walk and had decided to wear clothes.

The wolves sat down at the table and helped themselves to currant buns and lemonade. The cosy domestic scene through the cottage window, so entirely different from my childhood nightmares, was such a shock that I found myself back in my adult body, with Flash at my feet under the medlar tree.

The trip was supposed to let me discover how I'd changed and outgrown my fears. However, rather than being exorcised from my life, the wolves had chosen to stay in Thorpeness. Why? Taking Flash for a quick walk around the village, it slowly fitted into place. With a lake featuring characters from *Peter Pan* surrounded by fairy-tale houses, obviously they had felt they belonged here.

Strangest of all, I found I missed them and was swept away with nostalgia for the last time my fantasies were more real than my mother's reassurances. Rather than ridding myself of the wolves, I wanted them back; in fact, if I was ever to make the transition from journalist to writer I needed my childhood sense of make-believe again.

So I returned to my medlar tree and tried a second visualisation. The wolves opened the door of the holiday cottage with their bags packed. The boy wolf even had the windmill on a stick from the photograph. They stopped to look both ways before crossing the road and the closer they came, the more human they seemed. Weird.

In a reverse of the *Little Red Riding Hood* myth, where the woodcutter chops open the wolf and Grandma jumps out, a large slit grew in my chest and all the wolves climbed in.

This time, I'd be taking them home with me.

Recounting my experiences to Steve, he declared me the strangest person he knows.

Flash seemed to have enjoyed his visit to Thorpeness. In fact, he was so keen to bring back a souvenir that he rolled in something fishy-smelling on the beach.

— ❧ —

On my return to Hurstpierpoint, I found a letter from Relate informing me that my application was 'not being taken any further'. So I will not be escaping into the secure world of head of communication. It's back to the original plan. I will need the wolves more than I imagined.

23 April – Easter Sunday

My parents moved back to Bedford when I was seven. My father was born in the town and my mother moved there at seven too. They still live in the same house where I celebrated most of my childhood birthdays and blew out the majority of my candles. It was strange to be driving there with the dog that I had longed for asleep beside me in the passenger footwell.

On the journey, I started remembering the dogs that did their best to fill my childhood doggy void. My father's elder brother had married my mother's elder sister and with this double tie, a lot of my childhood was spent at their farm, a few miles outside Bedford. Their first dog was a Labrador called Bones, but what I remember about him was the void when he died. They looked after a few friends' dogs and then finally got another black

Labrador. My uncle called the puppy Jack and my aunt called him Spike. It was my first introduction to the complexities of relationships – because for a while he had two names – but my uncle disappeared and he became Spike.

The whole extended family would descend on the farm every third Sunday. I would gather up my younger cousins and disappear out across the fields, the dog always ahead – sniffing out rabbits or pheasants from the hedgerows – somehow gave shape and purpose to our games. In my dreams, Spike was my dog even though he was determined to go his own way. It was generally better to walk over the farm's land because if Spike got bored with us, he could safely peel off and return home. However, occasionally, we would venture further and I would have to coax Spike out of someone's garden, and on one occasion I chased him round a large apple tree while a cat taunted us from the lowest branch and its owner yelled at me from her back doorstep.

Of course, I would have loved to take Spike home with us, but he was a farm dog and as my mother would say:

'It wouldn't be fair on him.'

I would look out of the car back window as my father drove us home with the Top 20 Chart rundown playing on the radio. In my memory, it is always dark on the farm track away from the house – even though in the summer it would still have been light.

Twenty years later, it was me behind the wheel. I parked outside my childhood home and Flash woke up, his ears quivering, and sat bolt upright. I had never realised that something so simple could be so satisfying.

Flash was soon scrambling across my mother's polished parquet flooring and exploring their house. I was hardly through the door before my mother was simultaneously offering him a drink of water and a comfort stop. Flash was taken out into the garden on his lead, as trampling down the wallflowers and tulips would not have been appreciated. He lifted his leg over the apple tree which my sister and I used to climb – some of its branches still bear the crease marks from us hauling ourselves up and down. I couldn't help but think it would have been a great garden to bring up a dog. With a brick wall right round, which must be almost six foot, plus trellises covered with climbing roses, it would have been given an RSPCA five-star rating. However, there was no time for such reflections, and scarcely enough to gulp down a cup of coffee, before my mother suggested a walk:

'He's been cooped up in the car.'

My parents' home is opposite a large park so we took Flash 'once round' the perimeter path – the traditional Marshall family walk, which is normally undertaken with grandchildren after Christmas lunch. My mother was a little anxious when Flash lagged behind but, of course, he always caught us up. At the park pond, he had a bit of a nasty surprise. His Sheepdog tendencies came to the fore and he rounded the mallards into the water. Up sailed the cob swan, Flash put his nose down to sniff him and promptly received a pecking. I am afraid we all laughed as he came scuttling back to us for protection.

However, underneath the laughter, I felt uncomfortable. Flash, of course, would not have registered our amusement at his discomfort so it was not about him... I remembered a visit I'd organised to the National Portrait Gallery in 1998. Lewis Carroll, the author of *Alice in Wonderland* and *Alice Through the Looking Glass*, had been an early adopter of photography and the gallery had organised an exhibition about him called: *Through the Viewfinder*. My maternal great, great grandmother had a connection with Carroll and he had signed a first edition of *Alice Through the Looking Glass*. My mother had enjoyed looking at it when she'd been a little girl. I'd wondered whether Carroll had taken a photograph of our relative, so I'd arranged to visit the gallery with my mother, her sister and her brother. (I'd always thought my great-great-grandmother had been one of the children

Carroll had told stories to, but it turned out that she'd been his father's housekeeper – and indeed he had taken a photo which was displayed in the exhibition.) I'd never had the opportunity to watch, close up, how my mother and her siblings interacted – because there were always partners and other children around – but I was struck by how they all talked at the same time, how they contradicted each other and how they would laugh if one of them got something wrong. It was a cruel laugh – rather like the way we'd laughed at Flash for getting his nose pecked.

'Remind me about the story of you and the wasps,' I asked my mother.

'The four of us were out exploring and Michael (her eldest brother, who died over twenty years ago) had disturbed a wasps' nest – he was always getting us into some sort of trouble. The wasps came after us and we all ran away.'

'What happened to you?'

'Being the youngest, I was the slowest and I kept on calling out for them to wait for me, but they just laughed and ran faster.'

I could imagine just what sort of laugh that would be. The sort of laugh that distanced them from pain and vulnerability and shame. And there is only one way to fit into a family – and not always be on the receiving end of the laughter – and that's to join in.

Up until that moment when Flash met the swan, I had not recognised how the laughter had spread from one generation to the next.

After Easter Sunday lunch, roast beef and crumble using apples from the garden, Flash was rewarded with a longer walk along the embankment of the River Ouse. Afterwards, we visited my aunt because my mother wanted to 'introduce her to Flash'. We just missed my cousin, her husband and their daughter, who had headed home early to feed their pack of three dogs. My aunt had been the owner of Spike, my surrogate childhood dog, so I asked:

'Do you miss having a dog round the house?'

'I'd love to have a dog again,' she said with surprising warmth, 'but they are such a tie.'

'In what way?' I asked. After all, she was retired and living alone, and would probably enjoy the company.

'Such a responsibility.'

That phrase again – why is everybody so terrified of responsibility?

—— ❧ ——

In the evening, I told my parents about my trip to Thorpeness and asked to look through our holiday photos from the summer of 1966. There were a few black and white pictures in the official family album but not the photograph with my grandmother on the steps of the cottage. My father explained that it had been taken as a colour slide and, with a little persuasion, he dug out the old projector.

The images cast on to the pale blue woodchip wallpaper in the living room seemed to belong to another family. Were my parents ever that young and handsome? The sixties colours had the surreal brightness of a Jehovah's Witness pamphlet – or maybe it was just our makeshift blue screen. I watched myself transmute from a happy smiling baby with golden hair through to a rather sulky-looking boy in a brown stripy top at Thorpeness. He seemed far more interested in the red and yellow windmill he was holding than having his photo taken.

On the living-room wall, he is forever trapped in the summer hinterland between being a child and arriving at big school in the autumn. The Jesuits' maxim is 'Give me a child until the age of seven and I'm show you the man'. Yet the forty-one-year-old man looked at the seven-year-old boy on the wall and he saw a stranger. I knew all the furniture in the room: the writing desk, the floral sofa and the framed illustrations of flowers bought on my parents' honeymoon in Sidmouth. They should have been more familiar than, for example, the back of my hand. However, my hand has changed: hairs have grown on my wrists and been bleached by the sun, the veins have become bluer and more pronounced and I've got several scratches from my puppy's teeth. The past is the past and perhaps it is time to stop picking at the old scars.

When I was a teenager, especially growing up gay in a country where it had been illegal only a few years before, it was easy to feel misunderstood. When I was in my twenties, I was only too aware of the gap between how I needed my parents to be and how they were. In my thirties, they fell short when my partner fell ill and died. But in my forties, through owning a dog and revisiting my childhood, I am beginning to look at the past through fresh eyes. I understand better the pressures on my mother and father when they were growing up and have tried to step into their shoes more often. Perhaps the sign of being a true adult – rather than just passing eighteen – is giving up being angry with your parents for what they are not and accepting them for who they are.

My father got bored with showing slides. I'd been hoping to move on to the old home cine films but bowed to his wishes and instead we watched the new TV adaptation of *The Railway Children* with Jenny Agutter, who played the eldest child in the film, as the mother.

During the programme, my sister phoned to ask our mother for ideas for her and my father's birthday presents. When it was my turn to chat to her, she told me about an Easter egg hunt she'd arranged for Shadow using special dog chocolate and, oh yes, the children had eggs hidden for them too.

Monday 24 April

Last night, after the usual bedtime biscuits and hot-water bottle, Flash settled down in his basket in the kitchen. I thought he was going to be fine. However, five minutes after I'd climbed into bed in my old room, there was a terrible yelp from downstairs – as if he'd fallen asleep for a second but a nightmare had woken him into strange surroundings. He started whimpering – which I ignored – and then a few howls. I went down to check on him but that made him more distressed. Not wanting to set a precedent, and letting him wander round my room all night, I left him downstairs and after twenty minutes of further puppy grief, Flash fell asleep again.

He started whining at about six-thirty in the morning and woke my parents, but I was too exhausted to care. My mother, who has always been an early riser, went downstairs and let him out.

Half an hour later, I finally dragged myself out of bed and gave Flash breakfast. My mother volunteered to take him out again while I had tea and toast. They spent an age tracking the scent of one of the neighbourhood cats and I had a chance to open the morning newspaper and discover the most extraordinary coincidence.

At the end of a week tracking my nightmares about wolves, smiling from the morning paper was a picture of my other childhood nemesis: the gangster Harry Roberts. The Police Federation were reported to be complaining about his impending move to an open prison and his preparation for possible release. I had been wondering if Roberts was still alive and what exactly he had done all those years ago. The *Daily Mail* had all the details.

Harry Roberts, sixty-four, was sentenced to life imprisonment for shooting three policemen in Shepherd's Bush. Although his gang were quickly arrested, Roberts had gone on the run, sparking what was at the time the Metropolitan Police's biggest manhunt, and sleepless nights for my family. He was finally caught living in a camouflage den, made out of plastic bags and branches, near Bishop's Stortford, Hertfordshire.

When my mother returned to the kitchen, I thanked her for her grandmotherly duties and decided to bond a little over the stresses of raising children/puppies.

'Harry Roberts is in the news again,' I told her.

'Who?'

'You remember, the gangster who gave me all the nightmares.'

'But you had so many nightmares, it is hard to remember them all.'

The bridge I was trying to build was crushed.

I lapsed back into silence; exactly as I would have done as a child.

My resolution to be more adult around my parents hadn't lasted very long. However, my adult self inwardly smiled. Many of my clients were nurtured on guilt – which can be devastating – but over the breakfast table, where many Marshall family battles had been fought, I recognised how often I must have disappointed my mother (which is a milder emotion than guilt but can also be debilitating). No wonder I've been trying so hard to train Flash and to impress Jeff with our progress.

I had to stop myself from laughing because I could never have explained what I'd found funny or just how liberating it feels to understand the past or how giddy I am about the possibility of letting it go.

Friday 5 May

Without the practice run of dog-owning, I doubt I would have had the courage in my dog parenting abilities to own Flash. It seemed only right that Flash and Tyson should meet but I had put it off and put it off. First, I was worried that Tyson would teach Flash bad habits – like forcing his way through doors and counter-top cruising. Second, we have such a strong bond that many casual observers think he is my dog and I would hate for Flash to think he was being supplanted in my affections. However, at the same time, I have to admit that I've missed Tyson.

As I parked in Handcross village hall car park, Flash was on full alert. I went around to the passenger door, where he was waiting impatiently for permission to leap out. I gave it and he flung himself to the furthermost point of his lead, nose quivering, back and tail in one straight line. He knew something important was about to happen.

Even before I had pushed back the shrubs and walked down the path to Tyson's house, I could hear barking in the kitchen. Flash bounded forward. We were greeted by a surprised Sara, who had forgotten about our visit and was about to take her daughter to work. With Tyson still barking behind the kitchen door, Flash could not decide whether to turn on the charm, gambolling at Sara's feet, or to sniff at the crack under the door which excluded Tyson.

I knew it would have been a long time since Tyson had had a proper walk, so I volunteered to take both dogs into the woods behind Nymans National Trust property. Sara looked doubtful. Tyson pulls so much on the lead that she cannot control him.

'I've stopped taking him even to the shops in the High Street,' she confessed.

But with three months of dog training classes from Jeff under my belt, or should that be collar?, I felt I should be able to cope. Sara opened the kitchen door and a mortar bomb of black fur exploded into the living room. Normally, Flash would wait to size up another dog, but he instantly started grappling with Tyson. There was nothing malicious, but he seemed determined to put him in his place. Embarrassingly, Flash even tried to mount him. I had to admire his tenacity because Tyson was almost twice as tall and perhaps three times heavier.

After a short struggle, the dogs calmed down enough to have both their leads put on and I set off back down the path, a dog on either side. Before we'd reached the garden gate Flash had tried to nip across me and continue play fighting. I imagined what Jeff would have done and gave Flash an extra-sharp check on his lead. He obeyed and I inwardly sighed with relief.

Fortunately, the path into the woods was only 200 yards away but first we had to negotiate the traffic in Handcross High Street. Like a gladiator in a chariot, I was dragged past the countryside supplies store and the newsagent's. Crossing over a side road, I was waved on by a lady in a four-wheel drive who obviously spotted it was easier for her to stop than me.

Gaining confidence – after all, I was still upright with both leads firmly in my hand – I decided to assert control. Following the instructions from Jeff to stop dogs pulling, I stopped, stepped back and brought Tyson round in a circle. It worked. By the convenience store, I followed the same trick with Flash and had both my charges close to under control. The parked cars in the High Street made crossing over difficult, but with a firm push on Tyson's rear, I had them both sitting on the kerb, waiting. Except while I peered out to find a break in the traffic, Flash kept on leaping over to have a pop at Tyson.

Off the leads in the woods, the dogs were quite sociable. Sometimes Flash would lead an expedition into the undergrowth, followed by Tyson, and sometimes Tyson would charge up a bank of fallen leaves and Flash would follow. Most of the walk, however, they ignored each other.

Tyson kept running back to check I was still on the path. His vigour was impressive for an eleven-year-old and now rather portly dog. For the first time in days, it was not raining. The sun sent bright wedges of light through the trees, illuminating flecks of dust – almost like they were rays from our old home cine projector. For a moment, I could step back into the film and re-experience my first summer without Thom. A leaner phantom Tyson leapt into the lake, the water making his rough coat stand up like a lion's mane. Beside him walked a thirty-something man weighed down with pain, the dog's quiet companionship one of the few things that calmed him. I watched the memories but thankfully, they seemed to belong to somebody else.

By the time we emerged from the woods both dogs were covered in mud. Aware of Sara's spotless parquet flooring, I took a towel out of the boot and started to rub Flash down. Unfortunately, Tyson kept on leaving his 'sit/stay' by the car and kept egging Flash on for another bout of rough and tumble through the puddles. After five minutes of puppy wrestling, Flash was vaguely presentable and I turned my attentions to Tyson. Normally quite obedient, Flash would not sit still for more than two seconds while his precious master towelled down his rival. It proved impossible to dry and separate the dogs so I 'threw in the towel'.

Back at the cottage, Sara had returned and was preparing some lunch. I tried to mop muddy footprints off the floor and stop the wrestling hounds from knocking over her elderly mother. We managed about five minutes, with Flash lying at my feet and Tyson at Sara's, as we had a coffee, but every so often Tyson would try to inch a bit closer and that would trigger another rumpus.

Finally, I could stand it no more and suggested sending them into the garden to sort out top-dog status while we settled down for some serious catching up. Inevitably, the dogs wanted to return indoors and I asked to borrow a dog towel to dry Flash off.

'We don't have any,' explained Sara.

'So what do you do when Tyson comes in from the garden?'

'I leave him to dry off in the kitchen, but it's a good idea.' She ran upstairs and produced an old pink towel. 'From now onwards, this is the dog towel.' Except she allowed Flash to drip over her parquet and shut Tyson back in the kitchen.

'If Tyson was a good dog like you,' she told Flash, 'and could sit quietly, he'd be allowed through too.'

Sara's mother pursed her lips.

As the ultimate victor, Flash enjoyed the spoils of lying across my feet. His post-walk snooze was only slightly disturbed by Tyson's pitiful whines from the kitchen.

I had always known that Tyson seldom left the house but never how much time he spent cooped up in the kitchen. I longed to liberate him, to beg Sara to let me take him home, but I said nothing. My first responsibility was to my own family: Flash. He would hate not to be an only dog.

Tyson was finally let back into the living room for our goodbyes and I walked back down the path with heavy feet, but beside me, Flash had a spring in his step.

Saturday 9 September

Over the summer, my bond with Flash deepened and the pain of losing Thom no longer sat at the centre of my life. The shock of bereavement, however, is that it has exposed the fault-lines in my life. So I don't just want to feel better, I want to make certain that I've cleared everything out so there is nothing left lurking in the background to bite me. So I have made a big decision...

A maverick called Roger Palmer keeps a pack of wolves in the grounds of his home in the Berkshire countryside. He is trying to rehabilitate the wolf's reputation from 'Little Red Riding Hood' and 'The Three Little Pigs' by taking members of his pack to country shows and inviting schools to visit. His most unusual project is the 'wolf walk', where handlers and brave members of the public wander through a nearby wood with only a collar and lead to restrain what are, after all, dangerous wild animals.

I thought it would make a great article for the *Daily Express* and a chance to truly face down my childhood fears.

I've spent the last week trying to track down Kez, a volunteer at the UK Wolf Conservation Trust, who divides her life between the wolves and her job as a prison warden. I wonder which set of inmates are the most dangerous. After Kez gave long and complicated directions to the trust headquarters, I shyly confessed my fears about wolves and asked if I could bring Flash. No problem. He will have to stay in the car but can have a runaround later.

It was a beautiful morning and I was surprisingly calm. I followed the first part of Kez's directions without any problems but on reaching the sleepy village of Beenham, it became clear that I'd made a mistake. I stopped on a narrow lane to ask for directions from a father with a young son. The father shook his head in bemusement. There couldn't possibly be a wolf sanctuary nearby. A white pick-up truck barrelled up behind me and started aggressively hooting. I had no choice but to drive on and pull into a nearby pub car park so the maniac behind could pass. I had no idea where he was heading in such a hurry on a Saturday morning, but he had completely destroyed my equilibrium. I gave him a couple of V-signs and then hoped he had nothing to do with the sanctuary.

I called Kez from the pub car park and she told me to double back. I found the entrance and turned into what could have been any farm drive. Somehow, my imagination had insisted on a large triangular road sign declaring: 'Danger Loose Wolves'. I wondered what the Highway Code design would be – a man in silhouette having a limb torn off by a hungry predator? Flash, who'd been snoozing in the passenger footwell, sat up, his ears and nose quivering with anticipation. Either he'd sensed we were about to meet the ancestors, or was just excited by an opportunity to stretch his legs.

I'd hoped to find Kez, talk about wolves in general and then psyche myself up to actually see one. However, within seconds, I'd driven past the trees, which screened the farm from the road, and was confronted by a small enclosure. It was full of wolves and the fence did not look very high. My arrival set off a terrible howling. One of the wolves leapt on to the mound at the centre of their territory and flung his head back into the classic pose and gave a long mournful howl. I immediately understood the cliché: his blood ran cold. Flash was more alert than I'd ever seen him before. I gave him a quick stroke – mainly to calm myself down – but felt guilty about dragging my dog into my private psychological battles.

There was a small arrow pointing to a car park – except it was right next to the wolf enclosure. I could not get out there! So I continued down the track towards a couple of barns, hoping to find somewhere else to park. Instead, I came to a halt outside a *Country Life* – style farmhouse. I had probably gained only an extra fifty yards buffer zone from the wolves, but I treasured each of those yards. I walked round to the passenger door – to let Flash out for a pee – but I was interrupted by a woman shouting from inside the wolf enclosure:

'You can't park there.'

Somehow you don't argue with a woman brave enough to clean out a wolves' enclosure. I climbed back into the car and returned to the official car park. When Flash finally leapt out, he seemed far more interested in sniffing round the trees than the nearby wolves. With my back to my childhood foes, I found my mobile and called Kez again. The signal kept cutting out. I put Flash back in the car and saw a smiling young woman in her late twenties heading my way. We introduced ourselves and she took me round to the barns, where a group of volunteers were setting up a temporary souvenir shop with wolf T-shirts, bookmarks and mirrors.

'We have two different types of wolves: North American and European. For first time in 700 years, European wolves have been born in England,' said Kez, 'and it happened right here.'

'You're not thinking of reintroducing them to the wild,' I laughed nervously.

'No, our main aim is educational. That's why we took our wolf cubs from their parents at one week old. It's controversial but the only way to get them used to being handled by humans. They were returned at twelve weeks. So while we can only enter the parents' enclosure after we have tranquillised them, we can take our hand-reared wolves to schools and let children meet them.'

Under Kez's steadying influence, I was able to slot into my usual journalist role and ask questions:

'But why would you want to do that?'

'No healthy wolf has ever attacked a human being, they're naturally frightened of us. You can tell people the facts, but they don't really believe you until they've actually met one,' explained Kez.

I shuddered:

'It didn't help cure my phobia. I was taken to London Zoo in the sixties by my mother and if anything, the trip made everything worse.'

'All the North American wolves in England are descended from that pack.'

So thirty years on, I was about to meet my tormentors' great-grandchildren!

'However, there's a big difference,' continued Kez, 'between looking at a wolf through the bars of a cage and meeting one. Are you ready?'

I would have preferred to shelter amongst the wolf merchandise and do a full in-depth three-hour interview, but I managed to nod my head.

'Don't worry, we never take the alpha male on the walks,' continued Kez, 'he's far too territorial. In fact, there are only three people he'll let anywhere near him. Our wolves might be socialised, but they're still wild animals.'

'Of course, nobody has ever been bitten by them?' Mentally, I was begging her to agree with me.

'When a wolf bites someone it's always because the handler has made a mistake. It's never the wolf's fault.'

She rolled up her sleeve to reveal a small half-crescent scar.

'It was just a warning nip, but a wolf's teeth can sink through a puffer jacket, jumper and a shirt with no problem whatsoever.' She must have noticed how big my eyes had become. 'Nothing serious, if a wolf means to bite he could easily break your arm. C'mon, let's go over to their enclosure.'

I followed meekly behind.

On closer inspection, the enclosure was divided in two.

'These are the North American wolves, with lighter coats because of the different terrain.' Kez pointed at the wolves which had spooked me earlier.

Four sets of piercing yellow eyes followed me round the perimeter fence.

'That's Kodiak, the alpha male and pack leader,' explained Kez as the boldest and largest wolf bounded up.

I blanked him out.

'The European wolves are over there?'

I thought it better to start with my indigenous foe.

'They're much bigger because the North American wolves in this country have been so interbred.'

We walked over to the second grassy enclosure, my heart beating just a fraction faster. There was already a volunteer in with them – which was reassuring – and as soon as we came around their night shelter three eager faces pushed towards the fence.

'But they look just like dogs,' I exclaimed. With only a small stretch of the imagination they could have been three large German Shepherd dogs.

'That's why film makers always ask for the North American wolves – even if the movie is set in England.'

'So for once Hollywood isn't casting the Brits as the baddies,' I said.

'Why don't you greet them?' suggested Kez. 'Make your hand into a fist, we've trained them to think of it as a muzzle.'

I followed her instructions.

'Now push it through the bars.'

Amazingly enough, I found myself doing exactly as I was told. A rough tongue gave my fist a tentative lick. A set of large white teeth gently encircled my fist, just the same way that Flash would when he was younger.

I had come face to face with my nightmares. I'd seen for myself what big teeth wolves have and I had held my ground.

Kez chatted away with the women inside the enclosure about which wolves to take on the walk and the levels of experience of each handler. Everything was so relaxed, I took my cue from them and breathed easily for the first time.

Before the wolf walk, there was just enough time for Flash to have a run. We walked over to the car park and I let him out. He greeted us both enthusiastically.

'It's a shame he can't meet mine,' said Kez. 'She's a guard dog who had to be retired because she liked humans too much. She's fine, but a lot of dogs find her too rough.'

'Flash doesn't mind rough play,' I reassured her. So Kez's German Shepherd, Tara, was allowed out of her car and immediately bounded over to Flash.

I'd spent enough time watching dog etiquette to know that Tara was a little forward. Flash, being only nine months old and really still a puppy, much preferred strange dogs to stand or semi-crouch while they decided who should approach first. So he was a little worried when she almost knocked him over. We walked towards the paddock, which is about to be converted into a new wolf enclosure, with the dogs racing on ahead. Tara made another dive at Flash and rolled him over in the grass. He was a little winded and streaked off. Like an anxious parent watching out for the playground bully, I could tell Flash was concerned but not frightened. There was no need to intervene – just yet. Tara chased after Flash, but he was gaining confidence. He made his usual Sheepdog lunge at her neck and full of the joys of the chase, they streaked after each other. Flash had faced down his fears too.

With the dogs playing happily, I had the chance to compare Tara with the European wolves, which were larger, longer and leaner. There was not an ounce of spare flesh on their bodies and they moved with a grace that made Tara look like a six-month-old baby beside an Olympic decathlon champion.

All too soon, it was time to put the dogs back in their respective cars as the wolves were about to be taken out.

— ❧ —

One by one, four wolves were led out of the enclosures on long metal choke chains, towards a specially converted horsebox. After much shoving and pulling, all four wolves were safely stowed away and I was introduced to Roger Palmer (who turned out to be the man I'd gesticulated to earlier). I covered my embarrassment by going into professional journalism mode:

'How did you become interested in wolves?'

'I was on holiday in Canada when a zoo was closing down and looking for a new home for their pack,' he explained – as if for the three millionth time. 'So I asked my parents if I could have them.'

'How old were you at the time?' I asked, expecting for him to reply fifteen.

'Twenty-six.'

It sounded odd to ask your parents' permission but perhaps people who want to own wolves don't lead their life by the usual rules. Fortunately, Roger was more interested in planning the walk than being interviewed and I drifted away.

After a drive of about ten minutes, we arrived at a private wood and parked in a small clearing. Roger, Kez and the rest of the team started to unload the wolves. For each one, the policy was to have two handlers: somebody in charge and somebody to answer the public's questions. However, today, there were four wolves and only seven handlers.

'You can come with me,' said Kez. 'You didn't seem at all fazed by the wolves before, so you can be my second-in-command.' She grabbed hold of Duma – one of the North American wolves, which up to that point I had been trying to ignore.

'OK.' I tried to make my voice sound confident and manly.

'Why don't you get to know her?' suggested Kez, so I made a fist for her to lick. She was so keen on the idea of making friends that she tried to jump up and slobber over my face. Fortunately, living with Flash meant I saw this move coming and turned away. Following Kez's instructions, I carefully rubbed Duma's stomach because patting a wolf on the head suggests dominance. She certainly seemed to enjoy the attention. Yes, I was stroking a wolf and we were both enjoying ourselves.

The rest of the team had sorted themselves out into pairs and we were ready to go. From the way Kez handled Duma, I could tell she was the most experienced of the handlers. Although the wolves were generally allowed to roam, she kept a much tighter grip of Duma's lead and would stand for no nonsense – which was very reassuring.

About fifty yards down a woodland path, we discovered a tight knot of people. They gave the wolves a collective anxious stare, and perhaps it was my imagination but they seemed to huddle closer together. It was a relief to find people more anxious than me and I adopted the slight swagger of someone with an hour and a half's extra exposure.

'They normally find the person most frightened of them and give them a hard time,' whispered Kez to me. Duma's sister had already chosen a late-middle-aged woman and made a lunge for her handbag. Flustered, the lady dropped her wolf walk programme. She tried to laugh but I recognised the terror lurking in her eyes.

'Thank goodness she didn't get her bag, because I doubt we would have been able to retrieve it,' confided Kez in me. 'They were warned.'

Suddenly all the wolves ran through the gaggle of humans with their handlers running behind. I followed Kez, who explained:

'They're just checking out who's in their pack today.'

Finally, the wolves were ready to walk and we headed deeper into the woods. It was extraordinary to watch the European wolves in their natural habitat, their brown fur merging with the red English soil, the dark bark and the lighter bracken, until they were almost invisible. No wonder my ancestors had feared them.

The walk had been billed as lasting anything up to three hours, as Roger and his team had no idea which route the wolves would choose. Every so often he would find a clearing, talk about his animals and try to separate the fact from the myth. Slowly, each member of the group would come up and either stroke a wolf's belly or have their photo taken beside one.

Fortunately, Kez was performing the dual role of keeping an eye on Duma and answering the public's questions, so I had nothing to do but watch and learn. We were all feeling relaxed. It was a beautiful day and the sun streamed down through the leaves, dappling our path. It would have been easy to believe that we were taking four dogs for a walk – four very large dogs. Except, from time to time, a less experienced handler would run past, trying to keep up with their wolf; the sweat would be pouring off them. No wonder they needed two handlers per animal.

'Could you take Duma for a second?' Kez asked as she stopped to get something out of her shoe.

'If you're certain.'

I took hold of the lead. Duma, who had been a model wolf up to this point, did not seem to mind the substitution. We walked on, chatting about nothing in particular. I was so relaxed that when Duma started to head off into the bracken, without thinking, I gave her a quick check. Just like I'd been taught in puppy training – a gentle tug on the lead – except I had a fully grown wolf at the end of a metal chain. I had broken the cardinal rule of wolf-walking: let the wolf set the direction of travel. I tried not to panic.

I could hear Jeff's voice in my head.

'Your emotions go down the lead.'

I took an inward deep breath.

Miraculously, Duma responded to the correction just like a dog and focused her attention back on me and we carried on down the path as if nothing had happened.

How could I have been so stupid? I had checked a wolf. Stupid, stupid, stupid.

'Could you take back control?' I tried to keep my voice even.

Except the check had been so subtle, so quick, that Kez hadn't even noticed.

'If you're sure…'

My reply came out in a rush:

'Yes!'

About three-quarters of an hour later, we reached a large lake and I had a glimpse of how dangerous wolves could be. One of the pack found a rusting tin in the shallows. The female handler called out for help. Immediately, Roger and another handler were by her side. The wolf's jaws were so powerful it took two of them to force its mouth open and one of the handlers, a handsome man with a long blond ponytail, was left with blood all over his hands. He was quick to reassure us that he had cut himself on the can and not been bitten.

'Anyway, if she had really wanted to keep her treasure, it would have taken four of us to prise her teeth open,' he said.

I looked at the blood which seemed red against his pale skin and, in my imagination, the wolves licked their lips. I had a further reminder of their strength when another wolf decided to take an impromptu swim in the lake and leapt off the bank. His handler, a thick-set man who looked like a truck driver, was pulled into the water – like he was a ball of wool tossed by a kitten. He came to a halt in the mud with a bemused look on his face. Later, he showed me the marks imprinted by the chain on his forearm. His colleagues joked that nobody was a fully fledged handler until they had been baptised in the lake.

'At least I didn't let go,' he told me proudly, 'that's the most important thing.'

'What would have happened if you had?' I asked.

'She would probably have swum off. I doubt we would have got her back and probably she would have been shot by a farmer.'

'We've taught them their names,' explained Kez, 'and a few simple commands.'

'Just like a dog,' I chipped in. Perhaps I hadn't been so stupid to check Duma after all.

'Yes, but they are much more intelligent. A dog will repeat the task over and over, but a wolf gets easily bored and makes its own mind up. So who knows if she would have come back.'

Watching the wolves on our walk, I was amazed at the similarities between Flash and the wolves. When the wolves found an interesting smell, they would first rub the underside of their necks in it and then roll over on to their backs until they were entirely covered with this enticing perfume. After a swim in the lake, they would shake themselves dry and sometimes after urinating, they would scuff the soil with their hind legs.

'This is to cover their tracks,' explained Kez. 'It's something that domestic dogs still do – although it serves no purpose. It's just a behaviour that's left over from their ancestors.'

'If they're still so close, can they crossbreed?' I asked.

'Yes, but it's very dangerous. They have the power of a wolf and no fear of humans.'

By this point in the walk, our wolves were becoming equally relaxed around their human companions – a problem for anyone with lace-up boots. From time to time, they would sneak up and try to pull someone's laces undone. Any 'wolf walker' not quick enough, or confident enough, to shoo them away would have a wolf tugging at their shoes. It would have been funny, except the wolves were determined not to let go. Worse still, they would remember who was most frightened, most vulnerable and return, time and again.

After just over two hours, we had completed our circuit and were back at the horsebox. The walkers were asked to wait while the wolves were cajoled back inside the horsebox. When they were stowed away, the walkers returned to their cars and we went in convoy back to the centre for coffee, biscuits and souvenir shopping.

—— ❧ ——

When I returned to my car, Flash was, as ever, ecstatic to see me. I took him up to the paddock and gave him a runaround. Both of us had become less anxious about the wolves, because when we walked back towards the car he headed straight for their enclosure. Fortunately, he didn't cross the small ditch and approach their perimeter fence. I had been warned this would be seen as an act of aggression by the wolves.

I tried to call him back. I blew my whistle.

He stood transfixed, smelling the air, fascinated by the strange animals pacing back and forth on the other side of the wire.

Normally, I would never go after him – because it is better to train a puppy to come to you – but on this occasion the stakes were too high. I nipped back to the car for his lead. He stood still while I slipped it over his head and we went for coffee and biscuits in the barn.

'So what do think?' one of the handlers asked me. 'Are you going to become a volunteer?'

Although I had plenty of admiration for Roger and his team, I laughed and shook my head.

Later, after the visitors had left and the handlers were packing away the souvenirs, one of the wolves howled. Nobody else paid any attention and even Flash didn't look up from his exploration of Roger's shrubbery. Despite all my new knowledge and my close encounters, my blood still chilled.

Nevertheless, I have learned something important over the last nine months. By facing up to both my wounds and my deepest desires, I have made peace with the little boy running back to bed for fear his nightmares would gobble him up. He might never feel completely safe, but his needs don't need to control my life.

PART TWO

Old Flash

I haven't felt the need to open my diary for a long time. So I haven't recorded Flash's many triumphs over the past ten years – like coming second in the Handsomest Dog in the Village competition or his persistence at being the first dog in the neighbourhood to spot when a bitch was coming into season, and the last to give up trying, finally paid off.

The owner of Crystal, the Labradoodle in question, had not asked my permission to breed from Flash but had ambushed him when she knew he'd be out on his morning walk. So when Valerie and I caught up, he had already tied and the two dogs were stuck together. We were soon joined by a group of other dog walkers to witness both my mortification and the embarrassment of Flash.

'This is the point when we should get out a cigarette,' said my friend Lana, who met us on the fields with her dog most mornings.

'If the mother is a Labradoodle and the father is a Collie cross, what will the puppies be?' Valerie asked.

'Collie wolly doodle all the day,' I replied.

Likewise, I haven't written about our shared triumphs either. The theatre company who toured rural communities commissioned my play, *Ladies That Walk,* about a fifty-something woman with a dog called Dash (guess where I got the inspiration), who noticed everything that happened in the village beyond her husband's meltdown. It was my first success as a creative writer and subsequently about half a dozen of my plays have been performed.

So why did I stop writing in my diary? Perhaps Flash helped me to see the world differently and I started to feel different. Perhaps I only need my diary when I've problems because I made no entries when I met Ignacio nor when he moved in with me eighteen months later. Even when we had our civil partnership ceremony in 2008, and my parents came to celebrate with love in their hearts not just for me but for Ignacio too, my diary remained closed. So maybe a better question would be: why have I started up again?

At eleven years old, Flash is often mistaken for a younger dog. A white muzzle means the grey hairs don't show and chasing squirrels has kept him young. OK, he had a problem with a torn cruciate ligament. But after a couple of weeks' rest and retiring from dog agility – where he used to jump over fences, run through tunnels and leap over the A frame – he is back to normal: monitoring squirrel movements in the garden, watching out for the postman from his sentry point at the top of the stairs and investigating the hedgerows of Hurstpierpoint. When people claim he doesn't look his age, I smile and tell them:

'He does a good impersonation of a young dog.'

Recently, however, Flash has started behaving like an old dog. A little stiffness getting up in the evening has translated into a restlessness – as if he can't get comfortable anywhere. On our lunchtime walk yesterday, he was just as interested in marking his territory on the recreation ground and hunting for balls lost in the stinging nettles round the tennis courts, but he walked all hunched up. I've sorted of got used to him being behind me rather than two fields ahead but yesterday his gait was like the old ladies inching across the green to the post office – half pushing, half leaning on their ancient wicker baskets on wheels.

Late at night when I watched him heave himself up from his favourite spot in the living room – with his head propped up against Ignacio's piano – he was not really putting his weight on his hind left foot, almost as if it's a peg leg.

So after a long lunch at Terre à Terre vegetarian restaurant, to celebrate my fifty-second birthday, I took Flash to the vets. It was hard to understand the vet partly because he has a thick Italian accent and partly because he kept sweeping his long black locks away from his beautiful dark eyes. However, the upshot is that the cruciate ligament has repaired but the joint has calcified. Flash has arthritis and I should give him one dose of Metacam with his breakfast and buy some food supplements to ease his joints. The advice is for exercise as normal.

Monday 13 June

The Metacam has worked. Flash has stopped hunching and is putting his weight down. So when Ignacio was instructed to go on a one-mile run every day, as part of the preparation for performing his one-man show at the Edinburgh Festival this summer, I suggested that he took Flash with him.

They started with a short run round the back of Hurstpierpoint High Street. Fifteen minutes later, I was greeted by a dog wide-eyed with excitement – mouthing my hand like a puppy desperate for attention. He settled down against the bookshelves in my office and snored contentedly while I typed out the proposal for my new self-help book.

Tuesday 14 June

Ignacio and I had a dinner party to celebrate the third anniversary of our civil partnership and Flash slept peacefully under the table, curled up over my feet. In many ways, he deserved the treat of finishing the leftover paella. If it hadn't been for Flash, Ignacio and I might never have met…

Back in 2001, four and half years after Thom died, I had organised a supper party. One of the three guests had dropped out when he learned that I had a dog because he was allergic to them. Another guest had had two dates with this guy from Mexico and asked if he could bring him instead. I said yes and the rest is history.

There was an almost instant attraction between Ignacio and I and we spent the next weekend and most of the following weekends together. When I guiltily phoned my friend to tell him I had purloined his date, rather than pistols at dawn, his interest in Ignacio had been so low that he hadn't even noticed his absence.

At the beginning of our relationship, Flash had been jealous of Ignacio and tried to jump up every time I gave him a cuddle, but he soon got used to being third in the pack. When eighteen months into our relationship, Ignacio moved into the house full-time, Flash seemed to welcome the extra company. He was an honoured guest at the hog roast to celebrate our civil partnership, even though I made him wear a sign round his neck saying: 'PLEASE DON'T FEED ME'.

Tonight, when it was time for our guests to go, I got up to say goodbye and disturbed Flash, who'd been sleeping on my feet. He whimpered as he hauled himself up and seemed to drag his hindquarters into the garden for the last pee of the day. It was particularly shocking because this morning he'd happily chased Ignacio up the road for his second short run – and Flash is normally unwilling to go anywhere without me.

There is nothing more miserable than a dog in pain. I gave him an extra shot of Metacam and hoped a good night's rest would do the trick.

Wednesday 15 June

When I came down in the morning, Flash could only manage a parody of his welcome dance: a shuffle rather than the usual bounce. Instead of rushing down the steps into the garden, he gingerly lowered himself on to the grass. When I rattled his food (soaked with another dose of Metacam), he seemed uninterested. I stepped out of his room – where he usually eats – and on to the patio and tried again. He attempted to heave himself up on to the first step, sighed and gave up. For the first time ever, I took his food to him rather waiting for him to come and check what's in his bowl. When I phoned the vets, there were no appointments until tomorrow.

Ignacio is in an unpredictable mood too. He's been researching his diet – as part of his get fit drive for a month of daily performances in Edinburgh – and has decided to cut out all carbohydrates. So pasta, bread, rice and our regular five o'clock tea and cake are all off the menu. He has put his general grumpiness and restlessness down to sugar withdrawal.

Fortunately, once the Metacam kicked in, Flash cheered up enough to want his morning walk.

Thursday 16 June

It is like a miracle cure. Book an emergency vet appointment and your dog recovers. Although Flash is no longer the miserable pathetic creature from yesterday, he's not the robust companion whose health I've taken for granted.

It was a different vet and after he rotated Flash's knees and hips and massaged his spine, he had another potential diagnosis. Of course, it might be the cruciate ligament but more likely the hips or possibly the back. He recommended an X-ray and I booked Flash in for tomorrow.

Friday 17 June

Rather than cooking two different meals, I have decided to follow Ignacio's example and cut out as many carbohydrates as possible. So instead of my usual two pieces of wholemeal bread from the baker's in the village, I made myself porridge and added a sliced banana.

After breakfast, I took Flash for a quick pee and a poo walk – because he won't do the latter in the garden. The reactions of my dog-walking friends to Flash's condition made it hard for me to keep minimising his problems. Their words were full of encouragement, but their eyes said something different.

Although my porridge had seemed filling – and I had trouble finishing it – an hour later, I was ravenously hungry. Except, on second thoughts, I was probably getting the first pangs of sugar withdrawal. I longed for toast and peanut butter, but I had to take Flash to the vets, where they will sedate him to take the X-ray.

It was hard to concentrate on my work. I kept worrying about Flash and going downstairs to help myself to fruit to ease my carbohydrate cravings. When Ignacio warned his new singing pupil that his partner and the dog were around and not to be surprised if either of us put in an appearance, I felt an ache. I'm here but my constant companion has been sedated.

There was still no news about Flash after lunch when I set off to see my supervisor, Christine, in nearby Crawley. (Therapists have someone to talk about any problems with their clients and help us spot if our own personal material has left us blindsided.)

Arriving a few minutes early, I phoned the vets. Flash was ready for collection, but the X-rays suggest it could be either his hips or his back. I could tell from the tone of the veterinary nurse that it was serious. Although I was supposed to be talking about my clients, when Christine asked her standard opening question 'how are you?', I told her that Flash was sick. She wore her look of professional understanding and I felt embarrassed that I was more worried about my dog than my clients.

Fourteen years ago, Christine had been my supervisor at Relate – I have a private practice now – and I had to tell her that Thom was terminally ill and I could no longer perform my duties. I had started my explanation in a reasonably matter-of-fact manner but broke down into tears – probably the first time I'd cried in public since I was a boy. Once again, I needed the tissues as I talked about Flash because, in my mind, he and Thom are inextricably linked. I hadn't realised it at the time but after Thom died, I felt like a non-person. Flash helped fix my position in time and place, and was an integral part of giving me back my identity.

Tuesday 12 July

As I have Flash insured, the vet had recommended that I take him to a specialist for a second opinion and have a scan which will provide more information about the exact nature of his back problems. There was only one problem: the appointment and the scan would eat up all the insurance allowance for this year.

This morning, the specialist examined both Flash's back and the X-rays from my vet and agreed a scan would be a good idea – so he would know what kind of operation would be necessary. However, the cost of this treatment and the follow-up appointments would run into thousands of pounds and there would be no guarantee that it would cure his problem. Worse still, if there were any complications, my insurance would not cover these either (because I would have reached their fixed limit for treating any condition).

I'm a writer. I don't have spare money. I didn't want to keep Flash alive just for the sake of it, but I couldn't just simply give up. I wished I'd brought Ignacio so we could talk it over.

'There is always another option,' said the specialist.

'What's that?'

'Flash seems to be stable on the Metacam. So we could always wait and see.'

When I got home, Ignacio – who comes from Mexico – was horrified that the English would even consider spending so much money on their dogs.

'I could ask my parents for a loan,' I thought out loud, 'but could I put Flash through a painful operation with a long rehabilitation time?'

'He's almost twelve years old. How many good years would he have – even if it was an unqualified success?' Ignacio asked.

Fortunately, I had another option up my sleeve. One of the other owners at my dog agility classes had a similar problem with her Collie and recommended Galen Myotherapy – which is a form of canine massage, posture improvement and remedial exercises. The website talked about treating chronic muscular pain to enhance mobility and health. The treatment centre was only half an hour away from Hurstpierpoint, so I decided to take Flash for an assessment there too.

Wednesday 3 August

Flash seems to be responding to his treatments of massage and a light being passed over his inflamed joints – or perhaps that's my imagination. Julia, who founded the treatment, was amazed at how calm Flash was when I held him.

'The way he looks at you, I can tell he really trusts you.'

In addition to the regular trips over to Bolney for the therapy, I have been giving Flash remedial exercises – leading him over a series of broom handles and sticks laid out in the garden – to encourage him to pick up his back legs. As I will be going away from the end of the week – to join Ignacio at the Edinburgh Festival – I discussed how that would affect Flash's programme. The unknown quantity is who will be looking after him in our absence. Normally, he would go next door, but Valerie has not been well.

A year or two ago, she woke up to find her bedroom full of ambulance staff. Her husband Michael had not been able to wake her and called 999. With an English stiff upper lip, Valerie played everything down and life went on as normal. We still walked every weekday morning together and Flash and her latest Dalmatian, Buffy, were the best of friends. However, during Michael and Valerie's annual early summer holiday on the Greek island of Kefalonia, Michael had been unwell. Valerie was running up and down the stairs between his bedroom and the taverna below and collapsed on the stairs. The doctors advised her to take everything easy and Michael had become responsible for exercising Buffy. So Valerie and I have been discussing whether looking after Flash for a whole month would be too stressful and we came to an arrangement: she will take him but can phone Vina, who sometimes cares for him, to take over, if necessary. So far, so good… Unfortunately, Valerie and I have opposing views about Myotherapy.

She wanted to know if it has been approved by my vet and worries that the exercises Flash has been given are cruel. Therefore, I know she will not do his exercises or take him over to Bolney for further treatment. However, Vina is interested in possibly training in the technique and would be happy to oblige, if necessary. After discussing everything with Julia, we decided it would be fine for Flash to have a break and return for more treatment in September.

When I returned home tonight from seeing clients in London, Flash was not in his room. (When Ignacio is away, I take him round to Valerie and Michael in the afternoon, and they give him his supper and take him home sometime in the evening.) So I went next door to collect him.

'Please sit down.' Valerie is using her most serious voice.

I sit on the edge of the chair. I would rather take Flash and go.

'When Michael took Flash out after he ate, he kept straining to have a poo and he had a prolapse. It's really serious. I think you should reconsider going away.'

It's not just 'alternative' therapies where Valerie and I have opposing views. While her life revolves round her dog, I believe Flash should fit round my life.

'What's a prolapse?' I asked.

'It's where something falls out of place.'

I looked over at Flash, who was laid out on the carpet. He looked the same as when I left him a few hours before – nothing hanging out of his back passage.

But I don't want an argument. It's quarter to eleven at night. I've spent four hours listening to couples in conflict, and Valerie has done so much for me. When I first moved into my house and needed a plumber, she gave me a number and over the years has taken in parcels and paid the window cleaner when I was at work. When Thom was ill, she visited him in hospital while I was working away. Ignacio teases me that she is my second mother. Furthermore, she has had dogs all her life and Flash is my first.

So I thank her for her concern and tell her I'll fix an appointment at the vets for Flash in the morning and escape into the night.

Thursday 4 August

I took Flash on to the fields behind the house in the hope that his usual walk and usual place to poo would do the trick but to no avail. I took my mobile so I could phone as soon as the vets opened. On the dot of nine, heart racing, I tapped in the number.

Within the hour, Flash had been examined and given the diagnosis of constipation. When I asked if it could be a prolapse, the vet gave me a look he must reserve for hysterical owners and suggested that I add a small amount of liquid paraffin to Flash's food.

I drop in on Valerie and tell her the good news. Although she is still happy to mind Flash while I'm in Edinburgh, I decided to phone my dog-walking friend Lana for a second opinion. Nobody could be more devoted to her dog (a Border-terrier pup called Onion), but she is also a businesswoman (running a service that provides guardians for international students studying at UK boarding schools).

'This is a great opportunity for Ignacio to showcase his talents to people from all over the world. If we get good reviews he can tour it round the country for the next eighteen months. He can't perform every day for four weeks and promote the show to venues, reviewers and find an audience too. I also want to make connections for my new theatre project – a children's musical. However, if Flash needs me here…' I couldn't finish this sentence. We had a lot of money invested in this project – several thousands of pounds and over a year's work had gone into developing the play (and if I throw in the time it took me to write it, probably two years). There were thousands of competing shows in the Fringe brochure and the average audience for any performance – unless somebody was out promoting the show each day on the streets – was just two.

'You need to be able to concentrate on Ignacio without worrying that every one of Flash's ailments will be given the most dramatic twist possible.'

'No.' I exhale sharply. I hadn't been aware that I'd been holding my breath until that point.

'I could look after him if you like.'

'Would you? That would be perfect.'

Friday 5 August

I flew up to Edinburgh in the afternoon. I should have arrived in time for Ignacio's first preview, but it has been cancelled. There are problems with the lighting rig and the venue is not even sure that they will ready for tomorrow's performance either. I don't get many details because Ignacio isn't sure what's really happening and neither are the engineers who are running around with gaffer tape in their hands.

Thursday 11 August

We have settled into a pattern. In the morning, I make up a Tupperware box of cooked chicken and raw vegetables – we are still on Ignacio's caveman diet – for a packed lunch for us both. While Ignacio warms up his voice, I take a bus into the city centre and tour all the shows with an older or educated audience who might appreciate Ignacio in our play: *Caruso and the Monkey House Trial*. (The famous tenor was accused of pinching ladies' bottoms at Central Park Zoo and the audience are the jury deciding if he's guilty or not guilty. Ignacio plays all the parts – including the monkey.) When I find a group of likely festival goers, I approach the ladies – because they decide what shows to see – and ask:

'Are you looking for ideas of what to see at the festival for this afternoon?' Obviously, I am going to push Ignacio, but I will also pass on tips about other 'must sees' and recommend any good shows I've seen myself. But I have a pitch, an incantation, a prayer about our play and I give it over a hundred times a day.

Most of the show pluggers are students or being paid by one of the big venues, so I stand out. I'm personable and I believe in the show. On a good day, I can find thirty audience members and about ten more will somehow mysteriously hear about us and turn up. If I can keep this up, we might have an Edinburgh miracle and break even.

I have been reviewing other shows at the festival for a website called Fringe Review and I agreed to man our stall at the 'meet the press' event organised by the Fringe Festival. Just before the doors were opened and the hordes of other show pluggers were let in, I went round the other stands and secured a review with *The Scotsman* – the most prestigious outlet for the festival and whose opinions can make or break a show.

Each day, I stop for a quick lunch and meet up with Ignacio, who has been checking on our latest reviews. The best ones are photocopied and stapled on to the flyers I give out and I have another two hours to drum up an audience. I pitch the queue at the half-price ticket booth – which is near to the theatre – but by 4 p.m. it is too late to find anyone else and I rest my feet, eat an apple and watch the show at 4.45 p.m.

Afterwards, I help Ignacio pack up. The next show starts about fifteen minutes after we finish so we must get our set out, and allow the next company to get in, as quickly as possible. Ignacio changes, and we have coffee and discuss the show. I give him notes and generally bolster his confidence. We get the bus back to the outskirts, cook supper and – with parking restrictions suspended – drive back into the city in the evening to see a concert or someone else's play. We drop exhausted into bed at ten o'clock and the next day start all over again.

However, this afternoon, I got a text from Lana:

'I have fixed a vets' appointment for Flash tomorrow. I really think you need to be here.'

I gave her a call and discovered that Flash's constipation has turned to diarrhoea. She has had to clean up her kitchen on several occasions. I feel ashamed for putting both my friend and my dog through so much trauma and tell her I will return as soon as possible.

Friday 12 August

I caught a flight at 6.20 a.m down to Gatwick, took the train to Burgess Hill and walked to the vets for an appointment at 9.10 a.m. Flash had the honour of being chauffeured in James's jaguar: Lana and James's four by four is too high for him to climb into and out of.

When they arrived and Lana opened the passenger door, I was surprised that Flash leapt out. Perhaps he was thrilled to see me again, perhaps it was adrenaline or maybe he becomes more alive around me: his internal organs kick-start and pump his blood faster round his body. However, I only half registered the transformation because I was drained from having got up so early this morning.

The vet changed his medication and afterwards Lana confessed that she thought he might have needed to be put down. However, my brain can't quite take this in. I'm not just tired; I'm watching everything from behind a plate of glass.

Tuesday 16 August

Up in Edinburgh, Ignacio is playing to only a handful of people at each performance. The reviews have dried up because I used to spot fellow reviewers on my flyering tour of the city and pitch them *Caruso and the Monkey House Trial*. Ignacio has almost lost his voice. He sounds dejected and there's nothing I can do to help.

Meanwhile, Flash has had a stable weekend and is pooing regularly. It seems only yesterday when he was a puppy and I was constantly monitoring his bowel movements.

I am needed in two places, by two people I love desperately.

I can't ask anyone to look after Flash in their home – due to the potential incontinence problems – but my dog sitter, Vina, has agreed to come and stay in our house. There is only one problem, she can't cover Friday night to Sunday morning because of a family celebration, but my friend Kate will come down from London.

So when the vet gave Flash the all-clear today, I bought a ticket and flew back up to Edinburgh. I have blown the budget on flights, but it doesn't matter. Ignacio picked me up at the airport in the car and in a mirror image of the scene outside the vets on Friday, when he spotted me in arrivals, the shadows lifted and the light came back into his face.

Thursday 18 August

Despite Ignacio's fitness regime before the festival and his new healthy diet, his cold is not getting any better. We talked about cancelling the show – which involves operatic arias – but I have lined up several reviewers to come today. In the end, we decide to wait and see and I head off to flyer people going in and out of other shows.

Halfway through the morning, I got a text from Vina. Flash was in pain again and she was worried about getting him into the car to drive him to the recreation ground, where he strains but hasn't managed to go to the toilet since I left. She will take him to the vets (yet again) and will let me know what they say.

In the meantime, I get a call from Valerie.

'I'm really worried about Flash.'

'Vina is taking care of everything. You don't need to worry.'

'She's very nice but she's not trained to look after sick dogs.'

'But her daughter is a vet's nurse and she's been helping her.'

'What's going to happen when Vina goes away?'

Valerie has obviously 'just happened' to be outside her house when Vina has passed by, and has quizzed her.

'Kate is coming down to cover,' I explained

'How reliable is Kate?'

Valerie has a point there. Kate is great in an emotional emergency but is not the most practical of my friends.

'Look, I don't have the full story yet.' I didn't tell her I also had a sick partner as well as a sick dog. 'Let's speak again later, when I do.'

When Vina called, Flash's complaints ran from constipation to diarrhoea, from colitis to enteritis and yet another vet at the practice has thrown an enlarged prostate into the mixture. After discussing Flash's confusing array of diagnoses, Vina and I decided to get a second opinion from the vets where her daughter works.

I don't have time to phone Valerie because as soon as I arrive at the venue, there is a message to go up to the artists' dressing room. (I am normally banned before a show as Ignacio wants to focus on his performance.) He looked terrible and sounded worse. So I decided he didn't need Flash's latest health bulletin at that point. In a short croaky conversation, he told me he had decided to go on and I told him that I backed his decision.

I went down to the bar, where I tried to relax and be charming to the reviewers, when I had yet another text. It was from Valerie threatening to report me to the RSPCA for being cruel to dogs. I had to read it three times before I could take it in.

She thinks I am being cruel to Flash. She wants to report me? I am at the world's biggest festival of theatre and there is more drama happening offstage than on.

Replying to the text would just make everything worse, so I sat sullenly on the banquette and waited to see how compromised Ignacio's performance would be.

Just before I went into the theatre, the phone rang again. It was Michael, Valerie's husband.

'Valerie is very worried about Flash.'

I gave him this hour's update on his health and what is being done about it. I didn't mention the text.

Michael was concerned about Valerie's heart and the stress this is putting her under:

'She is worried that we'll have to sort everything out.'

Perhaps this was not an unreasonable fear, I have relied on them a lot...

'But I'm not asking her to do anything.' I was trying to keep the exasperation out of my voice because I know Valerie loves Flash too.

'You're right. She keeps inserting herself.' It was Michael's turn to dial down his exasperation.

There was a pause.

I was not going to break it.

'OK, I'll do my best,' he ended.

Good luck, I thought as I turned off my phone... and good luck, Ignacio.

Although the mime clowns who shared the dressing room with Ignacio had suggested using his illness in the show rather than trying to fight it, Ignacio did not follow their advice. Dr Footlights – the adrenaline of performance – did not work either.

Afterwards, I told Ignacio the latest developments with Flash. I'd pretty much decided to return home, but Ignacio convinced me.

It's times like this when I'm reminded how good it is to have a partner with whom I can talk everything over.

'I can manage on my own,' Ignacio croaked.

'But how?'

'I'll be fine.'

Friday 19 August

Fortunately, there was a seat on a flight that would get me into Gatwick around 6 p.m. It means I won't see my favourite writer – Alan Hollinghurst – talk at the Edinburgh Book Festival tomorrow. I was thrilled to get one of the last tickets but ultimately, it doesn't matter.

Matt, the vet at the practice where Vina's daughter works, rang while I was on the bus to the airport. He has given Flash a human painkiller. I will need to sign a consent form because it's not licensed for dogs.

'To be honest, I don't know what the problem is,' he told me. 'Before I order more tests, I would like to do a full review of his case.'

Surprisingly, I found his uncertainty refreshing. We agreed that I will secure all Flash's records and his X-rays and bring them over to the surgery on Monday.

Vina met me at Hassocks station and I almost expected to see Flash leap out of the passenger footwell of the car – like he does when Ignacio collects me – but she told me he was waiting at home.

When I got back and put my key in the lock, there was no barking. My heart was in my mouth. He has always been such a good guard dog and because he makes so much noise and seems to have two registers to his bark, many visitors are surprised to discover I have only one dog.

When Flash saw who had arrived, he rushed down the stairs from his lookout post on the landing and greeted me by mouthing my hand. All that energy I'd put into trying to stop this habit as a puppy and now it was the best thing ever.

'He fairly dashed across the green at lunchtime and he finally pooed,' said Vina.

Once again, Flash has made a miraculous recovery or maybe that's how it looks from behind the glass screen.

Kate decided to take a train in the morning, so the dog and I settled down to a quiet night in front of the TV.

Saturday 20 August

Flash yelped with pain when I let him out into the garden. I mixed his human painkiller – and I hope human strength – into his food and said a silent prayer.

The doorbell rang.

It was Valerie with a casserole dish.

'I have made up some chicken and rice for Flash. It's got lots of jelly, which he likes.'

I have lived next door to Valerie for long enough to know this was a peace offering.

I took the casserole.

'Flash is on different painkillers and the new vet is doing a full review on Monday.' She has done so much for Flash, she deserves to know what's happening.

'That's good. Keep me posted.'

I waited for a second, to see if she was going to mention her threat, perhaps even apologise.

Silence.

I know this silence. It reminds me of my parents who prefer to leave things unspoken or covered up with practical support and gifts.

The silence was building.

I don't take this from my parents any more...

Valerie had turned to leave.

'It doesn't help to threaten me.' Her text had felt like being stabbed in the stomach, into the already gaping wound of Flash's hunched back – slicing through the stitches around the Thom-shaped hole in my life. But she loves Flash too, she just doesn't know how deep my pain goes. So I leave it at that – six words.

Valerie's parting shot was almost over her shoulder:

'The doctors say I could die.'

While my parents have listened and changed, Valerie was beyond reach.

For my mother and father, my heart was full of love and respect, but as Valerie walked away, she built an invisible wall between our houses. Brick by brick, step by step.

I closed the door.

Later, I almost had to drag Flash up the road to the path opposite the doctor's surgery where we start the morning walk. I tried not to think about the millions of times I'd had to stop him from pulling me up the same street. He half managed a poo, but I had to grab a handy dock leaf and pull down the stool as he could not get in the right position to expel the last strand of grass that he'd eaten as a dog laxative. After he'd suffered that indignity, Flash was much calmer and began to walk better. Unfortunately, when he got home, the two steps from the garden into the house caused a frenzy of yelping.

I had no time to panic as I was about to be collected to pick up a hire car from Haywards Heath. Once I had wheels again, I drove over to Burgess Hill to collect Flash's records. Back home, I called my new veterinary practice. They had an appointment for later today but not with Matt (the vet who'd examined Flash yesterday). I didn't think I should have yet another opinion. However, I left my number with the receptionist and the senior practitioner called. We decided it would be best to wait till Monday when I could see Matt.

Kate finally arrived and I gave her a huge hug. Her daughter Alice, who came with her, is on a radical diet and has not eaten solid food for a month. She's been on 500 calories a day – basically, packets of powder (to which water is added) and a protein bar. I couldn't help but say: 'Oh dear' and immediately felt terrible as many people would consider Ignacio's caveman diet faddish too. For lunch, Alice ate the meaty lamb steak I'd bought from the butcher's in the village – and a little bit of salad I'd prepared – but the baked potato was beyond the pale.

Kate used to have food issues herself and spent her undergraduate years living on cigarettes, Cup a Soup and Kit Kats.

'With Flash so ill, have you been comfort eating?' she asked.

'I did have a blueberry muffin with my coffee at the airport.'

'Not a whole packet of biscuits?' Kate looked puzzled.

After lunch, we sat on the terrace and drank coffee and I was pleased that Flash decided to brave the steps to follow us out and lie under the table.

Alice asked about my books and whether I'd written anything about jealousy:

'That feeling of lying in bed with your boyfriend and loving him so much that you want to kill him so he can't ever leave you.'

—— ❦ ——

Later, I drove Flash up to the village green – our normal destination for his afternoon walk – and he went to the toilet three times. On the fourth occasion, I got Kate and Alice to mark the spot and I ran to the greengrocer's to ask for another bag. To celebrate his success, I took Kate and Alice up on to Devil's Dyke. When we arrived, Flash sat bolt upright in the passenger footwell so I let him out and he ran about greeting other dogs – no limping whatsoever – and he managed another poo. We have turned a corner.

It was a lovely evening, so I drove down to Shoreham to walk along the beach and stare into the backyards of the millionaires' shore-front properties. Although I let Flash out for a quick pee, I did not want to exhaust him so we went on the walk without him.

However, I couldn't enjoy the summer flowers growing above the tide line or the long shadows as the sun dipped down towards the sea. How can you go for a walk and leave the dog in the car?

Sunday 21 August

I'd put Flash's basket in the kitchen – so he doesn't have to negotiate the step from the utility room where he normally sleeps – but in the early hours of the morning, I discovered that he'd crept upstairs and was lying outside my bedroom door, so for the first time ever I let him inside and he slept on the rug beside my bed.

I made Kate some porridge – with bananas, blueberries, raspberries and strawberries – but Flash stayed in his basket. After breakfast, I drove Kate and Flash up the High Street, even though it is only five minutes away from my house. Unlike yesterday, Flash could hardly make it from one end of the recreation ground to the other. I sat on a bench and waited for Kate to come back from buying the Sunday papers. Flash was lying down, panting, at my feet.

'You two look the picture of tranquillity,' she told us.

Unfortunately, Flash yelped as he climbed into the passenger footwell of the car. Worse still, he yelped his way into the house – wailing like a police siren – and threw himself into his basket with a final yelp. It was like stones being thrown at the glass wall between me and the world. The glass cracked but it held. I've always thought this detachment was 'the splinter of ice in the heart of a writer' that Graham Greene (English novelist, 1904–91) described, which allows us to watch and store away events for future use. However, I am beginning to wonder if I am protecting myself and creating distance from my anxiety. I wanted to pace up and down, but what good would that do? I wanted to phone Ignacio, but he has enough on his plate. So I decided to bury myself in the newspapers. I would think about what to do when I'm calmer. Kate brought me a coffee and lit herself a cigarette. About half an hour later, Flash joined us on the terrace and did a tour of the garden – up and down the steps from the terrace – before settling down in his usual place: as close to me as possible.

After a Sunday roast of chicken with carrots and beans, plus roast potatoes for me, Alice wanted to go to Beachy Head because its reputation for suicide appeals to her gothic heart. We stopped off at High and Over car park – which I discovered with Flash on the third anniversary of Thom's death – and looked down over the Cuckmere Valley and the river doubling back on itself as it meanders to the sea. Flash was determined to come the whole way. He was also determined to get out at Seaford Head – where we parked for the famous view of the Seven Sisters with the lifeguard cottages in the distance. There were some pimped-up cars on display in the car park and we wandered around while Flash explored. I put him back in the car – even though this is one of his favourite walks, with rabbits to chase – because I didn't want him to overdo it.

Earlier in the year, Ignacio and I had been down to the sea from Seaford Head. Despite it being early in the season, I'd been in for a swim and Flash had followed me in. On the way back to the car, we'd seen a dog who had lost the use of his back legs and had been built a small chariot to keep him mobile. Ignacio and I argued about whether I would do that for Flash. I'd been appalled at the idea and Ignacio said I was cruel.

Kate and Alice enjoyed the view and despite the walk being only about twenty minutes each way, I was shattered (perhaps I'm out of condition, with Flash only taking small walks or maybe the cold I caught off Ignacio is getting worse). Alice was pleased to get back to the car too, but then she's only having 500 calories a day.

Our next stop was Birling Gap – where the National Trust have bought the hotel – and therefore splendid cake is on offer and notices to explain that the windows to the conservatory are professionally washed twice a week and apologising if the salt, rain and wind meant we could not see out.

We finished our excursion at Beachy Head. I let Flash out for a pee, but left him in the car again while we explored. When Alice went to the loo, I showed Kate where we scattered Thom's ashes and stared into grassy eternity.

Kate broke the silence:

'It's going to be the end of an era.'

Yes… but am I ready to face the world without Flash?

Monday 22 August

Around 7.30 a.m., I could hear people talking somewhere. Puzzled, I walked downstairs. Kate was already up and had switched on Radio 4.

'Didn't you sleep?' I asked.

'Look,' she pointed to the kitchen door. Flash was out of his basket and full of curiosity. Giving him his Tramadol late at night seemed to have done the trick. He bounded over to greet me and licked my hand. He had no problems going out into the garden for a pee and no yelps getting in or out of the car when I took him up to the recreation ground. He passed plenty of stools and on our return followed Kate and me outside on to the patio. While we drank coffee and chatted, he patrolled the garden.

'If we can just get the pain medication right and he's pooing normally, who knows? The massage and the exercises might help him and… I don't know, he could go on for a couple of months more,' I told Kate. Although in my mind, I meant years, not months.

Later, I phoned Ignacio and told him the good news. Maybe if the vet gives Flash the all-clear, and Vina is back from her weekend break, I can return to Edinburgh. Tickets sales are still poor, but Richard – the technician Ignacio uses when he tours – has arrived and will start flyering today.

After taking Kate and Alice to the station, I attended to my emails and watched the Libyan rebels' forced entry into Tripoli on the lunchtime news. On my way over to the new vets in Billingshurst, I decided to stop at the playing fields at Cowfold so that Flash could have his lunchtime toilet break. Unfortunately, he didn't really want to get out of the car. He only managed a few steps, hopping most of the way, hunched up like an old dog – not certain if he wanted to poo or lie down. After a few steps, he decided he wanted a rest and to lick his bottom. So I headed back to the car. Flash decided to smell round the posts that divide the playing ground from the children's swings and slides, so I followed bag in hand (but with little hope of him going). Finally, Flash managed to poo and walk a little better, but he yelped as he jumped back into the car.

The Billinghurst branch of the vets is just an outpost. When I entered, everything was quiet. I suppose I'd been expecting lots of bleeping equipment and the sense that there were miracles performed every day. I took a seat; I was ten minutes early. An elderly Retriever arrived for the appointment before mine. A man in his mid-thirties came out of the consulting rooms and greeted us both and our dogs. It was Matt, our new vet:

'How was Flash over the weekend?' he asked.

'Up and down,' I replied honestly.

The Retriever went in for his appointment but he was back in reception before I'd found my place in my book. It was our turn, but I doubted we would be so quick.

Matt was calm and everything you'd want from a vet. He opened up Flash's notes and read them slowly. Next, he switched on his light box and looked at the various X-rays. The upshot was that bone spurs growing in between the vertebrae are probably interfering with the signals being sent from the brain to the hindquarters.

'Does Flash sometimes look out of it?'

I was not certain what he meant.

Matt showed me how Flash's back right foot had a crease where he puts it on the ground. His back left foot, the one that he's been avoiding using, does not have one. Matt used a technical term, but it went in one ear and out the other. However, I was aware that somehow Flash has gone from not using his right hind leg to not using his left. It was not just arthritis (as the previous vet has suggested).

'I don't think his prostate is particularly enlarged for an old dog, but that could have caused the problems pooing. He has a heart murmur. He has problems with his intestines. His pain could be caused by a whole range of problems, but generally, I think it's more likely that they are all down to the same thing: spondylosis – the degeneration of the intervertebral discs.'

Somehow, this sounded right. We had been firefighting, emergency to emergency, vet to vet, and in this simple ordinary room, it suddenly became clear.

'So there's nothing really that you can do for him?'

'You can up the dose of painkiller to three a day and you can reinstate the Metacam, as that is a muscle relaxant and we can make him comfortable. And if he was doing well on the prescription food, let's continue with that… but I'm afraid…that it's not take two pills a day and he'll be better.'

'No, all I want is honesty.' Which is true. You know where you stand with honesty. Although one part of me craves for 'take two pills'.

'I'd been wondering if I could go back to Edinburgh.'

'You could… and carers like Mrs Bird are very good.'

So that's Vina's surname. Wasn't that the name of the housekeeper in the Paddington Bear series I'd loved as a child?

'However, you know more about your dog than anybody else,' Matt continued, 'and you can give me the most information.'

'And I suppose only I can make the final decision.' The words were in the room.

'You'll want to be there to say your final goodbyes.'

'I'm not certain.'

But, of course, it's not going to come to that. I had extra medication and Flash was walking quite well round the surgery. Matt finished his examination by putting a gloved finger up Flash's bottom and found faeces – something he didn't find before. So that's good. His temperature was normal. That's good too.

While Matt was writing up Flash's notes, he stopped for a second and turned round.

'I've been really impressed by how much information you've been able to give me.'

It's like he's talking in a code that I don't quite understand but I was too tired, too busy trying to digest all this new information, to work it out. I said nothing.

Back in reception – while waiting for the prescription food and my bill – I watched two black Labrador puppies who'd just had their first injections. One minute, they were twisting in different directions and the next fast asleep on the linoleum floor. They looked so unformed. All those adventures ahead of them. Flash, however, was more interested in the cat in the basket, which has come in to be neutered.

Afterwards, I drove into Billingshurst to get some more milk. The library was across from the car park. I could not face my current book – a thriller for teenagers that my agent has recommended – and decided to find something else to help me self-medicate. Afterwards, I bought some plums and cherries from the local farmers' market shop and a date and walnut cake from an 'artisan' bakery. When I got home, the house felt really empty without Kate and Alice. Suddenly, I realised that I hadn't thought any further than the vet's appointment. The whole weekend had been centred around getting to this point.

Perhaps it was completing my list of tasks; perhaps it was all the dents in the screen from Flash's hunched back, to his problems with toileting and obvious pain; perhaps it was Matt's straightforward honesty or maybe the impossibility of cake and books making me feel better again, but the sheet of glass between Flash and I shattered. I was left staring directly in the eyes of all the love, all the fear and all the alone. I took a gulp of air. There was something else? Something worse… I hadn't been taking Flash's problems seriously. I had minimised and pushed them out of sight. Isn't that exactly what my parents did with my grief over Thom?

— ᘓᘐ —

I confirmed an appointment for my associate therapist in London tonight and answered a letter sent to my website. On the edge of my consciousness, I heard small paws climbing the stairs and a small yelp as Flash deposited himself in his usual place on the landing (where he can survey both the front door and my office door). I left my office and went over and gave him a stroke.

'I won't leave you again. I'm sorry,' I whispered in his ear and marvelled at how silky his fur felt on my cheek.

Later, I phoned Kate, who was sympathetic.

'I don't know what's going to happen but Flash copes better with me around,' I told her.

I tried to contact Ignacio to let him know that I won't be returning – but no reply from his mobile. Lana has read on Ignacio's Facebook page that I'm back in Sussex and sent a supportive message. So I phoned and gave her an update. While we were talking, Flash crawled into my office and laid down in his favourite place by the bookcase. Lana told me not to worry what Valerie is thinking, I have to concentrate on Flash and what is right for him. The conversation changed to her previous dog Jake – a Collie – who died about a year ago:

'I know I keep drawing parallels with Jake but if you want me to come with you…' The words hung in the air.

I hadn't really thought of what it would be like.

'We'll be terribly brave and hold it together,' she continued.

'Until afterwards, when we'll be like rejected contestants on a TV talent show: weeping and hugging and generally carrying on,' I tried to joke.

Tuesday 23 August

When is it time to let a dog go? Perhaps I shouldn't use the euphemism. What I mean is when is it time to put a dog down? One minute, I think Flash is fine and the next I know I'm fooling myself.

This morning, he was quite alert when I came down and opened the door to his room, but I suppose that shows how low my expectations have dropped. Normally, he would have run to the door, leapt up once, twice and spun round in his anxiety to be out the back door and analysing the morning garden smells. But today, I was pleased that he stepped out of his basket when I was just a step away. There were no yelps as he picked his way down the three steps on to the grass, where he just sat: no sniffs, no curiosity – nothing. So I started to prepare his breakfast – a full tin of prescription dog food, his pain relief and the full dose of Metacam. I called him, but he was not interested. He just sat on the grass in the morning drizzle. I stepped out on to the patio, trying to tempt him in with the slightly stomach-churning smell of tinned meat. (While I have been lecturing Kate and Alice about factory products, where you have no idea what's been put into the product, I am happily feeding the same stuff to my sick dog.) When Flash didn't respond, I retreated to the kitchen and started on my own breakfast. Through the window, I watched Flash pee. A long, long pee against his favourite bush – rather than evenly distributing his scent round the neighbourhood. The rain was getting worse. I went out in my slippers on to the sodden grass with Flash's bowl and tempted him into his room. He ate ravenously – as if he expected this will be his last meal – and slumped down in his basket. I called him through, but he was not interested. A few moments later, my spirits soared: through the frosted glass in the door between the kitchen and his room, I could see that he'd stood up and cocked his head to one side. I opened the door and he bounded through.

When I brought my porridge through to the living room, Flash watched me from his usual place by the piano. I picked up the book by Virginia Woolf that I got from the library. Her stream of consciousness novel, *Mrs Dalloway*, feels right for today, with its combination of everyday – buying flowers for a party, the bustle of London traffic, the window displays of ladies' hats and gloves in Bond Street shops – with the shadow of loss (from the First World War) and madness hovering off and on the page.

Another of my favourite novelists is Michael Cunningham. I went to see him read from *The Hours* at Charleston Farmhouse (the home of Woolf's sister Vanessa Bell and the venue for an annual literary festival). Cunningham's novel is based on

Mrs Dalloway and has Virginia Woolf as a major character. I'd arrived early for the event – with a friend who'd looked after Flash when I'd been away working in Romania and who also loved *The Hours* – and had a picnic by the pond in front of the farmhouse. When it was time for Michael Cunningham's talk, we packed up the debris and went to put the dog back in the car. As the public streamed into the talk, we had to wait at the gate.

'Dogs are not allowed on the property,' said an efficient-looking middle-aged man with a name tag.

I had been about to give my usual defence: what harm is he doing? But when I turned round Flash had fallen into the pond and was desperately trying to claw his way back on to the footpath. I leaned over and pulled him out by his collar. There is nothing more miserable than a wet dog in disgrace. The official spun on his heels and marched off to check ticket stubs. Flash shook himself and I had to bundle him into the car in the sure knowledge he would sit on my seat and leave a damp patch for the drive home.

This morning, I couldn't imagine Flash falling in a lake. I couldn't imagine him doing very much. When I finished breakfast, I went and put my bowl in the dishwasher, but Flash did not follow me through. I had my shower, got dressed, put my boots on and got ready to take Flash for a walk. No response. I went back to the living room. Flash was still lying by the piano. I gave him a stroke. He looked alert; he rolled over so I could tickle his tummy. I walked into the hall and opened the front door. Still no response. I had my answer: a dog that doesn't want to go for a walk is a dog that's had enough.

Just to make sure, I called his name and he came bounding out into the front garden and picked up a stray tennis ball. Perhaps I had been too hasty… At the recreation ground, he was anxious to get out and greet the day. He trotted over the grass, king of all he surveyed. Was that a squirrel in the distance? His body was alert and he was not dragging his feet. Except, he was straining to go to the toilet and produced only half the amount of faeces that I would have expected.

When Flash jumped back into the car, it was like he couldn't gauge the distance. Perhaps he couldn't get enough spring or – as the vet suggested – the nerves between the brain and his hindquarters have been scrambled. With a yelp, Flash pulled himself into the footwell and we drove home. Although he had no problems getting out of the car, he plonked himself back beside the piano and did not come upstairs for his morning work of sleeping in my office while I type at the computer.

I sent an email to Lana, asking her to come round at lunchtime for a second opinion, but I sort of know the answer. It is no longer if, but when…

Wednesday 24 August

I have made an appointment for Flash with Matt this morning. Lana has offered to take us – partly so I will not be alone but mainly because she believes I will be in no fit state to drive back. I have no idea what to expect but I accepted her offer.

When I came down this morning and waited for the coffee to percolate, I looked out into the garden and the tree where – all those years ago – I'd imagined Flash turning and looking at me and saying 'I belong here.' I put another load into the washing machine and crossed over the step he could no longer manage as an old dog. The step where I used to sit and cuddle him on my lap when he first arrived and I was helping him know this was his room.

I offered Flash the chance to go into the back garden, but he just looked out of the door. He made a half-hearted attempt at eating his food. I spent the last fifteen minutes, before Lana arrived, sitting on the back doorstep with Flash resting his head on my feet. I tried to make every one of those minutes count, but my mind kept going back through all our past adventures – winning my agility club's annual competition back in 2003; how he thought that a moat covered with algae was grass and fell in, and the time he chewed through his lead at Fountains Abbey so he could follow me into the café. I tried not to worry about what would happen when we arrived at the vets or whether I would always remember the exact weight of his head on my feet.

I looked at my watch: I still had ten minutes, but I was restless. I had not eaten any breakfast. I would have an apple. I fetched it and returned to the step to eat it with Flash. When I had finished, I offered him the core and he looked up at me with his trusting eyes. Although he had refused his breakfast, something that I had just finished and offered from my hand still held appeal. He slowly ate it and I wished that I had given him all my apple cores to finish.

Lana was a couple of minutes early. I heard the car and opened the door from Flash's room into the front garden – so she wouldn't ring the doorbell and get Flash excited. He could hardly stagger or hop down the passage. He landed in the front passenger side of her car with a yelp. It was definitely time. Lana had decided she and I should be calm so Flash wouldn't know there was anything to worry about. So we talked about TV programmes and the new larger office she's buying for her company in the village.

To keep stress down to a minimum, we had decided that all three of us would wait for the appointment in the car – so we could keep Flash quiet and not upset the other patients and owners in the reception area. So when we arrived and parked the car, I phoned the receptionist to let her know we were outside. A few minutes later, Matt came out to greet us and Flash sat up. So

I let him out of the car and he started to explore the lawn outside the practice.

'He doesn't look too bad,' said Matt.

However, while I was filling Matt in on the last forty-eight hours, Lana followed Flash round the corner and watched him lift his leg. She reported that he had lost control of his back legs and had fallen over.

Whereas I'd been worried about how we'd get Flash up the steps into the vets – as he doesn't like to be lifted – Flash entered under his own steam. He just followed me trustingly into the surgery, but that summed up Flash, he'd follow me anywhere.

Matt asked whether I wanted to be there while Flash's life was terminated. I remembered Valerie telling me how she felt it was her duty to be present when her Dalmatian Lily was put down. Faced with the same decision, I decided she was right. I nodded: I would stay.

Next, he asked whether I wanted: a) to take the dog's body home with me and bury it myself; b) to have him cremated and the ashes scattered at a special dog memorial; or c) to have him cremated and have the ashes returned.

I chose the last option and also bought a cardboard spout to facilitate scattering the ashes – which seemed like an unnecessary complication – but at eight quid, why not? (Although, I expect that's what the manufacturers hope.) Later, I discovered when the receptionist asked Lana if we were taking the body she replied – without thinking – 'I hope not.'

What happened next is a daze. I have odd patches of memory… Flash is on the examining table, but I don't know how he got there… Matt has left the room to give us a few last moments together… I should be making them count. I should be in tears, but I am blank… I could say something to Flash but how can I reassure him?… So I stroke him… He hardly registers me… I try to say something but my voice cracks and fails…

I try to muster some mental energy to lighten his way, but it's all burnt out...There is a knock on the door. I say enter... I might have been offered more time with Flash, but I can't be sure... Matt has a nurse with him. Somehow, I know it is Vina's daughter. Matt explains what will happen. Something about two injections? I don't know... The nurse has kind eyes... Somehow, Flash is given enough tranquilliser... the life creeps out of him and after that, I am blank again...

Later, Matt asked if I would like to be alone with the body. In the same way that I had wanted to escape as quickly as possible from the hospital after Thom died, I needed to be out of that consulting room before the walls closed in on me.

However, I must have asked Matt to write down the word I didn't know from Monday – in case Valerie or anyone else wanted to know about Flash's problems. I have it here on a piece of paper: proprioception.

Somehow, I was told that Vina's daughter had cried after leaving the room because she'd grown attached to Flash while I'd been in Edinburgh. Matt had given her the option not to assist but she had been determined to be present. Of course, I was pleased the final act had been performed with such tenderness, but the kindness could not reach me.

Like the morning after Thom's death, when I found his brother and his best friend crying in the kitchen, I was detached. Like when Thom's ashes were scattered and everybody else was crying, I had no tears. I should be practised around death. I should be open to the deep intimacy of this moment. But standing beside Flash's mortal remains, my heart was still blank.

Thank goodness Lana was waiting outside to give me a hug and provide a bridge back to feeling human again. She was right: I couldn't have driven. I asked her to stop for coffee and cake at some roadside restaurant. We took it out into the garden. Although I always joke there is no occasion that does benefit from a piece of cake, I have found one. The cake tasted of nothing and did nothing to ease my pain.

On my return, I walked round the house. Flash has left hairs everywhere. I swept up the ones round his basket but they're also at the top of the stairs where he used to survey the world and on the rug beside my computer where I'm typing this. I went across the road to let my neighbours, Jackie and Michael, know that Flash had been put down. They invited me in and I told them all the details. I tried not to look at their dog Betty asleep on the living-room rug. Jackie is Valerie's best friend. I know she will pass on the news. I can't face telling her myself.

After lunch, I expected to be followed into the kitchen by a dog looking for scraps, but of course there was none. Nobody to take for a walk. While Thom had arrived from Germany with eighty-seven boxes, Flash was wonderfully minimal. I gave his food and treats to Lana for Onion and his medicine to Betty across the road. I threw his old smelly blankets and his drying-off towels in the bin, cleaned his bowls in the dishwasher (something Ignacio would probably not have allowed) and rounded up all the tennis balls he'd found on the recreation ground from the garden and put them – along with a new tuggy and his lead – in his basket and stowed everything in the garage.

Even with the most obvious evidence of Flash removed, I couldn't stay. I went online, found a flight to Edinburgh and drove up to Gatwick to return the hire car.

Friday 26 August

I have been pounding the pavements drumming up an audience for Ignacio. It has been good to have something to do. I had breakfast this morning with my friend Chris – who is director of New Writing South, an organisation for writers to which I belong – she is up at the festival making contacts and seeing shows. Before I sat down, she looked concerned:

'How are you? You've lost a lot of weight.'

She was right. I have taken in my belt by several notches.

I tell her about the caveman diet. I cancel the toast that comes with my full 'Scottish' breakfast.

She was not so easily thrown off the topic.

'Are you sure you're OK?'

Ignacio has put the news about Flash on Facebook. Beyond telling my parents, I have told nobody.

I didn't know his death would hit me so strongly.

Monday 29 August

It was the last performance of *Caruso and the Monkey House Trial*. There were not many festival goers around but I managed to drum up a respectable house. Looking at the ticket sales reports, we have generated enough revenue to pay our rent at the theatre and we will be owed some money – but not enough to pay for our accommodation and food while up in Edinburgh. So a loss but not too much.

We decided to bring the car into the city, so we could pack up the set and leave straight away. We had a debate about whether it was August Bank Holiday in Scotland (as well as England) and whether the parking restrictions applied or not. We were wrong because we came out of the theatre to find a ticket on the car. Ignacio took the first shift of driving back to Sussex and I took the second. We spoke briefly about how strange it would be to return and not go round to Valerie or someone else to collect Flash, but we didn't dwell on it.

It was late by the time we got back to a quiet house. We unloaded the car and Ignacio put on a wash. I had gone upstairs for some reason and as I crossed the small landing at the top of the stairs, where Flash used to lie, I sensed a presence. A packet of dog energy curled in the corner with its eyes watching me. I felt it more than saw it.

I stopped. I turned and looked. Of course, there was nothing actually there. Nothing I could see or touch and I know this sounds fanciful, but I saw a ghost dog. The ghost of Flash. He was at the top of my stairs but when I looked directly, he wasn't there any more – and yet, he still hadn't gone.

I didn't say anything to Ignacio. He has been scarred by a childhood in the Opus Dei (an ultra-orthodox branch of the Catholic Church) and has no time for my superstitions. So I didn't really begin to unpack my encounter until I opened up my diary. So what happened? I know it wasn't my writer's imagination placing my departed dog on the stairs. It wasn't some deep longing that had conjured him up but something more... So what? I don't know. Ghost dog is the best I can manage. It wasn't frightening. It wasn't comforting. It was just a surprise. But perhaps it shouldn't have been because Flash always wanted to be close to me – even in the last few weeks when his health problems meant he'd retreated into himself. Until he'd get a fresh burst of energy and be back at my side again. It was always like the sun coming from behind the cloud. So perhaps that's what I experienced on the landing. A final shining moment.

Tuesday 30 August

Memory seems too slight a word. It is almost a physical sensation. When I get up in the morning, there is an irresistible pull to open the door to the utility room. Although I know there will be nothing there, I still open the door and prove to myself it's not all been some big mistake.

While yesterday I sensed Flash's presence, this morning I picture a ghost dog mouthing my hand, twice turning round to face the back door, feet scrabbling on the tiles, ready to charge into the garden. Later, the ghost dog watches me prepare lunch from its vantage point by the kitchen door. I can also hear the sound of his paws against our wooden floors and the click of his name tag against his collar buckle. I can almost smell the damp fields clinging to his fur. I wish I could still register the exact weight that the solid dog used to surrender on to my feet when he curled up across them… because it is never going to happen again.

I still haven't said anything to Ignacio because he's already asked:

'Are you going to mention Flash every time you throw away the fat off a steak?'

And anyway, it's not that I believe the house is haunted – beyond that brief moment yesterday when, as Kate would say, the veil between the two worlds thinned. No, it's more an overhang from the sixth sense of every dog owner, which knows where the dog is in the house even when we're not in the same room.

I have become a character from Philip Pullman's trilogy *His Dark Materials*, where everybody has a daemon – an external soul that manifests as an animal.

Flash has captured my heart and now I am bereft.

Wednesday 31 August

Flash inserted himself so successfully into my life that he inhabited every part of my day, but no time more successfully than the transition from breakfast to starting work. For almost twelve years, I would take Flash for a forty-five-minute to one – hour walk over the fields that surround Hurstpierpoint. It had not only provided exercise and a round-up of the local gossip, but I would often find the answer to some knotty problem with the article or book I was writing.

Yesterday, without a morning walk, I couldn't settle to write. It would feel like a crime to go for a walk without a dog, so I decided to go for a run instead. It is many years since I have run anywhere. Even though I could scarcely make it up the slight incline into the village without my legs feeling leaden and my chest tight, I put on an extra spurt whenever I saw dog walkers I know. They will guess what has happened and I am not strong enough for condolences.

My parents phoned this lunchtime. Ignacio answered and spent a long time talking to my father. When he passed the handset to me, my father said:

'We've had all your news. I'm glad Edinburgh went well. Would you like to talk to your mother?'

'How are you doing?' she asked.

I told her about the ghost dog.

'If dogs could come back, Flash would certainly try.'

She was right. He always wanted to know where I was, to chase squirrels and to wait for our next adventure.

'We've been thinking about him because he was like one of the family,' she continued.

And there is no greater praise for a dog.

However, I have been left with all sorts of difficult questions. What happens to dogs when they die? If there's an afterlife for dogs, what about rabbits and mice and fleas? I remembered the books I read when studying meditation. One was about a man who achieved merits for his next reincarnation – despite a dissolute life – because at some point in the past he'd been a dung beetle swept past a statue of the Buddha in the gutter after a rainstorm. So I wondered how many merits Flash accumulated while he sat in the car outside the meditation room in Brighton with the giant Buddha painted in gold leaf.

Although I want to honour the ghost dog and let it be (for as long as it needs to be here, or until I can let it leave), I wonder if it is not a ghost but the desires of a newly born puppy looking for a home… But I want to rent a room for us up in London, so there is less coming and going to my counselling practice and Ignacio and I can enjoy the richness of cultural life in the capital (and few people will want a puppy who might pee on their carpet). So I'm a complete mess, pulled in every direction.

When Ignacio collected me from the station in the evening, after seeing my clients in London, the ghost dog leapt out of the car, danced round my feet and veered off to sniff the bushes in the station car park.

I got into the car and kissed Ignacio on the lips. His love is always sweeter after a night listening to people argue.

'I was thinking of Flash and how he would know from the sound of gear changes or something that we'd reached the station and his head would pop up expectantly,' Ignacio said.

'I was thinking of him too.'

He squeezed my hand.

Monday 5 September

As normal on a Monday night, I took Skip (a dog who belongs to friends in the village) to the agility class and felt the pull of a real dog at the other end of the lead.

I had a wobble when I opened my mouth to tell Carol (the organiser) about Flash. I'd almost bottled it – because Flash has been retired for over a year so nobody would have asked where he was. Perhaps if I didn't say anything he could live on in her imagination (and everybody else's), but it was now or never.

'I'm afraid I've had to have Flash put down.'

She nodded. She'd been another member of the class when I first brought Flash as an eighteen-month-old – progressing from puppy training, to basic obedience, to agility (which better suited Flash's temperament).

'Could you pass the word around as I can't face telling everybody.'

Another nod. She looked down at her feet.

'One of ours is heading in that direction.'

We looked into each other's liquid eyes.

'Will you get another one?' She asked the question that's been skulking round the perimeter of my conscious mind.

'I don't know.'

I doubt Carol believed me. Perhaps she could sense the dog-shaped hole in my life. Perhaps she knows from bitter experience how much you can miss a cool nose and a warm tongue.

When I returned Skip to his owners, I went in for a cup of coffee and told Simon and Mirella about the last week. They shared their story of letting their last dog go. It was good to run my hand through Skip's wiry coat and to return smelling – as Ignacio's mother would say – of the dog of another house. However, I turned down their offer of borrowing Skip from time to time.

Tuesday 6 September

Two weeks after I'd taken Flash to the vets for a final time, a cardboard box came through the post. It was labelled 'Flash Marshall' and there was a short poem:

Your presence we miss,
your memory we treasure.
Loving you always,
in our thoughts for ever.

I could not help but think of Thom (who was cremated in Germany and his ashes put in the mail too). However, while it took a lot of deliberation to decide where to store Thom's urn before his family could come over to help scatter him, it was reasonably straightforward deciding what to do with the box with Flash's remains until the weekend (when we'll have time to properly honour him).

'What about putting it in his room?' Ignacio suggested.

And that's the big difference between last time and this: I am no longer alone. I have someone with whom to discuss my problems.

I put the box on top of the cupboard in the utility room, amongst the laundry detergents and the metal box where I keep what used to be Flash's bedtime biscuits but are now Skip's agility rewards.

Friday 9 September

Over the past week, I've ran further and further in the morning. I've been along the Millennium path – part of my normal walk with Flash – and I've had my heart filled with the velvety beauty of the South Downs on a sunny late-summer morning. The ghost dog has been tugging less. I've stopped looking for Flash where I used to tie him when I come out of the Co-op store and I can look the greengrocer in the eye (one of the shops which allowed Flash inside). I know he wants to ask why I'm dogless but basically knows and fears the answer. I've bumped into other regulars on the morning walk, received their condolences and reached down and stroked their dogs.

Today, I felt ready to run the full course of Flash's regular morning walk. As I ducked under the overhanging trees to go down the steps opposite the Health Centre, I pictured him in his puppy incarnation dancing through the shadows in the narrow alleyway down to the fields ready for an adventure. I remembered old Flash sniffing, crouching, straining and failing to toilet. But I was moving too fast for the sorrow to catch me out. I remembered taking Thom to the airport to fly back to Germany for the very last time, running back to move the car from short-term to long-term parking. The exhilaration of being able to move at speed again, to be free of the wheelchair.

But then on my morning run, I was out of the dark alley and into the light. The Weald. The empty fields. The occasional horse. The smell of rain sinking into the ground. Running. No ghost dogs. No sick partner. Alive.

There was no pain when I ran past the place where I used to meet Lana on the morning walk, where Flash had been ambushed by Crystal (the Labradoodle) who was in season and her owners were determined to breed from her. I sped along the lanes, past the houses with well-tended front gardens and through the gates that I'd walked in rain, sun and six inches of snow.

I had reclaimed the fields behind the house.

When I returned home and showered, the papers still hadn't arrived. *Mrs Dalloway* had too much madness, death and destruction, so I decided to read the news online. Except, I wondered if there were any crossbreed puppies for sale.

Ignacio came down for breakfast and found me sighing over a picture of ten puppies that someone had managed to get to face the camera at the same time.

'What are you looking at?' he asked me.

'Nothing,' I replied guiltily.

Ignacio looked over my shoulder:

'We haven't even scattered Flash's ashes.'

After lunch, I had my supervision session and talked about my loss. Christine wondered how much loss is at the root of many of my clients' problems too. Instead of facing pain, it seems part of human nature to distract ourselves – but in the long run that makes everything worse. Is that what I'm doing by considering getting another puppy?

Although I didn't reach any conclusion in my supervision session, I did come away ready to scatter Flash's ashes. It helped that the weather has changed – there's been a lot of rain – and it's the sort of afternoon where Ignacio and I might have stopped work early and taken the dog up on to the Downs.

Around 4 p.m., Ignacio and I drove to Devil's Dyke, where the sky seems bigger and Sussex is laid out before you: small villages, ploughed fields, the sea on the horizon and mile upon mile of green. I'd chosen Devil's Dyke partly because of Flash's Sheepdog inheritance (he loved acres of open space and he would charge joyfully into the distance) and partly because it is not somewhere I go every day. Something I don't tell Ignacio is that the Downs form a link between Thom (scattered at Beachy Head) and Flash (who was such an important part of my recovery). Ignacio is conflicted enough already about what we're about to do. On the short drive from our house to the Downs, he has alternated between 'You know, I'm probably going to get emotional' and 'In Mexico, when a dog is ill, you bribe a policeman to take it away and shoot it.'

When we parked and got out of the car, there was a fresh breeze and great dollops of sunshine were breaking through the banks of clouds. I picked a few blades of grass, tested the direction of the wind, then returned to the car and retrieved the box with Flash's remains from the passenger side footwell where Flash himself always used to travel.

When I'd first held the box, I'd felt no connection to Flash, but something has changed: I had a sense that I was about to take Flash for a walk. I could sort of understand why Lana decided to keep the ashes of her dog Jake. For a second, I wondered if I should hold on to Flash's remains for a little longer and take them for a few more walks. Except, in some sane part of me, I knew that sounded weird and although Ignacio was supportive about making a small ceremony, there were limits.

The perfect day to scatter his ashes was also the perfect day to walk a dog. So there were several dog walkers and a young Westie came bounding over to greet us. My heart was in my throat as I bent down for him to lick my hand. We agreed to wait until we were alone but there were two Spaniels behind the Westie and a man throwing a frisbee for his Labrador.

'What about over there?' suggested Ignacio. He pointed at the remains of a brick wall sticking out over the west-facing escarpment.

I peered down at barbed wire, a discarded Coke can and a few empty crisp packets.

'It looks like we're dumping him in a ditch.'

So we walked on further, feeling more and more uncomfortable.

The frisbee-thrower was walking back towards the car park, turning every so often for a last throw for his dog, and then we were finally alone.

'Here is as good a place as any.' I did the wind test again and opened the box.

Inside there was a cylindrical tube, a card offering deepest sympathy (with the date of Flash's cremation: 25/08/11) and a flyer offering us a 15 per cent discount on a casket, urn or a memorial for our garden.

Unlike Thom's urn (which needed a knife to prise off the top), the lid of the cylinder slid off easily. I pushed down on a serrated circle and peered at the gritty grey remains. Dog, human, it all looks the same.

'Ashes to ashes,' I wanted to quote the Bible or at least some Shakespeare, but it seemed too much fuss. Then I remembered the condolence card from my cousin Sue, who had seen my play about dog-walking and reminded me that very few dogs had such a literary heritage. What's more, lessons from owning Flash found their way into my first self-help book: *I Love You But I'm Not in Love with You* – and that's been translated into fifteen different languages. So perhaps he doesn't need more than what I did say:

'He was a very loyal dog and wanted nothing more than to be with us.'

I slotted the cylindrical spout into the box, tipped it over and gave it a shake. The wind caught the ashes – like the fumes of an illicit cigarette on a street corner. I passed the cylinder to Ignacio and he scattered a little more and passed the box back to me. A few more puffs of smoke and Flash was gone for ever.

We hugged each other and for the first time, we cried together. I wanted to hold Ignacio for ever but that's not possible. Instead, we stood and stared at the springy grass, the white, yellow and purple downlands' flowers and several kinds of thistles which had been painted grey – their tiny hairs capturing a dusting of Flash.

A group of middle-aged walkers strode across the grass slopes discussing: 'What is wort as in ragwort and St John's wort?' I wished I'd listened to my mother when I was a child so I'd learned the names of the wild flowers at our feet and could rejoice in the poetry of their names: cinquefoil, scarlet pimpernel, pale flax, vetch and clary. Instead, we gathered up the box, card and flyer and headed back to the car.

On the journey down to Brighton seafront, for a funeral tea at Hove Lawns Café, we traded reminiscences about Flash. However, as he was such a well-behaved dog, we quickly ran out of funny stories and instead listed everywhere he'd been with us: Scarborough and the Stephen Joseph Theatre where he'd been banned from Ignacio's dressing room (but the management had found a foster home outside the town for him) and the other theatres where he'd stayed in the green room while Ignacio had performed. There were our trips to Caernarfon, Stamford and the

Yorkshire Moors. After Ignacio's first English Christmas lunch in Norfolk – which had been cooked by my cousin Wendy, who was sadly lost to breast cancer two years ago – he had eaten so much, he thought he would burst until we stirred ourselves to exercise Flash and Wendy's three dogs. Finally, we remembered all the times we'd taken him 'once round the park' in Bedford with my parents.

The wind had dropped by the time we'd reached Brighton and found somewhere to park, so we left our coats in the car. There were more dogs on Hove Lawns but this time it didn't feel so painful. I had tea and a piece of carrot cake (which looked nice but tasted too sugary now I'm on my low-carbohydrate diet) and Ignacio had a bottle of sparkling water and a plate of chips (of which I ate half).

We didn't talk about Flash but discussed Ignacio's next tour and other plans for our future. And that seemed right: better to seize the last of the summer sun, the joy of the children rollerblading on the seafront and the cries of the gulls trying to steal food from the bins behind the café – than to dwell on the past or what might have been.

Writing in my diary, late at night, I was struck by the tragedy of being a dog owner. It's not fair that we can live for three score years and ten but our constant companions don't make it much past the ten. But on second thoughts, that's also the dog's great lesson for us: impermanence. Nothing lasts for ever and perhaps dogs have been put on the earth to remind us of this inescapable truth.

Which brings me to the most important question of all: how do I keep falling in love if, over the long haul, the destination is always erasure? But if Flash has taught me anything it's that I only get out what I put in and what I'm willing to allow in. I could be sad, depressed or angry, but much better to be like a dog and sniff the air, look around with curiosity and run and run and run. Because all I have is this glorious moment.

I finish typing and climb into bed beside Ignacio.

AFTERWARDS

It is a tribute to Flash and how he was an intrinsic part of our lives that Ignacio and I decided to get another dog. While Flash had always been 'my' dog – when Ignacio would ask him to do something he would always look at me first to check it was OK to obey – this would be 'our' dog.

So the day after scattering Flash's ashes, I arranged for us to look at three sets of puppies and a slightly older puppy that needed rehoming. Once again, I wanted a crossbreed rather than a pedigree dog. In order for it not to seem that we were replacing Flash, who was a Collie/Spaniel mix, I lined up a litter of Collie crossed with German Shepherd and another of Spaniel crossed with Beagle puppies. However, when we went to assess the older puppy, a beautiful mix of Labrador and Collie – who immediately captured my heart – Ignacio complained that he had Flash's eyes. I knew exactly what he meant because that's what had appealed to me!

After many miles and many cute puppies, the final litter was the ones I'd being sighing over when Ignacio had come down for breakfast and discovered my treachery to Flash's memory. They were a five-eighths red fox Labrador, a quarter Vizsla and one-eighth Spinone. They had been lovingly bred by a family who wanted to keep one of the puppies. They were nothing like Flash and they would be ready to leave their mother in a month's time. Ignacio named our puppy Pumpkin and he has grown to be a handsome and clever dog who brings us endless joy.

I continue to keep a diary and honour the part of Flash that lives on in me: loyalty, curiosity and living in the eternal now.

'The Power of the Dog'
Rudyard Kipling (1865–1936)

There is sorrow enough in the natural way
From men and women to fill our day;
And when we are certain of sorrow in store,
Why do we always arrange for more?
Brothers and Sisters, I bid you beware
Of giving your heart to a dog to tear.

Buy a pup and your money will buy
Love unflinching that cannot lie –
Perfect passion and worship fed
By a kick in the ribs or a pat on the head.
Nevertheless it is hardly fair
To risk your heart for a dog to tear.

When the fourteen years which Nature permits
Are closing in asthma, or tumour, or fits,
And the vet's unspoken prescription runs
To lethal chambers or loaded guns,
Then you will find – it's your own affair –
But…you've given your heart to a dog to tear.

When the body that lived at your single will,
With its whimper of welcome, is stilled (how still!).
When the spirit that answered your every mood
Is gone – wherever it goes – for good,
You will discover how much you care,
And will give your heart to a dog to tear.

We've sorrow enough in the natural way,
When it comes to burying Christian clay.

Our loves are not given, but only lent,
At compound interest of cent per cent.
Though it is not always the case, I believe,
That the longer we've kept 'em, the more do we grieve:
For, when debts are payable, right or wrong,
A short-time loan is as bad as a long –
So why in – Heaven (before we are there)
Should we give our hearts to a dog to tear?

Previously...

MY
MOURNING
YEAR

*A Memoir of Bereavement,
Discovery and Hope*

ANDREW MARSHALL

Praise for *My Mourning Year*

'In a way, [this is] Andrew Marshall's best self-help book. He does not offer steps or guidance for how to navigate the mourning process; instead, Marshall uses his experience as anecdotal evidence that a person can survive and learn to live again after being affected by a tragedy'

– Lambda Literary

Our GP agreed to call round. This was not a good sign. OK, when I was a kid and sick in bed with a bottle of Lucozade, a box of fruit gums and Mummy suggesting that I might like to listen to *Desert Island Discs*, the doctor would make house calls, take my temperature and say: 'Keep him warm and give him plenty of fluids.' Times might have changed and Thom's stomach might have swelled up but he is still fit enough to be in charge of the laundry, still fixing his own low-fat meals and still getting out of bed most days.

This morning, he put on tracksuit bottoms and a sweat shirt, and came down to the living room. Rather than lying down on the sofa, he opted for the Corbusier chaise longue – that he'd once given me for Christmas – as it was easier to roll on and off. He looked really bloated, like he was six months pregnant. I wondered if it was wind. Maybe that's what Thom thought. I had a quick look round, cleared away a couple of newspapers. The place looked presentable. The doorbell rang and I showed the doctor through but cannot fill in the next bit. I remember he did not take off his coat and I don't think Thom got up. It would have been too awkward. Did the doctor examine him? He must have done. His diagnosis was bleak.

'I'm afraid that you have only weeks to live.'

I waited for Thom to react. He didn't.

'Your liver has failed and the ascitic fluid has leaked into the abdominal cavity.' He tapped Thom's stomach. 'You can hear the fluid move.'

Thom appeared mildly interested. I was still trying to process the first statement. I had to concentrate.

'What's ascitic fluid?'

'A clear liquid.'

I felt like a first-year medical student.

Dr Toynbee's eyes were sad. Thom's were unreadable. I can't understand why I didn't ask if there was any treatment. What about draining off the fluid? Could they give him a diuretic? The next bit is blank too. But I remember talking to Dr Toynbee in the hall. For some reason, I didn't want Thom to hear. Dr Toynbee was already making polite goodbye noises. I had questions. His hand was on the front door. It was now or never.

'When you say weeks, do you mean weeks adding up to months? After all, we've all just weeks to live…' I wanted to start running on the spot or fall to the ground and do twenty push-ups.

'About a month.'

'Will it hurt?'

'There are worse ways of going.'

'Will I be able to take care of him at home? He wants to stay here.'

Dr Toynbee looked at the track lighting in the hall.

I let him escape. There's only so much honesty I can swallow.

I found Thom in the kitchen. We must have exchanged a look but here again is another blank. Later, I remember him standing in the living room, by my grandmother's bureau, when he asked:

'So where would you like to take one last holiday?' He tried to make it a joke.

For a second, I imagined renting one of those weatherboarded cottages in Maine, New England – nothing between us and the North Atlantic beyond miles of sand dunes and reeds. I'd take long walks along the beach and Thom would learn to paint watercolours. However, I could also picture cylinders of oxygen on the veranda and bags of clear liquid that needed emptying and tubes everywhere.

I shrugged and Thom looked embarrassed. Who were we fooling?

'I suppose we'll have to tell people the truth,' I finally said.

'I want a second opinion.'

Suddenly, I could breathe again.

I had a magazine article to finish. So I escaped upstairs and closed my office door. Downstairs, Thom switched on the TV and had breakfast.

There is an abyss between us far greater than up stairs and down stairs. It opened up sometime towards the end of last summer, although it's hard to be precise because terminal illness creeps up on you. We'd driven out of Brighton on the cliff road, past Telscombe, where last year Thom had spent his summer sabbatical – between finishing work in Germany and starting a business or finding a job in the UK. It was a beautiful day and we could have parked the car and climbed down the steps, negotiated the wall by the pumping station and trekked across the rocks to the gay beach. However, Thom would have been exhausted just by the stairs. We were a team, in this together, so I told him to drive on. But I think we both realised the difference: I could choose whether I went to the beach or not, but Thom had no choice.

So why didn't I go downstairs and talk about the doctor's diagnosis? Why didn't I ask: 'How do you feel about the news?' Perhaps I dare not stretch out my hand, in case Thom pulls me down into the darkness too.

He might be going to die but I want to live.

Wednesday 4 February

Thom has phoned Herdecke hospital in Germany and asked to be admitted as soon as possible. While we wait for this second opinion, everything continues as normal. The bloating is not too bad and although Thom's spending longer in bed, he seems reasonably cheerful.

So far this week, I've been up to London to schedule more music for the bar at the Café de Paris and yesterday did an interview with

BBC Radio Suffolk. I'm not certain where I found the energy. I saw my private counselling client, and fortunately she has decided that she does not need any more help. I wish I felt the same.

Thom's been talking to Walter (his best friend) on the phone in Germany. I'm telling nobody about the diagnosis until we know for sure. Last night, he banged on the bedroom floor. I was watching *Coronation Street*, so I went up reluctantly. I offered to read another story from *Winnie-the-Pooh* or perhap's we could discuss what I've started to think about as 'the situation'. Thom shook his head; he wanted me to sit with him.

I cannot just sit.

This morning, I caught the 8.40 train to London for my weekly recordings of *Agony* for the cable channel Live TV. The scenarios that the production assistant faxed were as outlandish as ever: 'My teacher says he'll give me good grades if I go out with him'; 'My girlfriend's pussy gets in the way of our loving' and 'My boyfriend wants me to dress up like Geri Halliwell from the Spice Girls'. We had recorded two shows when the producer came striding on to the hot set:

'Nice outfit, Andrew.' I was wearing an orange jacket and a saffron shirt. 'Except, can you stop recommending counselling all the time. It's so downbeat.'

'Right, Pearl,' I nodded enthusiastically. I might be on the bottom rung of show business, but I am determined to cling on. She gave the thumbs up sign and retreated back to her control box.

I turned round and looked up the set with its large sixties pop art heads of beautifully made-up at girls with diamond-shaped tears rolling down perfect cheeks. It was my way of reminding myself that this show was all about appearances.

'Only three more,' said Kate. (Agony Aunt to my Agony Uncle.)

I sat bolt upright on the red sofa, held my stomach in and hoped the lights did not shine off my bald spot.

ANDREW G. MARSHALL

ARE YOU RIGHT FOR ME?

Seven steps to getting clarity and commitment in your relationship

BLOOMSBURY

ANDREW G. MARSHALL

BUILD A LIFE-LONG LOVE AFFAIR

Seven steps to revitalising your relationship

BLOOMSBURY

ANDREW G. MARSHALL

HEAL AND MOVE ON

Seven steps to recovering from a break-up

BLOOMSBURY

ANDREW G. MARSHALL

RESOLVE YOUR DIFFERENCES

Seven steps to dealing with conflict in your relationship

BLOOMSBURY

ANDREW G. MARSHALL

LEARN TO LOVE YOURSELF ENOUGH

Seven steps to improving your self-esteem and your relationships

BLOOMSBURY

ANDREW G. MARSHALL

HELP YOUR PARTNER SAY 'YES'

Seven steps to achieving better cooperation and communication

BLOOMSBURY

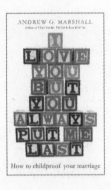

ANDREW G. MARSHALL
Author of I Love You but I'm Not in Love with You

I LOVE YOU BUT YOU ALWAYS PUT ME LAST

How to childproof your marriage

ANDREW G. MARSHALL

I LOVE YOU BUT I'M NOT IN LOVE WITH YOU

Seven Steps to Saving Your Relationship

BLOOMSBURY

BLOOMSBURY

ANDREW G. MARSHALL

How Can I Ever Trust You Again?

INFIDELITY:
From Discovery to Recovery in Seven Steps

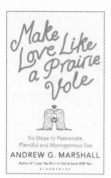

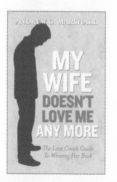
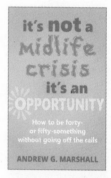

ABOUT THE AUTHOR

Andrew and Flash

Writing as Andrew G. Marshall, Andrew has written nineteen self-help books about relationships – including the international bestseller, *I Love You But I'm Not in Love with You*. His writing has been translated into twenty different languages. He still writes for newspapers like the *Mail on Sunday* and leads a team of therapists in London and Berlin. There is more information about his work as a marital therapist at www.andrewgmarshall.com

The Power of Dog is the second volume of Andrew's memoirs. You can read more about the death of his partner and the first steps in his recovery in *My Mourning Year*, which is also published by RedDoor Books. For more about this book and pictures of Thom, go to www.mymourningyear.com

For more pictures of Flash, go to www.andrewgmarshall/flash